"This book creates a joyful and effortless system that blends mind, body and spirit to create a comprehensive life. The exercises throughout the book are thought-provoking and will open the reader up to become more intentional and tuned-in to living their lives. *Soul Mission, Life Vision* is a must-read for people who are ready to enjoy the journey of their lives!"

—Terri Levine, Master Certified Coach and author of the international best-seller, *Work Yourself Happy* and *Coaching for an Extraordinary Life*

"*Soul Mission, Life Vision* is infused with the loving authority and humility of one who clearly knows his own mission and has the rare gift of being able to guide others in manifesting their soul intentions. Alan Seale has woven together three golden threads: the seasoned teacher's awareness of the questions, challenges and promises of seekers; the mystic's intuition and ability to channel Spirit; and thirdly, the scholar's penetrating understanding of ancient wisdoms. Be prepared to read with underliners and journals close at hand. I will certainly be recommending this book to clients, students and friends."

—Gloria D. Karpinski, author of *Barefoot on Holy Ground* and *Where Two Worlds Touch*

"A comprehensive, in-depth guide for life alignment, this book will be of great value to many. Alan Seale continues to make thoughtful and heartfelt contributions to the emerging New Age."

—Rick Jarow, author of *Creating the Work You Love*

SOUL MISSION * LIFE VISION

SOUL MISSION LIFE VISION

*Recognize Your True Gifts
and Make Your Mark
in the World*

Alan Seale

**Red
Wheel**

First published in 2003 by
Red Wheel/Weiser, LLC
With offices at:
500 Third Street, Suite 230
San Francisco, CA 94107
www.redwheelweiser.com

Library of Congress Cataloging-in-Publication Data

Seale, Alan
  Soul mission, life vision : recognize your true gifts and make
your mark in the world / Alan Seale.
    p. cm.
Includes bibliographical references.
  ISBN 1-59003-013-3
    1. Spiritual life. I. Title.
  BF624.S43 2003
  291.4'4—DC21
              2002152833

Typeset in Aldus

Printed in Canada

TCP

10 09 08 07 06
  8 7 6 5 4 3 2

To JP, with much love.

CONTENTS

Acknowledgements   xi

PART I—*How Life Works:*
Understanding the Human Experience   1

Introduction   3

Chapter 1—The Journey Begins   11

Chapter 2—Choosing Freedom: Claiming Your Life   25

Chapter 3—Creation by Intention   39

Chapter 4—Entering the Silence: The Gift of Intuition   45

Chapter 5—The Laws of the Universe   57

Chapter 6—The Human Energy System: Chakras   85

PART II—*Identifying Mission, Creating Vision*   113

Chapter 7—Soul Mission   115

Chapter 8—Life Vision   127

PART III—*Paradigms, Mind, and Thought*   139

Chapter 9—Paradigms: Hidden Keys to Creation   141

Chapter 10—The Universal Trinity of Creation:
Concept, Form, Action   153

Chapter 11—The Power of Mind and Thought   159

Chapter 12—Taking Stock of Your Present Situation   179

Part IV — *Manifesting Your Vision, Living Your Mission*   191

Chapter 13—The Manifestation Wheel   193

Chapter 14—Manifestation House 1 Intention   199

Chapter 15—Manifestation House 2: Peace   207

Chapter 16—Manifestation House 3: Energy   219

Chapter 17—Manifestation House 4: Guidance   229

Chapter 18—Manifestation House 5: Empowerment   239

Chapter 19—Manifestation House 6: Action   253

Chapter 20—Manifestation House 7: Surrender   267

Chapter 21—Manifestation House 8: Legacy   275

In Conclusion: The Journey Forward   281

Bibliography   287

Acknowledgments

THIS BOOK WAS A GIFT from Spirit. My relationship with Spirit as mentor, guide, and support grew each day I wrote. I am profoundly grateful for this opportunity, and offer my gratitude and love to Spirit for this extraordinary year of creation and birth, promise and fulfillment.

I also want to thank all of you who participated in "Paradigm Shifting" and "Soul Mission ✷ Life Vision" classes over the last year. Your willingness to share your journeys, celebrate your victories, and face your challenges, offered deeper understanding of the process of identifying mission, creating vision, and manifesting dreams.

Many thanks also to those of you for your time, energy, and love in reading all or parts of this manuscript, and for offering invaluable feedback: Beth Barrett, Sandra Bilotto, Dr. Kathleen Calabrese, Sue Evans, Shari Garrett, Dr. Michael Heggerty, Daniel Karslake, Gerry LeBeau, Rev. Joel Rosow, Rev. Dr. James M. Seale, Mary Dudley Seale, Dr. Arlene Shrut, and Devin Wilson.

Tremendous admiration and thanks to the whole team at Red Wheel—especially Jan Johnson, Robyn Heisey, Jill Rogers, and Chris Wold. Your support and belief in this project is a marvelous gift.

And finally, my deepest thanks to Johnathon Pape for your constant love and support. Thank you for endless hours of working through every page with me, and your commitment to helping me find just the right words. We made the journey of this book together—a journey that fed and sustained us both. The journey continues, and the gifts continue to unfold.

Part I

HOW LIFE WORKS: UNDERSTANDING
THE HUMAN EXPERIENCE

INTRODUCTION

 THIS IS A BOOK about you—a journey into Self and into the world. It is about your dreams and aspirations, your daily life, your future, your relationships, your thoughts, your beliefs, your intentions, your priorities, your wisdom, your spirituality, and, ultimately, your freedom. It contains ancient and timeless tools, support systems that can launch and sustain your process of self-discovery and life creation in the 21st century. It propels you forward on your personal spiritual path and empowers you to recognize and fulfill your soul's mission here on Earth. In short, this book is the owner's manual you never received when you entered this world, offering both the theory and the practice that can lead you to getting the most out of your life—physically, emotionally, mentally, and spiritually.

This book opens a passageway to the soul so that you may know its truth and mission. From the truth of your soul, you can recognize and examine the paradigms or belief systems by which you define and create your life, and then make the necessary shifts in those beliefs to allow the soul to accomplish its mission. At that point, you release yourself from the ties that bind you to limiting beliefs and behaviors so that you can dream without restriction. Recognizing your true gifts and the ways you wish to share those gifts, you then see clearly your role in the world, the path toward making your mark and establishing your legacy.

Within this larger journey into Self and the world, there are many smaller journeys and opportunities. First, there is the opportunity to learn about choice and decision. Our formal education process does not teach us a method for making choices and decisions. As a result, we tend to be forced into decisions by circumstance rather than by our own initiative. With this book, you will learn to make choices out of desire and personal plan, rather than out of circumstantial necessity. Choice can be proactive rather than reactive.

This book will help you understand more clearly that action without clear intention, decision, and aligned thought ultimately produces less than full-potential results. Intention is a key factor in the manifestation process. Aligned thought means that your inner desires and outer actions are in harmony with one another, and that they are both in alignment with the larger, universal flow of life.

Conscious awareness is expanding rapidly in our culture. More and more people are realizing that they must fit their life into their spirituality rather than trying to fit their spirituality into their life. Your life is your spiritual journey—recognizing the flow of Love in your life. I speak of Love with a capital "L" as the creating and sustaining force of the universe. You might also call it "God" or "Spirit" or "Universal Mind." Kahlil Gibran said in *The Prophet*, "All work is empty save when there is love . . .[for] work is love made visible." I rephrase that statement so that it says, "All *life* is empty save when there is Love, for *life* is Love made visible." It is a conscious choice to live in the constant flow of Love. What is important is that you find your way into that flow and live every moment within it.

The following passage by Martin Luther King can be found in *A Testament of Hope: The Essential Writings of Martin Luther King, Jr.* by James Washington:

> Personal power, properly understood, is nothing but the ability to achieve purpose. There is nothing wrong with power if used correctly. One of the great problems of history is that the concepts of love and power have usually been contrasted as opposites—polar opposites—so that love is identified with resignation of power, and power with denial of love. What is needed is a realization that power without love is reckless and abusive, and love without power is sentimental and anemic.

Power is an essential component of creating your life as you want it to be. Through exploration of Self, you will learn how the universal flow of Love can move through your being to manifest the highest possible creation of you. Through your power, you can share your valuable gifts with the world. When you recognize that power and Love are one and unleash that force into your life, anything is possible. You may desire a loving relationship, to be a better parent, colleague, or boss, to be a healer, to increase your income tenfold, or to become a celebrity. How you use your power force of Love in the world is completely up to you.

All of us together are making up a big play called "Life." In tandem with Spirit (or God, or whatever you choose to call the great creative and sustaining force of the universe), each of us gets to choose the role we wish to play and even write our parts of the script, which will be influenced by and have influence on many other players and their scripts. What part do you wish to play? What is the script you wish to write?

This book is about knowing Self and which role you want to play, how you want to develop your character and create your life, and then doing it! It is so easy to let life be dictated by the needs and wants of others or the demands of a job. The more you know who you are and the more you live that true identity, the stronger and clearer are your perceptions and sense of reality, and the less you are swayed by forces that go against your nature. You have the power to make your own choices, and to create your life as you want it to be.

Paradigms are belief systems that shape our lives. You will recognize your core beliefs or paradigms and the ways they affect or shape your life as well as discover hidden paradigms you didn't realize were there or that you thought were inconsequential. You will see how your paradigms create the lens of perception through which you view and experience the world, and you will develop tools to shift them in order to have a clearer, less distorted view.

Through this book, you will gain an understanding of the principles of energy vibration. Whether or not you are aware of it, you are constantly creating your future path by your thoughts, words, attitudes, and actions. Our journey together is about looking carefully at your current creations, comparing them to what you really want to create, and then shifting your thoughts in order to create or manifest what you desire.

This book will help you achieve a "big-picture view" of life—to see life within a global and perhaps even universal context, not just within the box of your current situation. As you get clearer about your soul mission and shift the paradigms that limit you, your view of life gets much broader. Ultimately, this is a journey of freedom. In the end, that's what the soul is always seeking—to fly freely and experience fully. Along the way, you learn that freedom is a matter of perspective more than a matter of circumstance. In the course of working through this book, you will have many opportunities to realize what freedom means and looks like in your life, and to take the necessary steps to move closer to it.

This book is not just about your life looking the way you want it to look on the outside. It is about being who you want to be, doing what you want to do, having what you want to have, on every level of existence, all the way to the core of your being. Inspired by your soul mission, you will learn to create a vision—clear, unobstructed, unlimited—and then transform that vision into reality.

Michelangelo is credited with having said, "The greatest danger for most of us is not that our aim is too high and we miss it, but that it is too low and we reach it." This book is about reaching high. If you miss it the first time—even many times—it doesn't matter. Each time you miss, you learn, stretch, and grow, gaining a better understanding of the vision and how to reach it. When we have small vision and reach it easily, there is no stretch, no growth.

What we are really talking about is what I call full-spectrum living—embracing, celebrating, and fully participating in all that life has to offer as well as all that you have to offer life. It means being willing to experience life on many levels of feeling and awareness at once. The journey to full-spectrum living is a process of uncovering your soul's intent, and preparing your body and mind to carry it out. It is full-blown manifestation of you. In her book, *Barefoot on Holy Ground*, Gloria Karpinski refers to manifestation as "spiritual technology." That is exactly what we are studying and utilizing—the technology of the spiritual Self that is simultaneously human and divine.

Developing your spiritual technology may mean radical shifts in thought, belief, habit, lifestyle, relationships, and career. Or it may mean subtle shifts in awareness to fine-tune the process. Wherever you are is where you begin the journey of this book. Regardless of where you are, you are still Spirit made manifest in human form. Simply by opening your mind and heart to the idea of full-spectrum living and limitless potential of Self, you are well on your way.

Whether you are a novice at full-spectrum living, have been moving in that direction for some time, or are a master in many areas of your life, the process is still the same: be open, be clear, be responsive, be patient, and take the next step. Ultimately, you must trust that you have arrived at this point through a divine process, even if the process has not led to where you might have expected. Wherever you are right now is the right place, because you have opened to the possibility that there can be more to your life.

Our journey together has four parts. The first part is an exploration of the human experience—of how life works—a journey into Self. We cannot know what our soul mission is if we don't know who we are in the first place. You might say, "I know who I am. I am [name], and I am a [profession], and I share my life with my [family, spouse, partner, pet, friends]." But when you peel away those external aspects, who are you deep inside? What is important to you? What do you think and dream about?

Through the first part of the book, we will make our way to the heart of your being so that by the time we get to Part II, you have a deeper sense of who you are at a soul level. In Part II, you will identify your soul mission and write your soul mission statement. This statement will then be the springboard for creating your life vision and writing your vision statement.

In the third part of the book, we will look at the concept of paradigms and how they shape our lives, most often without our realizing it. We will explore the power of the mind and the importance of disciplining thought for creation.

Finally, in the last part, we will work with a Manifestation Wheel to turn your life vision into reality. We will have moved from self-discovery, to declaring mission and vision, to utilizing the mind and thought for creation, to at last living your mission and manifesting your vision in your daily life.

This book is not one that you can simply read, hoping that the concepts will soak in and personal change will happen. While just reading will certainly stir up new thoughts and ideas, in order to get the most out of this book, you will need to do your work along the way. This requires time and commitment, but I can assure you it will be one of the best investments in yourself you have ever made. This is not because my words are so important. It's what my words trigger in you that is important. A powerful synergy will occur when you synthesize the information in this book with your own inner guidance, personal revelation, and life experience. That synergy can lead to profound personal transformation and the full realization of your soul mission—your reason for being.

Resistance or fears may arise at several places along the journey. It's all right—in fact, expected. Fear and resistance are just signs that you are crossing over into unknown territory. You don't know what will happen, how others will respond, who you will become, what changes may occur in your life. If you never experience any resistance or fear, or at least have a sense of apprehension, you are probably not challenging yourself enough to be truly all you can be. So, when fear or resistance comes up for you, acknowledge it, respect it, take a deep breath, and go on.

There are four particular junctures where, in classes and private coaching work, I see fear and resistance arise most consistently:

→ At the beginning of doing this work;

→ At the point of actually writing a soul mission statement;

→ At the point of committing to the first significant paradigm shift;

→ After goals are set and it is time to take action.

These feelings surface at these particular junctures because by making those statements or engaging in those processes, you are actively and intentionally stepping into your creative power.

Claiming your power often means that your life—or at least some aspects of it—will never be the same again. Your sense of Self will change; you will grow into your fullness and recognize yourself as the unique and important being that you are. You will embrace the responsibilities inherent in claiming your place in the world. Relationships will change—some will dissolve, others take on new forms, while others will remain solid and secure. The ways in which you move in the world and interact with others will change, for you will be thinking, feeling, and doing from a sense of purpose. You will live your life from a place of clarity for which few choose to strive. And, most importantly, you will experience new levels of freedom.

You may not realize that freedom right away, but when you assertively step through your fear and resistance and stay the course that every fiber of your being tells you is yours, you embark upon the most profound and miraculous journey in the universe—the journey to freedom through Self. When we become pioneers and explorers of our own inner space, we set off on the ultimate freedom path.

Throughout this book, you will find exercises in the forms of meditations and activities as well as "Questions to Ponder." "Ponder" is not a word that we hear much anymore. Its lack of use is a reflection of our fast-paced times. To ponder is to sit with a question, issue, or situation for a period of time—a few days or even weeks—and allow clarity and understanding to unfold.

As you come across the "Questions to Ponder" sections, pause to reflect on them, and then keep those questions fresh in your mind for a few days. Spend time with them in contemplation and meditation. Much of your growth, development, and transformation will come through your ponderings, letting them show you their place or role in your life. The exercises will serve as catalysts for that growth and transformation, and are an integral part of the process.

With private clients and students in classes, I suggest that they spend an hour a day in silence, meditation, and reflection. I ask that they write in a journal for at least 15 minutes a day, which can be a part of that hour. Journaling can be a powerful tool in your process of paradigm shifting and manifestation. The journal can become an amazing partner, offering tremendous insight into your experiences. The hour can also include exercises from the class or from our individual work.

I suggest that you develop this same practice. Take an hour a day and give yourself the gift of *you*. We will talk much more about silence and meditation in chapter 4, but you can begin now. Enter into the silence, write in your journal, do the exercises from the book as you come to them one by one. If this is not a part of your daily schedule already, I can promise you that if you commit to the discipline, it will change your life. It will give you the opportunity to break through armors you've been wearing, perhaps for years. It will allow you to peel away layers of what you think of as protection and dip down into the beautiful and profound inner silence. This silence is the place where you can know Spirit within you.

And so we begin a journey of learning together, growing, shifting, rearranging, and transforming. How we do it all will be made clear one page at a time. So, be open, be clear, be responsive, be patient, and let the journey unfold.

The Journey Begins

WHAT WE CARE ABOUT—our hopes, dreams, values, and aspirations—are often buried deep in the unconscious. Most of us were raised in a society that supports making deals with ourselves and others in order to survive. We trade what we care about in order to get what we think we need. Or we trade what we care about for what we are told we are supposed to want. We are socialized to place a title, recognition, or a position above that which might give us pleasure, satisfaction, or fulfillment. Yet, deep inside, so many people are asking, "Is this it? Is this what I've been working so hard for? Is this what I really want?"

An early part of our journey together is to help you uncover your true identity from a soul level, your true sense of Self. This leads you to discover and accept openly and fully your personal gifts and talents, your wildest hopes and dreams, your personal sense of purpose, and the gifts you wish to share with the world. It involves an honest look at your life, what works and what doesn't, which of your paradigms are serving you and which are keeping you from achieving what you desire. At its core, this is a journey of personal transformation. In this chapter, we will discuss the "how-to" process of discovery and transformation and lay the groundwork for your soul-mission quest.

Personal transformation does not necessarily mean "doing the job better," moving into a higher income bracket, getting a promotion, or improving a skill. Any of those things and much more may happen as a part of your journey, but they are all part of your "outer" life. Personal transformation is an "inner" life process that begins at a fundamental level. It is about becoming your *true* person rather than a new person. It means reevaluating who you are, what you do, why you do it, and with whom or for whom you do it. It is the greatest gift you can give to yourself and to the world, because ultimately you are giving the gift of you in your highest and most fully developed form. It's the gift of stepping out of the mindless rhythm of daily life to see the bigger picture and the hidden agendas and meanings behind all that you are and do as you present yourself to the world. It's about recognizing all that you are capable of as a divine creation. It's about knowing yourself completely, and through that knowing, being able to harness all of your power and love. It's about living as a dynamic and creative being in the universe.

Transformation means shifting paradigms. Paradigms are belief systems or structures that, consciously or unconsciously, shape every aspect of your life. James Ray, author of *The Science of Success*, defines "paradigm" as "the sum total of our beliefs, values, identity, expectations, attitudes, habits, decisions, opinions, and thought patterns—about ourselves, others, and how life works. It is the filter through which we interpret what we see and experience." For example, a child who is constantly criticized for everything he does develops the belief that he can't do anything right. This becomes a paradigm that says, "I will always be a failure." On the positive side, the new college graduate who has great success in her early professional life develops a paradigm that says, "I am confident and capable, and can succeed at anything I choose."

We begin forming our paradigms unconsciously from life experience during infancy and early childhood. (We will talk about how that happens in chapter 9.) Through adolescence and early adulthood, those paradigms begin to shape our lives. As time goes on, new paradigms form as outgrowths of the original ones and the life experiences they have shaped. It becomes a circular process. Experience leads to paradigm formation, which leads to more experiences, which lead to new paradigm formation.

We can easily go through life oblivious of the whole process, wondering why we are where we are and why things didn't turn out the way we thought they would. Transformation, however, is a conscious process—one that demands our intention and attention. Personal transformation means change. And if you want to change your life, you must first change your paradigms.

I invite you to look closely at your life and recognize where you are perhaps stuck in a box of limited thought, as well as to acknowledge and celebrate where you experience freedom. What do you allow to define your life? If your job defines your life, you have allowed the job to become a box for your life, confining you to its parameters and limitations. However, if you see your life as a moving, breathing, dancing essence of Love that uses your job as a vehicle for expression, you are free. Your job serves you rather than you serving it. If you allow your religion to define your beliefs and lifestyle without your conscious choice, your religion has become a box and a lens through which you perceive and process life. If, however, your religion is a living, breathing, flexible structure through which your sense of spirituality dances freely and finds its home, you are free.

Any belief system, lifestyle, or spiritual practice lies somewhere on a spectrum that is at one end complete liberation and at the other a deadly trap. A free life is one that is ever expanding, renewing, discovering, revealing, and becoming. It is your choice as to how you create your life, and how much freedom or limitation you wish to live with.

When we live within limiting paradigms, we tend to make uninformed choices. We see choices as black and white or either/or, recognizing very few possibilities. For example, one such limiting paradigm might be that in order to achieve personal gain, someone else must lose or be pushed down. Another might be the assumption that something is impossible simply because we haven't yet been able to accomplish it. We hold on to paradigms and preferences based on habit, not on what we really know in our heart of hearts that we want. We have gotten used to certain patterns in our lives, and are reluctant to shift those patterns. However, we are living in delusion if we expect our lives to get better without making an effort toward personal change.

Perhaps the most limiting paradigm of all is that our way is the best way. When we have found something that works for us—a belief system or way of doing things that we perceive has made our life better—we feel compelled to get others to believe and live as we do. However, there are many paths on the road to enlightenment. Rigidity, too many rules, or too-tight structures leave little room for individual expression and freedom. And that's what this journey is all about—expressing your individual, divine essence as a soul set free to experience the ecstasy of doing what it came here to do.

Gandhi said, "We must be the change we wish to see in the world." His words are an important key to this journey. Ultimately, we cannot change anyone or anything outside ourselves that does not wish to be changed. However, we can change ourselves, our perceptions, and attitudes. By disciplining thoughts to create new paradigms, we free ourselves to construct a world we wish to live in. If we want our world to change, we must first change ourselves.

Changing yourself begins on the inside. If you are unhappy in your job, simply changing your job will not necessarily make you happy. Unless you address the root of your unhappiness, which is probably a much deeper issue than just your job, the chances are good that you will draw another job to you in which you are once again unhappy. When you come up against conflict in relationship, walking out of the relationship may seem like a quick solution. However, the same fundamental conflict will continue to come up in subsequent relationships until you address the inner conflict that the outer situation is mirroring. It is like going in search of a new mirror because you don't like the reflection you see in the old one. Changing the mirror will not change the reflection. Only a change in you will create a new reflection in the mirror. Rarely is there a time in our lives when a problem we face does not reflect an inner issue that we need to address. The challenges we face in our outer world help us see the challenges we need to recognize and work through in our inner world.

So, how exactly are we going to do all of this shifting, changing, growing and transforming? The answer is in a step-by-step, systematic process. And the first step is to look at our concepts of process.

Although our Western, rational thought process tries to make it so, life is not linear. It never was, but the slower pace of past generations created the illusion that life was a linear process. A hundred years ago, one could expect that, at least in appearance, life would flow in a straight line from point A to point B to point C. This is not the case in the 21st-century world. As time seems to be speeding up and life is becoming increasingly complex, we more easily see life in its real circular or spiral pattern. This is not circular as in geometry, but rather a flow of moving in and out of truths, concepts, life circumstances, lessons, and thoughts. A century ago, you could expect to be born into a family, follow the accepted educational or vocational training for your gender and social standing—raise children and keep house if you were a woman, or go to work for the family business, a factory, or other establishment if you were a man. If you followed this path, you could expect to live out your life in relative security. Security went beyond having a stable income source; it included knowing the rules for living, and being certain that no one would change them without you knowing about it.

Today, you are born into a family, begin an educational or vocational training path of your choice—regardless of gender—and may take time to explore many possibilities before settling on a career path. In fact, you may change career paths a number of times within your professional life. We rarely find someone who begins at point A even knowing what points B and C will be, let alone exactly what the path is to get there. It seems that we start at A, have some vague idea of what and where B might be and begin the journey, only to have many other opportunities and possibilities come up long before we ever get to B. If there are 10 steps to a process, chances are we begin with step 1, then move to step 2, then maybe to 4 or 5 before returning to pick up 3, and then on to 6, and so forth, as we make our way to complete all 10 steps. We may also do more than one step at a time. Or, we may complete the first several steps and realize that we are being instinctively called to another path and set of steps entirely.

In today's pop culture, people speak of living "in the box" or getting "out of the box." "The box" refers to a carefully-constructed box of beliefs or circumstances that create a feeling, albeit often false, of safety and security. The reality, however, is that "the box" doesn't work anymore. The rules of life are changing so fast that it often seems there are no rules anymore. What a liberating feeling and what a tremendous challenge, all at the same time! I saw a poster years ago with a quote from Thomas Edison: "There are no rules here. We're trying to get something done." I share that quote with every new group of students as we begin our work. Letting go of the rules sets the soul free to create as it wishes. The ego, however, longs for a structure that sets boundaries and makes the rules for us.

Full-spectrum living involves being willing to start from scratch, listen to soul mission, and create your own set of rules. It involves creating a structure for life that provides stability while at the same time sets us free. Then ego can feel secure once again. The difference is that this time the structure and rules were created by soul rather than by outside forces that may or may not be in harmony with your true mission. Role models for how it has always been done, for "in the box" living, abound. However, role models for full-spectrum living built on freedom and soul mission are much harder to find. We must be our own role models, and find our own way. And the way is a circular process—in, around, and through, weaving the web of our lives. We must learn to listen to the wisdom of our soul and trust its guidance.

Although we may not recognize it as so, our education process is circular. Reflect back on your schooling; most everything you've ever studied you first began to learn about at a fundamental level in the first few grades of school. From then on, you kept coming back to the same subjects, each time adding a new layer of knowledge and understanding. In kindergarten and first grade, you first began to know the alphabet and then began the first levels of reading. Each year you continued to develop your reading and comprehension skills, in part by formal education, and in part by simply using those skills on a daily basis. In those early grades, you learned about numbers and how to add and subtract. As time went on, you studied multiplication and division, geometry, algebra, and you have continued to work with numbers your entire life. In each subject, year by year, you learned more details, refined more skills, and developed deeper understandings of concepts. You kept coming back around to the same basic subjects and taking your knowledge and skill to the next level. Yet every new level of study required that you remember everything about the previous levels. Sometimes you had to go back to review previously learned concepts so that you could take the next step on the learning ladder.

The same is true with this book. We will learn some fundamental concepts, and then keep coming back to those concepts and looking at them from different perspectives, exploring them at deeper levels, and understanding them more fully and completely. Your linear self will say, "You've already talked about that." But your circular Self will say, "Good, I'm glad we're here again. I want to understand this concept more fully and apply it to where I am right now."

Our Western cultural tendency is to think of learning as acquiring knowledge, developing a skill, memorizing facts, taking in information. However, learning can be so much more. Learning, at its highest level, is personal transformation. Learning at this level involves questioning views, opinions, and beliefs, acknowledging areas of our lives where we need to grow and expand, and opening to the possibilities that lie within our boundless potential.

Learning is a proactive process. It involves moving forward, not standing still. It involves developing awareness through personal experience, not just reading about it in a book or collecting facts. To really know something in a dynamic way, it has to get into your cells. You must have integrated that information into every aspect of your life. In our 21st-century world, the facts are always changing, or being influenced by other facts. When we embrace the concept of circular flow in the learning and development process, we can move forward at an astounding pace.

I define "Spirit" as the all of the everything that is. It has no particular form yet it embodies all forms. You may call it God, Love, Universal Mind, Creative Force, Great Mystery—whatever term you are comfortable with is the term you should hold in your mind when I say Spirit. I have worked in partnership with Spirit for many years. That partnership has evolved to the place where I live in constant dialogue with Spirit, not only in my daily meditation practice, but in my activities, as well. The dialogue began in my early days of meditation simply as a sense or feeling of Spirit being present. In time, I began to feel as though Spirit was communicating ideas or thoughts to me. As I got more comfortable in receiving that guidance, our communication expanded to include words and visual images. I heard a "voice" speaking to me and saw inner "pictures" or "movies." As I disciplined myself to focus and receive from Spirit, many beautiful teachings were given to me—teachings that I knew I was to share.

My first book, *Intuitive Living: A Sacred Path,* is about learning to live in the constant awareness of the interactive presence of Spirit, and includes many of those teachings. I believe that intuition is one of our greatest gifts. In its most highly-developed form, it is the voice of God or Spirit within you. Everyone has the gift of intuition. If we choose to refine that gift, we develop the ability to live in the constant awareness of Spirit or divine guidance. One of our focuses in this book will be to open to that voice within, and let Spirit and your soul guide you in this journey of transformation, paradigm shifts, and manifestation. For some of you, the belief that you can tap into divine guidance within yourself and trust it to guide your life will be a paradigm shift in itself!

Several years ago, Spirit began leading me into a much deeper examination of the spiritual laws that govern the universe and the manifestation process. It began as I started asking questions within my meditation like, "What is reality?" "Whose reality is it?" "Who creates it?" "What is my personal involvement and responsibility for it?"

My first big lesson was to embrace the concept of inner reality versus outer reality. There are many factors that influence my outer reality—others' desires and needs, others' feelings and opinions, my past actions and decisions, my vision of the world and how I project that vision into physical manifestation. It may seem at times that I have very little control over my outer reality. The fact is that I cannot control the actions, needs, or opinions of others. What I can control is me.

Spirit made it very clear, however, that before we went any further, my concept of control had to change; I had to learn more about spiritual discipline. I was somewhat taken aback by this directive from Spirit since I considered myself a disciplined person spiritually. After all, I had developed and maintained a daily meditation practice for many years; I lived my life in constant dialogue with Spirit, and thought I was good at responding to Spirit's guidance. But as we just discussed, learning and growth are circular processes. Spirit was guiding me to learn on yet a deeper level that through discipline I could experience freedom—a freedom that could then lead to a completely new and much more dynamic concept of control.

This is a concept that I understood long ago in my life as a singer and voice teacher, but now I was being asked to apply it in my daily life. On the surface, it might seem that the paths of discipline and freedom would lead in opposite directions. Not so. In order to have the ability to do absolutely anything I wanted with my voice with no tension or restriction, I needed a solid vocal technique. When I first began crossing over from a classical singing career into cabaret and other genres, I began with improvisational singing. At that point, I realized that because I had disciplined myself for so many years to build a solid technique, I had the freedom to let Spirit sing through me. I never questioned whether or not I could actually sing what was coming through. I just did it. Through that incredible freedom, I found that I had more control over my instrument than I had ever known. The dynamic range and variety of colors in my sound seemed unlimited. Control was now a matter of thought, not a matter of muscle or force. An idea immediately became a sound. And it was all because of discipline.

Now Spirit was talking to me about the discipline I needed to free myself so that I could create and control my inner reality. I could choose to let the outer reality of my various life circumstances continue to create an inner emotional roller coaster, or I could discipline my thoughts and attitudes to create an inner sense of peace, tranquility, and general happiness. Spirit made it very clear that this was my choice, no one else's, and certainly not Spirit's. I could choose to create my inner reality to be whatever I wanted it to be. I could tangle myself in the outer dramas of life, or I could bask in the inner stillness of my soul.

Another gift from Spirit during this same time was a new understanding of "life lessons." I was being very hard on myself for not being able to move through certain big lessons of my life more quickly. Then Spirit stepped in to show me that I was not fully grasping the concept of life lessons. The key word here is "life." We all come in with several big lessons to learn in this lifetime. When we can understand that the learning of those lessons is a life-long journey, we can be much gentler with ourselves, and allow ourselves the process. Those big lessons continue for the duration of our time here. They aren't meant to be learned quickly and then let go, for then we would only be learning the lesson on one or two levels. Life lessons are those on which we spend a lifetime working. Each time the lesson comes around again, our understanding and learning goes to a new level. Again, it is a circular process.

How do you fully engage in that process? With discipline. Discipline of daily meditation and/or contemplation, in whatever form works for you, in order to hear the inner voice of Spirit and your soul. Discipline of thought to create a positive and peaceful inner reality. Discipline of action to support your unfolding Truth.

Through discipline you can find freedom. When you have the discipline to listen to and respond to your soul, you are free. You are living your truth. Then you have found a new control over your life and you can live in alignment with the universal flow, listen to your soul as your divine Self, and create a rewarding life of joy, peace, and fulfillment. You can experience full-spectrum living. And you will know that, regardless of the dramas unfolding around you, you can choose to stand in your own inner reality and be at peace in the truth and essence of your being.

This path toward freedom through discipline is the path of the spiritual warrior. We may have a stereotype of a warrior as someone with a painted face, ready to fight. But that is not the nature of warrior energy. The warrior is one (male or female) who has a mission and is committed to that mission, regardless of what obstacles may appear. The spiritual warrior stands firm in his or her truth and is committed to personal growth and evolution. The spiritual warrior welcomes the challenge of new ideas and opinions, and weighs them against soul truth, adopting only those new beliefs that are in harmony with their soul. The path of the spiritual warrior is a high calling, for it demands commitment and discipline. But the rewards are great.

During the preparation of the second edition of *Intuitive Living*, Spirit offered these words on what it means to be a spiritual warrior in the 21st century. This teaching became the catalyst for this book.

✳

You are a spiritual warrior of the new dimension of time. We say "new dimension of time" because that's what the 21st century is. Time takes on a new meaning. For those caught in a 20th-century reality, life will be a struggle. They will not understand why they can't grasp hold of their lives and move ahead. However, for those who are willing to let go of old paradigms, the new dimension of time will become not only clear, but also a great friend and ally.

Let's step aside here to talk about "ally" and your relationship with the universe. Too often, you and your Western society are at odds with the natural flow of universal energies. You then begin to look at change as your enemy rather than as your friend. The more you have invested in your current or past realities, the greater the challenge of living, for time in your linear and spatial dimension is moving on. Current realities will give way to new realities, just as the past gave way to the present. Being grounded in the moment—in the present—now has a new meaning.

Being grounded in the 21st century means sinking into the rushing wave, fastening your feet firmly in the footholds of the rushing and shifting tide. You have a saying that "life is like a roller coaster." You haven't seen anything yet! And please don't interpret this statement as gloom and doom! Not at all. You are in for a great ride, if you plant your feet in the footholds of the shifting tide and let the ride begin. However, if you don't commit to the ride by fastening your feet to the floorboard, or if you try to stand still while the roller coaster is in motion, you are going to have a rough go of it. Please consider the racing times, the shifting nature of the universe to be your ally, your friend. You can get on this universal wave and ride it into your dynamic new paradigms and future. Or you can resist change, hold tightly to the past and old ways of thinking, and be forever out of sync with the world around you.

The spiritual warriors of the 21st century will live fully in every chakra. (Chakras are energy centers in the body. We will discuss them in chapter 6.) And every chakra will fill every other chakra. The Love of the heart will live in all. The grounding and life-force of the root chakra will live in all. The creative/sexual power of the sacral chakra will live in all. The power and strength of the solar plexus, the truth and freedom of the throat, the vision of the brow, and the wisdom of the crown will exist in every chakra. The energies of living will reach higher and higher levels of intensity. You will recognize and live your essence in a very new way. Your life on the outside may look the same, but your relationship to it—your paradigms of living—will be vastly different.

Spiritual: infused with the breath and breadth of the divine.

Warrior: one who is willing to live personal truth no matter what! Against all odds.

Who are you? Are you a spiritual warrior? Are you a leader of the masses simply by how you live your life? Are you willing to let go of the old paradigms even though the new ones are not firmly in place and, in fact, may never be firmly in place again?

As you move into the 21st century, your reality becomes more and more circular, not linear. It is more and more about relationships between souls, and relationship of ego to soul. Ego must surrender to soul for this ride into the new dimension. The new paradigm is an ever-evolving one. It has been said that the shift from the Piscean to Aquarian Age for the Western world is a shift from solar plexus domination to more heart-centered living. But that is only the beginning.

The shift is ultimately to be in total-being-centered living. As we said, you will live fully in every chakra all the time, not bouncing around from one center to another.

Your lives must move on to ever-evolving processes. Never again will you be able to plant your feet on firm ground and say, "Here I'll stay," not if you want to ride the wave of the new dimension of time—not if you want to set free and live the life of the spiritual warrior that is you. Accept movement as your new way of life. No, not just accept— celebrate! Celebrate the ever-shifting, growing, evolving paradigm that is your life. Then you can be a spiritual warrior.

This is the first step; plant your feet in the shifting tides. Ride the wave with your feet fastened into the wave itself, not the ground beneath. Live in the current reality that is always changing. And you will hear your call, see your path, and know the journey of your soul.

✳

Our outer lives are constantly changing. People come and go. We move from place to place. Creation and manifestation are ongoing processes. Inside, however, our essence remains the same as it has always been. It's just that we keep uncovering and discovering who we really are. We may think we are changing at the soul level, but it is actually our awareness that is changing. It is our awareness that is evolving so that we recognize our true nature. As our awareness develops and we know ourselves more fully, we more easily recognize our path in the world, and the gifts we wish to share.

As you step onto the circular path of the spiritual warrior, recognize what you've already accomplished, the work you've already done. You bring a certain awareness and understanding to this journey. At the same time, it is important to be willing to be a beginner. Acknowledge that perhaps there are things you have to learn that will be completely new concepts to you, or at least new ways of looking at those concepts. Even if you read along and say, "Oh yes, I've heard all of this before," take the risk to put your attitude aside, let down your guard, and become a fresh and open mind, a sponge ready to absorb the gift and magic of your soul-mission journey.

Living this journey demands a great deal of patience, especially when the life you have been living, the lenses through which you have looked at the world, and the roles you have chosen to play are not in alignment with your soul mission. It takes time, energy, focused concentration, commitment, and patience to master a new way of living, even if it is the path of your soul. We are creatures of habit, and any habit takes time to change.

As you move through your circular process, it is all right to lack the answer to every question, or the knowledge of what your next step should be. This "not knowing" can be the beginning of a fuller opening to Spirit if you are willing to surrender to that divine guidance. Restating a memorized fact is not the same as really knowing it, deep in your being. You have to live the journey, open to Spirit, and the answers to all questions will be revealed in their own time.

When you work intuitively, you pass through many levels of conscious awareness at once. At first, you may feel that it is all you can do just to be aware of your immediate circumstance, what is apparent to the outer senses. However, the more you develop your awareness of multiple levels of consciousness, the more your inner senses come alive. Whatever you may be experiencing in your life at any given time is mirrored at deep, personal levels as well as at expansive, universal levels. As a shift occurs on one level of awareness, all other levels are affected.

Finally, soul mission involves developing and refining your craft of living—becoming a master craftsperson at life. We don't develop our skill or artisanship at anything by simply reading about it, listening to instructions, or watching someone else do it. We become master craftspeople by diving in with our hands and feet and learning the "feel" of the skill, and living through our mistakes. This is the journey of soul mission—becoming masters at living our essence and truth. Mastery then continues to unfold through all of our days. The master of life is one who, even after perfecting skills, continues to refine, explore, experiment, and learn.

When you reach mastery, you are living your essence, living out your personal truth. We can become caught in thinking that developing craft means being the best we can be in our profession or in a particular skill. But we are talking about a much bigger picture here. We are talking about the integration of all aspects of your life, the magical dance that occurs when you experience complete harmony within Self. It is a journey of discovering your legacy, and then perfecting your craft of living in order to most effectively leave that mark. Love and intuition are Spirit's gifts to you. Listening to your soul and Spirit, and being the vehicle for the flow of Love through your life is your gift to the world.

Already there are many thoughts and ideas taking hold in your mind. Let them play in all of your senses—inner and outer—and you will be amazed at the shifts that occur. Transformation is a constant dance between taking in new ideas and integrating them into your being. So step up to the music! The dance has begun!

Activity: Chapter Reflection

Before you read on, take a few moments to reflect on the concepts discussed in this first chapter and write about them in your journal. What in particular spoke to you or was important for you to hear? What in particular did you learn about yourself, your journey, and your inner spiritual warrior? Think of someone with whom you can have a conversation about your insights. Talking about it will help solidify your ideas, thoughts, and discoveries, and perhaps bring new thoughts for your pondering.

Choosing Freedom:

Claiming Your Life

 WHEN WE BEGIN the soul-mission quest, I like to explore four important words. They tend to be trigger words, in that they often provoke powerful reactions. You may be very comfortable with these words. However, you may also find that at least one of them brings up emotional discomfort or personal issues. The way you relate to them will tell you a lot about where you are as you begin your soul mission expedition. The four words are:

Freedom

Success

Power

Love

Before reading further, take time to complete the following exercise. What you learn may surprise you.

Activity: Cluster Writing

You will need at least 10 sheets of paper and a pen for this exercise. You will not want to have to stop in the middle to go search for paper, so be sure you have plenty from the start.

In the center of a blank piece of paper, write the word "freedom" in large letters and draw a circle around it. Then, as if free associating, write on this page every word that comes into your mind. Just cover the page with words. When you come to a stopping point and you seem to have no more words for "freedom," take a clean sheet and write in the center the last word that you wrote on the first page. Draw a circle around it, and continue free-associating with that word, writing every word that comes to mind. Continue this process, starting as many new pages as necessary, until you begin to feel that you are coming up to a personal issue or new revelation. At that point, go to yet another fresh page and write, in paragraph form, anything that is coming to you.

When you have completed this entire process with "freedom," then, one at a time, go through this writing exercise with "success," then with "power," and finally with "love."

Freedom, success, power, and love are very important in your journey toward your soul mission. The soul seeks freedom in order to explore fully itself and its growth. But freedom can take many forms. What does it mean to you? Where in your life do you feel that you need to experience more freedom? Is freedom something you believe you are allowed to or can have? Freedom from what?

What does success mean to you? To some it means making hundreds of thousands or millions of dollars a year. To others it means touching just one other person's life in a meaningful way. Success is whatever brings you happiness and fulfillment. What are your personal standards for success? How do you feel about success? Do you feel you deserve it?

Are you supported in your quest for it? Do you have a plan for how to achieve it? When you think of success, do you think of it only in terms of career, or do you look for success in every area of your life? Do you feel that success is possible for you?

Power is a major challenge and issue for many people. Remember Dr. King's statement, quoted in the Introduction (p. 4), about the importance of balancing power with love? Our journey includes transcending the cultural perception of these two concepts as separate so that we see them as one. When we open completely to the flow of Love, the creating and sustaining force of the universe, and harness and focus it for our human creation, we are standing in our ultimate power. There is no separation. What we are talking about is the metamorphosis of ego power to soul power. For ego and soul are simply vibrations on a continuum of energy that is our essence. Ego is the lower, less-refined vibration that is limited in its perception. It can only see a "close-up view" of any situation. Soul, on the other hand, is a very high, super-refined vibration that offers a "big-picture view," a very broad and clear perspective on all aspects of life. We will go into this concept of ego and soul more fully in chapter 5, so if you aren't quite grasping it now, don't worry. It will become clearer as we go along.

As we are willing to expand beyond the limited view that separates love and power, we undergo this dynamic metamorphosis from self to Self. We then can blossom into the limitless Power of the liberated soul. That Power is Love.

Where are you with the concept of power? Do you embrace your personal power? Are you afraid of stepping into it? Do you even recognize who you are as a powerful person? Do you recognize the potential of who you could be if you were willing to undergo this dynamic metamorphosis from self to Self?

By now, things may be stirred up not only in your thoughts, but also in your body. Throughout this book, we will talk a lot about the body, the human energy system, and their roles in our journey toward soul mission. But for now, just feel your body's reactions to the exercise you have just completed. Do you have particular physical sensations anywhere in your body in response to this work? Do you feel particular emotional responses such as excitement, anxiety, resistance? Do you feel them in specific parts of your body? There is no right or wrong response. What is important is that you become aware of your feelings and emotions, both physical and mental.

The fact that you have chosen to read this book is a clear indication that the spiritual warrior in you is ready to move, ready to step boldly into full-spectrum living. The rest of you, however, may have some resistance or hesitation. It is time now to bring all the parts of you to the table, the parts of you that are primed and ready to go, as well as those that will find a hundred reasons why retreat is in order. Let the warrior in you prevail, and hear this powerful teaching from Spirit.

———————— ✳ ————————

Greetings. Let us get right to the work at hand as you continue to experience many shifts in your conscious awareness. You must understand that freedom is a choice and a state of being, not a circumstance. If you wish to be free in your life, you must first choose freedom. If you continue taking actions that you think will set you free but have not yet chosen freedom, you will never be free. The action or step in and of itself may bring a temporary sense of freedom, but in the end, you will not yet be free. Intention is the key; declaring your intention and claiming your life; declaring your beingness; choosing and committing to sit in the flow of Love in every moment.

Enlightened living is living in the constant flow of Love in every moment of your existence. For most people, this way of living does not just happen all by itself. You must choose it. Otherwise, you will move in and out of that divine flow. Choose to be in the flow of Love. From within that flow you can easily choose freedom. There are no obstacles. Although your circumstance may appear to be the obstacle to freedom, this is not so. The real obstacle lies within your belief. Choose freedom. Choose Love. Choose stillness, centeredness, and peace. Then all filters or lenses of perception fall away and all becomes clear. The choices you need to make in your physical or outer circumstance become clear and are easier. Until you choose and declare your freedom to yourself, you will not know freedom in your life.

There are two fundamental orientations to life—human and divine. The human orientation will have you believe that actions will create results. The divine orientation will show you that thoughts create results. Your thoughts and choices in thought create life. Choice, however, is the most challenging step. Working through the mental limitations of the human orientation can only bring limited results. Step into a divine orientation for living and choose your life circumstances. When your thought is clear, focused, committed, and aligned with soul, life circumstances manifest as you desire.

Here we move into the relationship of Love and power. When you stand in the flow of Love and choose freedom, you are in your ultimate power. Just as Love is a state of being, so is power. Standing in Love, you stand in power. Embracing both your power and your Love, a synergy is created that is extremely dynamic. And then anything you desire to create is only a matter of declaring it, and calling it into being.

Making choices is the first step in paradigm shifting. You have the option of letting your paradigms shift over time in a passive way, allowing years of life experience to create your paradigms, or you can choose the paradigms you wish to live with now. This accelerates the journey, and moves you into the position of active cocreation of your life with Spirit.

Choose your belief systems rather than let them choose you. This will first be a mental process. Once you have made the decision mentally, you have begun the process of paradigm shift. The process continues as you make that decision in every cell of your being. Your cellular mind is the ultimate mind. Here is where the paradigms really exist. They begin as mental thoughts, but then make the transition to becoming your core beliefs—cellular belief. Making the choice is the first step. You can choose your paradigms. Then, every day you choose those paradigms again, and they evolve in your beingness, evolve in your cells, until your energy system vibrates to a new set of beliefs. Vibration is the key. Your brain may be vibrating to a new idea, but until your every cell is in vibrational alignment with this new thought, you have not made the paradigm shift. You are still held by an old belief system.

Enter into the flow of Love. Sit deep in your soul and know the power of your being. Allow your soul to guide you. Your soul is already in perfect harmony with the universe. Your soul is already living your divine purpose and being. But your soul may be buried under old *thoughts, habits, fears, and beliefs that are not serving your divine nature. Choose a divine orientation to life, and know the fullness of your being.*

✳ ────────────

Where in your life do your choices need to be different? Where are you stuck in old belief systems or paradigms that are keeping you from your full potential? Paradigm shifting, manifesting dreams, and sharing your gifts with the world all begin with making choices—choosing to live who you really are at your essence—choosing to experience life fully and freely. Spirit is clearly telling us, wherever you are stuck, choose freedom now!

At the beginning of this chapter, you did an exercise on the word "freedom." Look back to see what you wrote in that exercise. Everyone's concept of freedom is different. Does freedom mean to you more free time, release from the stress of a job, more money? In other words, was freedom an "outer" concept? Do you find yourself making deals with yourself, like, "If I get a new job, I'll be free," or "If I make more money, I'll be free," or "If I just get out of this relationship, I'll be free"? When Spirit speaks of freedom in the context of this teaching, it is freedom of the soul—freedom to be and create and soar in the ecstasy of a life that recognizes what it is here for and lives that dream.

George Kinder, financial planner and author of *The Seven Stages of Money Maturity*, wrote, "Freedom is like the soul. Without it we are nothing. Lived in its presence, life becomes transformed. . . . Our first obligation in this world is to discover the circumstances in which our souls flourish. This is the truest and deepest meaning of freedom—living under the conditions that make us most truly ourselves."

At whatever level you are starting to work with the concept of freedom, Spirit makes it clear that you don't find it by action alone. Instead of making deals, choose to be free inside now and then blossom in whatever job you choose. Choose to be free inside now and notice the great abundance that begins to flow in your life, monetarily and otherwise. Choose to be free inside now and watch your relationship move into its true place in your life. Then you will know whether you needed a shift in attitude or whether the relationship is to take another form.

When we feel something isn't right in our lives, few of us go inside to recognize what is happening within the many layers of Self, or look at our outside life as a reflection of our inner being. This is because we have been taught that if something isn't right, we should look outside and see what pieces can be rearranged, what part can be replaced, what person it can be passed on to in order to just "fix it." This kind of change is only superficial and temporary, because no inner shifts have occurred. In fact, we will tend to attract yet another circumstance that reflects our inner state. When we go inside and make the choice for freedom now, we have taken the first step toward claiming that freedom.

Inner examination is the first step, followed by inner choice. In order for any action to affect real and lasting change, it must be preceded by conscious choice. This may be the most important concept for you to internalize fully as you work through this book.

Why is choosing freedom now so important? It is a statement of intention. Declaring your intention to be free immediately begins to open your perspective, setting vibrations in motion to allow you to recognize and fulfill your unlimited potential. When you are clear about purpose and intention, the universe seems to come rushing to your side to support you in your soul-mission journey. Synchronicities happen all around you. You run into someone on the street who has the professional connection to help you. You get a phone call from an old friend and discover you are on similar quests. You keep running across information you need without having to look for it. Your creative energies are racing and new ideas and thoughts are flowing. Everything seems to be happening very fast, yet it is completely manageable at the same time. You begin to call your life into being. Now you are embracing your power—the power that is Love flowing freely through a liberated soul. As time goes on, your outer world may change entirely, but only because it now reflects your inner world.

Does this mean that everything will then be easy, that there will be no more challenges or conflicts in life? I'm afraid not. In fact, you may feel that you are coming up against even more challenges and conflicts. This is because you are so much more aware of the many facets of your life. Your response to the challenges, however, will be very different. You will be able to see the gift in the challenge and accept that gift. Once you have accepted the gift, the challenge becomes an opportunity for growth and expansion of Self, and you are able to meet the challenge with grace.

Choice is something we must do for ourselves. No one else can choose freedom for us, just as we cannot choose it for someone else. The same is true with Spirit. Spirit will not choose for us. We have been given the gift of free choice. Spirit will wait for us to exercise that right. We might wish that Spirit would just "take care of it," but then we would not be engaged in a cocreative process. Spirit is always ready to work with us in our life creation, to be involved in a cocreative project with us for the manifestation of soul mission. But Spirit will not create our lives for us. Instead, Spirit will help us to have whatever life we appear to want to create. Spirit is there to support and inspire us once we make the conscious choice to walk the freedom path, but we must first take whatever turns are necessary in order to set foot on that path.

Henry David Thoreau said, "If a man does not keep pace with his companions, perhaps it is because he hears a different drummer. Let him step to the music which he hears, however measured and far away." Hearing the inner drummer is an essential part of claiming our life. As the inner drummer comes into our conscious awareness, we begin to recognize our personal truth and break away from mass consciousness. That breaking away can take enormous courage. It is much easier to conform to the group mind rather than break out and create what we really want. Discipline, commitment, and courage are required.

Remember that this is a circular journey. You have a revelation in consciousness, and while it develops in your awareness, you are struck with another revelation. As you integrate the first revelation, you begin to develop the second one, so that there is a constant process of birth, development, integration, and living as you claim your life. It is not a one-shot deal. You don't just claim it and then you're done, like claiming your prize at the raffle, taking it home, and putting it on the shelf. Claiming your life is a daily, ongoing process. Choosing freedom is a daily, ongoing process. There will always be obstacles and challenges that could threaten to take control of your life. When you meet those challenges centered in your essence and truth, you find the courage, strength, discipline, and commitment to stay the course. This is the path of the warrior: to live personal truth, *no matter what.*

Making a difference in this world—and even in your own life and the lives of those around you—may very well mean rocking the boat. So, rock! From time to time I have a student in class who some might consider difficult. They challenge me, ask a lot of questions, or perhaps are not afraid to share any part of their journey into the shadow Self. These students are always gifts, because they "stir the pot"—they keep the rest of us thinking and questioning. They challenge the rest of us to go into the shadows of Self, and to bring every part of us to the Light. In their forthrightness, we are all challenged to come out of our own "truth" closets.

Choosing freedom and committing to living your soul mission can be a lonely journey if you are surrounded by people who are stuck in their lives, unwilling to look at another possibility. When others try to hold you back, it can be for any number of reasons. They may love you so much that they "want only the best for you." But their view of what is best may be limited. They cannot see the bigger picture. Or they may be afraid that you will change and they won't know you or you won't love them anymore. Assure them that this is a journey you have to take, and that the real you isn't changing at all. You are just growing in your understanding of who you are. That doesn't change your fundamental love for them. Others may try to get you to conform because they are threatened by your commitment to being all you can be. They see too clearly that they are stuck, but do not want anyone to challenge them to do anything about it. In their minds, it is easier to just let things be as they are. No one rocks the boat, life remains predictable, and they feel in control. This perception is all illusion, but a carefully guarded illusion!

Take the initiative to find people who have also chosen freedom and are claiming their lives as their own. Surround yourself with people who are not afraid to take the bold step that will move them on to the next level of awareness and freedom. Let those who would hold you back fall away from your life as they naturally will. At a time when you are just taking your first steps onto the freedom path, you need lots of support and encouragement. Otherwise, it is too easy to fall back into old patterns.

On Friday evenings in New York City, I lead a Spirit Circle. These are beautiful evenings of meditation guided by Spirit, followed by soul readings for all in attendance. One evening in the meditation, Spirit brought a teaching about living "true to form." We sometimes use that phrase in the context of someone acting true to form. It might be used in a positive context, saying that an athlete's outstanding performance was true to form, meaning that she was living up to her past record or reputation. Other times this phrase is used as a comment on someone's behavior or action that did not meet with approval. However, Spirit offered a much broader understanding of true to form. Spirit talked about our "form" being the human manifestation of an aspect of God. Put simply, our form is God. Being true to form means *being* the God that is within you.

Spirit is telling us that being true to form means honoring the God-self, speaking every word from the God-self, breathing every breath to feed the God-self, taking every step in service of the God-self. This is being true to the form of you—the divine being that you are.

Where in your life are you being true to form? And where are you being true to something else? When you are living true to form, you are living your greatest potential, and therefore offering the best that you can be to others. You are living your soul mission in its full spectrum. However, when you are not true to form, you deny the best of you to both yourself and others. The greatest form of service you can give to others and to the world is to live true to form.

In another Circle, Spirit talked about inhabiting all of our being—fully inhabiting all of Self—expanding and evolving into all of who we are. For just as we choose from the inside out, so must we also claim our life from the inside out. By routine, we rarely inhabit all of who we are—physically, mentally, emotionally, spiritually. An essential part of being true to form is learning to inhabit all of Self. Self with a capital S, the fullness of who we are, is the gift of the Creator. We come into this lifetime, every one of us, with the possibility and potential to know ourselves fully. And the fullness of Self includes and, in fact, is our divinity. In expanding into the whole Self, we grow into our divinity and humanness. To be fully human is to be divine. Our responsibility in good stewardship of the Creator's gift is to develop, explore, expand, and evolve into all that we are in order to fully know Self, and to fully experience Love as it makes itself known to the world through us.

Questions to Ponder: Inhabiting the Self

The intention of the following questions is not to imply judgment, but rather to help you observe your life objectively, and take stock of your relationship to various aspects of your being. Although each of these questions can be answered superficially by "yes" or "no," go deeper. Look for your full response.

Physical

Am I comfortable with every part of my body?

Can I sense all of my body? Do I have a full body awareness?

Is my body healthy and in balance?

Do I get proper exercise, nutrition, and rest so that my body stays fit?

Do I spend time with people who support me in this aspect of my life?

Mental

Do I work to continually expand into the vastness of my mind?

Do I continually learn and grow by questioning and exploring my ideas, beliefs, and paradigms?

Do I spend time with people who both challenge and support me to be all I can be, from a mental perspective?

Emotional

Do I allow myself my feelings? Do I give voice to those feelings?

Do I question and explore my feelings in order to live within a clear emotional perspective?

Do I spend time with people who support my emotional growth and exploration, and with whom I can share my emotional life?

Spiritual

Do I spend time daily in meditation/prayer/reflection?

Do I continually question and explore spiritual beliefs, seeking always to uncover my truths as distinguished from those I have been given?

Do I integrate the physical, mental, and emotional aspects of Self into my spiritual Self? Do I recognize that the spiritual Self is, in fact, the whole Self, and that all other aspects of me are simply aspects of my larger spiritual Self?

Do I spend time with people who support me in my chosen spiritual path, and with whom I can share my spiritual journey?

What have you learned about yourself in reflecting on these questions? Do you live true to form? Where do you need to make shifts in your life in order to fully inhabit all of you and live true to form?

Choosing freedom in this moment and claiming your life are the foundation for inhabiting all of Self and for living true to form. In the next chapter, we will talk about the creation process within our lives and the importance of clear intention. When your underlying intention in all of life is freedom and living true to your divine form, you can create a fulfilling and rewarding life that serves soul mission and brings you what you truly desire.

Activity: Chapter Reflection

Before you read on, take a few moments to reflect on choice and freedom as they relate to your life. What in particular in this chapter spoke to you or was important for you to hear? What did you learn about yourself and your journey? Think of someone with whom you can have a conversation about your insights. Talking about it will help solidify your ideas, thoughts, and discoveries, and perhaps bring new thoughts for your pondering.

CREATION BY INTENTION

 WE ARE CONSTANTLY creating every aspect of our lives every day. This can be a conscious or unconscious process, but just like the passage of time, creation continues with or without our intentional involvement. In this chapter, we will look at the process of creation and the importance of stating clear intention for what you wish to create.

Many people think of creation as the beginning of the universe or what an artist does. But we speak of creation here within a much larger context. Every thought, feeling, word, or action creates some kind of response. We can either choose to continue creating our lives as they are now, or to recreate them in another form. Through self-discovery and manifestation of soul mission, we constantly rebirth Self, peel away layers that mask true essence, and create our lives.

When we do not state our intention clearly, we allow our lives to be created for us by outside influences, such as friends, family, jobs, or society. We become just another ordinary person leading a very ordinary life. That may sound all right on the surface. But when you consider that each of us represents an aspect of the divine manifest in extraordinary human form, doesn't it seem as if we're selling ourselves short by moving through life without intention and conscious creation?

When we want to change any part of our lives and create something new, old patterns and habits must die. There may then be a period before we have manifested the new patterns and the new creation becomes firmly established. During this transition, life can seem like chaos. We may feel we have lost control, experience emotional upheaval, and do not know what is going to happen next. However, chaos can be the catalyst for great creativity, launching us to new vistas of the imagination.

It may make us very uncomfortable as it disrupts our habitual patterns of being, but it can also show us amazing new possibilities, ones that we might never have seen had we not allowed ourselves to let go of control. Chaos can be a vital part of the creation and transformation process. If we will allow the process to unfold, letting go of "how we've always done it," a new order will soon form, and a new level of development will be reached.

Your intention is critical in creating the life you want to live. Clear intention sets up patterns of energy that attract similar patterns in physical reality (we will discuss the Law of Attraction in chapter 5). Those energy patterns begin to draw to you all that you need in order to fulfill your intention. Everything will begin to fall into place, and you'll see results.

What is your intention as you begin this book? Do you want a career change, a new or improved relationship, to earn more money, to travel, to be more at peace with yourself? What prompts you to look at your paradigms? What is your yearning deep inside? Why are you bothering to do this very profound self-discovery and self-realization work? There must be a reason.

As you proceed through the work, your reason and intention will evolve. At times, they may shift every day, as you experience revelations at a fast pace. At other times, you may go for weeks or months with the same clear intention, steadily moving toward your vision.

Intention focuses your mission and propels you toward the manifestation of your vision. It is most powerful when it is guided by soul, not by ego. Then there is complete alignment of being, and the dance of life flows like a beautiful and graceful ballet. Without clear intention, everything else about the process lacks clarity, and the dance is awkward.

Your intentions are strong energy systems in and of themselves. They speak much louder than actions or words. Your intentions stay with those with whom you interact much longer than your physical presence. Therefore, keeping intentions pure with Love as their foundation is of utmost importance to the conscious spiritual manifestation journey.

What is your intention about the shape and size of the container that is your life? We aren't talking about height and weight. We are speaking of the container of Self that you offer up to the universe to fill. The universe will fill whatever container you present. There is no judgment here that a larger container is good and a small one bad. It is simply your choice about what size and shape container seems to fit your soul's mission. Some people recognize that their mission is to take care of one person for their whole life, while others feel that their mission is to hold political office or be an international performer. One might appear to be a small container while the other is a large one. But the size and shape of the container are not the only consideration. There is also the energy that pours through the container. It can take much more concentrated energy to take care of one individual's every need for many years than to be in front of thousands of people on a regular basis. The universe will fill whatever size container you offer, with the appropriate concentration of energy. Your job is to put forth the container, to offer yourself to be filled and let the divine mission unfold.

Creation involves change. Any fundamental change we wish to make in our lives must be preceded by a paradigm shift, and that happens from the inside out. Our society tells us that the road to success begins with setting goals, stirring motivation, and assessing abilities and performance. But there is a fundamental piece missing in this formula. That piece is *You*—the essence of you, your soul. Personal learning and growth are important keys to paradigm shifting and creation. Many people claim to be committed to growth and change in their lives, but follow the societal model of working on the outside only.

The journey toward true soul freedom and success begins with looking in the mirror for a close examination of Self. It begins by uncovering the truth of what really matters most to us in this world, and acknowledging that there are things that we really do care about, both for ourselves and for others. This realization immediately helps us move to the bigger-picture view of life, seeing ourselves as a part of a larger whole, and recognizing our oneness with all of creation. We begin to see a divine flow of movement in our lives and in the lives of those around us. We see the value of the human spirit and the interaction of Spirit in our lives. We become more inspired to take care of and honor our own individual needs, and to serve the needs of others with whom we share this Earth, both now and in the future. Stewardship of self, talent, and the gifts of Earth and Spirit are an essential part of this journey.

When we do the inside work, the outside begins to take care of itself.

We have embarked upon a remarkable inner journey. Creating lasting change and manifesting major life dreams require much more than setting goals, creating plans of action, and then following through. Creating lasting change requires transforming your processes of thinking and interacting with Self, Spirit, and others around you. Then you can set goals and take action.

A part of the journey of spiritual manifestation is the creation of a sacred space within which to live out the soul mission. Once again, intention is key; we must create that space consciously. However, it is important to understand that sacred space is a concept much more than a place. A place feels sacred because of what it invokes in you. If it is our intention, we can make every place that we occupy a sacred space simply by our intention to be there in the flow of Love and recognize the unfolding of divine soul mission.

Throughout the first part of this book, you are learning about how life works, who you are, and how you fit into the big picture. Chapter by chapter, and exercise by exercise, you gain insight into your soul's mission. Out of that mission will grow your life vision. This is an evolutionary process that begins wherever you are right now. Don't worry if you don't know what your soul mission or your life vision is. They will show themselves to you as you do your work. What is important at this point is that you set out on this soul mission journey with clear intention. With clear intention and commitment to the journey, your mission and vision will unfold.

What do you want to accomplish by taking this journey? Take time now before reading on to write your Declaration of Intention for what you want out of reading and working through this book, and make your commitment to the extraordinary journey that lies ahead.

Activity: Declaration of Intention

What you are about to write is for you. You may choose to share it with a friend or partner, or you may not. This is your personal declaration of how you intend to focus, what you intend to accomplish, and the shifts you intend to make in your journey through this book. Don't worry about how clearly you are able to state particular hopes and aspirations right now. This is a place to start, an exercise in beginning to clarify intention. Your intention, as well as your aspirations, will get clearer with each chapter.

After you have completed writing your Declaration of Intention, keep it in your journal to reflect on from time to time. As your intention evolves, do not alter it as you've written it here. Instead, rewrite your intention in its newly evolved form each time, so that you are able to look back and see the progression of your journey.

Congratulations! You have taken a very important step toward living your soul mission and manifesting your dreams. Simply by declaring your intention, you have set the manifestation process in motion. The rest of the book will weave powerful tools and techniques into your journey.

Activity: Chapter Reflection

Before you read on, take a few moments to write what you gleaned from this chapter on creation and intention. What in particular did you learn about yourself, your journey, and your use of intention? Think of someone with whom you can have a conversation about your insights. Talking about it will help solidify your ideas, thoughts, and discoveries, and perhaps bring new thoughts for your pondering.

Entering the Silence:

The Gift of Intuition

"Silence is golden." We have all heard that saying, but how many of us partake of the "gold" on a daily basis? How often do we make a point of removing ourselves from the noise of life, both inner and outer, and just sitting in the silence? The silence is golden in a multitude of ways. In this chapter, we will journey into the silence so that you might discover the gifts it holds for you.

During the process of creating my personal life vision, Spirit spoke these words to me:

❋

Inner space is ultimately what freedom is all about. It is about knowing that within you is room for every experience, every heart, every aspect of life. Inner space is the final frontier. Your society may tell you that the final frontier is outer space among the stars, but inner space is the real magical galaxy. The stars, solar systems, and planets that dwell within you are the new frontier to explore. There is a sun within your solar plexus. Go to that sun and see and experience the solar system that revolves around that sun. There are unknown yet inhabited regions within you. Go find them. Seek them out. Speak with the voices there. They will show you the way to God. And you will know your freedom. Freedom in your being is the true freedom. For even though every outer circumstance of your life may indicate that you are free, if you are not free to travel throughout all of your inner spaces, you are not free. Freedom means that there is no place within you that you have not traveled, no place within that fear keeps you from going.

Silence is the gateway to your inner space. Enter into the silence and travel the highways and air space of your soul. Explore the far reaches of your inner universe. When you can fly freely in your inner world, your outer world will become the perfect mirror of your inner freedom.

✳ ─────────

To introduce you to the silence and to your inner space, take a few moments to do this very brief breathing meditation.

Meditation: Breathing into the Silence

Close your eyes and focus all your attention on your breath passing in and out through your nostrils. As you focus on your breath, you will find your entire rhythm slowing down and becoming steady and peaceful. This may take a little time if you are very tense or stressed, but be patient. Just breathe. Smile as you breathe and you will notice your whole body relax. That's all there is to the exercise—just close your eyes, breathe, and focus all your attention on your breath. Your body and mind will respond automatically.

Throughout your day, take a few moments to do this exercise. Your breath can be your best friend for helping you enter the silence and find your quiet center. It will help you remain calm and focused all day long. You can do this anywhere—on the job, in between appointments, while working out, and while dropping off to sleep. Let your breath show you the way to your stillness and quiet.

Scientists have estimated that the average person has approximately 60,000 thoughts every day. For most of us, they are the same thoughts, played over and over again, day after day. We tend to get stuck in a pattern of inner chatter. Much of the time, however, we are not even aware that the inner chatter is going on. When we get very quiet, we start to become aware. The chatter can become maddening, not only because you realize that you have those thoughts playing over and over in your mind, but also because you can't seem to stop the playback. For this reason, many people choose to avoid getting quiet, to avoid the silence. Dealing with the outside world, no matter how challenging, seems less daunting to them than facing the inside one.

Entering the silence is another essential part of the soul-mission journey. We have talked about the importance of living in an expanded awareness. Entering the silence is the first step. If you discipline yourself to sit quietly and let go of your battle with the chatter, it begins to disappear. You begin to learn to enter the space between your thoughts. These spaces, short as they may be at first, are the passageways into the inner sanctum of your being.

Your inner sanctum is a place of stillness and peace. Whether or not you have ever found it, it's there. I call that place your Point of Stillness. It is deep within the heart of your being. It is peace, quiet, rest, essence, truth, soul—it is the real, unadorned, unprotected, unassuming you. At first, it can be a disarming place. You may feel vulnerable and exposed, because you are not used to opening to your essence, even in your relationship with yourself, much less with others. However, the more time you spend in your Point of Stillness, the more you experience a sense of peace and serenity that perhaps you've never known. You begin to recognize your oneness with all of creation. Paradigm shifts can happen simply by spending time in this deep center of your being.

We tend to think of ourselves as isolated beings, separate from one another, and especially from one another's experiences. But as you enter into the depths of your heart and soul, you begin to realize that we are all one. We all breathe the same air, drink the same water, and come from the same Source. We all experience joy, love, pain, and anguish. The outer circumstances of our lives may be different, but the inner feeling is the same.

It takes the deep quiet to begin putting you in touch with your connection to all of creation. Then you can begin to understand the great laws of the universe (chapter 5) and how they play out in your life. As you understand those laws and work with the energy system of your own body (chapter 6), you can work with Spirit in cocreative partnership. This partnership is available to all, but called into action by very few. As we move deeper into the journey, entering into the silence is the most important tool we have, the most valuable skill we can develop, the gateway to accelerated understanding. For in the silence we can hear the guidance of our soul and Spirit. Through the silence, we recognize the full spectrum of possibilities and find our wings for free flight.

Very few of us were taught to sit in the silence and enter into the Point of Stillness. In fact, probably no one ever even suggested that there was such a place. We may have been taught to "pray"—to ask for what we desire or for guidance—but few of us were actually taught to just sit in the silence, listen, and enter into a dialogue with Spirit or God.

The first question is inevitably, "How do I do that?" There is no one way. There are many methods and techniques. One is not particularly better than another. The right way is the way that works for you. You might count your breaths, repeat a mantra, enter into reflective silent prayer, take a silent walk by a river, or sit on a mountaintop communing with nature. Everyone must find his or her own way. If you do not have a reflective/meditative practice already, the exercises in this book will help you begin.

If you sit by the ocean or a large lake and watch the surface, sometimes the waters are calm, sometimes rough. However, that is only the surface. Deep down, the waters are very still and quiet. On the surface, there may be no hint of the calm deep below, but it is there. At the same time, in the depths there may be no hint of the troubled surface, yet the turmoil appears very real. In the deep waters of our souls, all is quiet and still, regardless of what is happening on the surface. On the surface, we may be overwhelmed with anxiety, stress, or agitation. However, deep inside there is a place of peace and stillness. This is your essence, your truth.

At first, the silence may seem overwhelming and terrifying. What we perceive to be the reality of our feelings and emotions might be so uncomfortable that we would rather return to the chatter. The chatter is what we know. It keeps us from the "difficult" stuff, and therefore feels safe. The silence, however, is unknown territory. We don't know what to expect. It's easier to return to the familiar. But if we are willing to endure the discomfort for a while and discipline ourselves to stay the course, the layers of feelings and emotions, hurts and pains, and the dis-ease within our being begin to drop away. We enter into the Love that is our core.

Entering the silence is healing. We are not talking about the kind of healing for which we go to the doctor. That is a cure. We speak of healing as entering into wholeness. Ram Dass, in his book, *Still Here*, draws the distinction very clearly: "While cures aim at returning our bodies to what they were in the past, healing uses what is present to move us more deeply to Soul Awareness, and, in some cases, physical 'improvement.'" In a 1994 lecture at an Omega Institute conference in New York City, author and teacher Stephen Levine defined healing as, "entering with intention and awareness that which you have avoided and run away from." If we want to get in touch with our soul mission and then live that mission, we have to be willing to get in touch with our soul! And for so many of us, soul has been put on the back burner for too long. We've been so busy keeping up with "life" that somehow our real soul yearnings couldn't come to the surface. From time to time, when we got glimpses of soul, we might have said, "I know I need to get there. I know there is more for me in this life. And if I can just get through . . ." In chapter 3 we talked about making deals with ourselves. If we really want to uncover soul mission, develop a vision for our life, and then manifest that vision, we have to stop making deals. We have to "enter with intention and awareness that which we have avoided and run away from." Whatever shadows lurk inside must be exposed to the light. Simply by walking in, by "entering with intention and awareness," things shift and the healing begins. We come to wholeness. We come to Self. We begin full-spectrum living.

When we can align our outer desires with the desires and purpose of the soul, the manifestation journey becomes easy. We move toward inner peace and harmony. When outer desires are not in alignment with soul purpose and desire, however, life seems like a constant struggle. Awareness is the key. As we develop in awareness, we gain a fuller perspective of Self. And awareness begins in the silence.

Meditation: Point of Stillness

Sit quietly with your eyes closed, back straight, feet flat on the floor or legs folded in a lotus position, and hands resting comfortably on your lap. Take a few deep breaths, allowing your body to relax, and then let your breath find its own natural, relaxed, easy rhythm. Begin paying attention to your breath as it passes through your nostrils. Bring all of your attention to that point of focus—breath passing through your nostrils. There is nothing else in your conscious awareness except your breath.

You may notice a great deal of chatter going on in your mind as you attempt to focus solely on your breath. It's okay. Just notice it. Then step by step, layer by layer, go beneath the chatter. Let your breath help you drop deeper in your consciousness. On the inhalation, feel as if the floor of your current layer of awareness opens, and on the exhalation feel yourself float down to the next deeper, quieter layer. Continue this process until you realize you have come to a place of absolute quiet and stillness. You may have to pass through many layers of outer chatter before you finally reach this place. It's all right. Don't worry about how long it takes. Just keep breathing and floating down to deeper and deeper layers.

As you are floating deeper, you may notice that you begin to feel calmer, more centered, and more grounded. You may feel your heart open. You are simply opening to you—your essence. You may become cognizant of several layers of awareness and consciousness at once. You may begin to understand on a whole new level the meaning of "still waters run deep"—that on the surface there is lots of chatter, but the deeper you go, the quieter it gets. Take your time to float for awhile, and then when you feel as though the meditation is complete for now, open your eyes.

The ancient philosopher and mathematician, Pythagoras, said, "Learn to be silent. Let your quiet mind listen and absorb." The 17th-century French philosopher and scientist Blaise Pascal said, "All man's miseries derive from not being able to sit quietly in a room alone." Throughout history, religious teachers, philosophers, scientists, and artists have spoken of the necessity of quiet and reflection. Although sudden realizations and revelations may occur to us during the course of our daily activities, it is in the silence that we develop our awareness to the point of being able to recognize those revelations when they come. Without highly developed awareness, many opportunities that life offers us for personal growth, development, and understanding pass us by. Through the silence, you can enter into your inner universe and, with time and discipline, expand your awareness to encompass the far reaches of existence. While the silence itself may bring many revelations in your understanding, when you take your outer world experiences into the silence, you find that your awareness fans open and you have far greater comprehension of your experience.

There are three basic forms of meditative/reflective practice: Eastern, Western, and New Age. Our point here is not to discuss the many methods and techniques within each, but to see how each form has something to offer us at different times. The Eastern form, commonly known as meditation, is reflective in nature. The object is to quiet the mind, have a one-pointed focus, remove all thought from conscious awareness, and reach absolute inner peace through stillness. The Point of Stillness Meditation falls into this category. The Western form, known commonly as prayer, has an agenda, dealing with specific things for which you seek guidance or want to discuss with God or Spirit. Many of the exercises/meditations in this book fall into this category. The third form, New Age, is more cosmic in nature. It can involve astral travel, journeying to past lives, guided fantasy, and exploring other realities.

A well-balanced meditative/reflective practice can include all three forms. There are times when we need to quiet the mind, find our center, and be in absolute silence and stillness. This brings balance and harmony to our entire being. It is amazing how things fall into place in our lives when we become centered within Self. There are other times when we have an agenda—a project we are working on, a concern, something in our lives that we don't understand. Then, the Western form can be very helpful. It is through a combination of these first two forms that we establish our mentor relationship with Spirit, and develop our intuitive gifts. Finally, there are times when we need to rest or to escape reality. New Age meditation can offer new perspectives on our lives by taking us to other realities through guided fantasy, or simply by letting Spirit take us on a journey.

Our work in this book will utilize all three forms at different times. In the fast pace of our 21st-century world, we need to be open to the meditation form that will best facilitate our journey in the moment. As you learn to sit in the silence, listen, and develop your relationship with Spirit, you will learn to move among the three forms easily, often integrating all three.

While developing a technique for meditation is important, don't get caught up in the "method" or wondering, "Am I doing it right?" Technique is the vehicle that takes you to the silence. By repeating the same process for entering meditation and getting to the silence daily, you develop your technique. Repetition is the key. As you do something repeatedly, the body and mind respond increasingly faster. Soon, simply your intention to meditate and your focused attention will take you very quickly to the silence, and you will know that your technique is in place.

Within your meditative/reflective practice, you discover your own personal sense of spirituality. Spirituality is one of those words we toss about a lot, but never really define. Spirituality is simply the exploration of your spirit that is at the same time human and divine. It doesn't matter whether you follow your own free-form sense of spirituality or an established religious tradition. Regardless of the form, the path is an inner one, not a predetermined outer structure. We all ultimately have to find our own way home to our hearts, which then takes us straight into the arms of Spirit. When you are committed to taking this journey with full awareness of Spirit and its interactive presence in your life, the path is easier to follow.

In addition to your hour-a-day of reflection, meditation, and journaling, choose a time in the next week when you can devote at least one full hour only to silence. Sit in a chair, under a tree, wherever you wish, but do not do any activity during this period. Take just one hour during the week for absolute silence with no journaling, no exercises. Just you and your soul. You may find that you want to build an hour of silence into your schedule on a regular basis. In time, you may find it very useful to go on silent retreat periodically. Having two or three days in the silence can be a very powerful and transformational experience.

The Buddhist tradition includes the practice of mindfulness. To be mindful is to have all of your attention and awareness focused on what you are doing at the moment. It is as simple as that. However, we live in a culture that rewards multitasking. The more tasks you can do at the same time, the more you are valued by "the system." Unfortunately, the more tasks you do at once, the more each one suffers, and the more your mental "circuits" go on overload. No task can be given your full attention and care.

The practice of mindfulness means doing only one thing at a time.

When you are eating a meal, you are just eating—not watching television, reading a book, or having a heated discussion. When you are sweeping the floor, you are sweeping the floor—not listening to music to keep you entertained or talking to your friend on the phone. Your linear self would say, "What a waste of time. I can do three tasks at once, get three times as much done, and have more time to play later." However, your soul would say, "At last, peace and stillness. She is finally centering herself in the beauty of this task."

Soul wants to give full attention to every detail of life. But it is not the kind of full attention that we usually think of—crossing every "t" and dotting every "i." To the soul, full attention means being fully present in the flow of Love through that activity. When eating your meal, you are nurturing and feeding your body, the house of your soul, and the physical manifestation of an aspect of God. When you are sweeping your floor, you are honoring your sacred dwelling place. Care and attention to the moment feeds the soul. When you slow down to do just one thing at a time, you become fully present there. You get to fully experience the moment. You enter into full-spectrum living. And you recognize how that activity or task is related to your soul mission. Every task, when done mindfully, feeds your soul mission, because you are living your life from a place of focus and intention.

Deepak Chopra says that the best way to prepare for the future is to be fully conscious in the present. Think about mindfulness and your life. How are you at multitasking? Are you willing to try single-tasking? Enter the silence every day, and feel the silence bless your very existence. And become mindful of every moment in that blessed existence.

The silence and a practice of mindfulness unlock the gates of intuition. Intuition, in its most highly developed form, is nothing less than the voice of God or Spirit within us. It is one of the greatest gifts we are given for this life. It is a talent that everyone has to some degree, and can be developed to guide and direct our lives in powerful and transformative ways. If we want to work in full partnership with Spirit for the cocreation of our lives, we must develop our intuitive gifts as fully as possible so that there can be open pathways of communication—communication not only between ourselves and Spirit, but also soul-to-soul communication with others.

Guidance from Spirit is around you all the time. There are signs or messages for you everywhere, from "coincidental" or "chance" meetings with someone on the street, to a topic that comes up in conversation, a newspaper or magazine article that comes across your desk, dialogue between two characters in a television show, or even billboards on the highway. When you are open to receive, Spirit will find many ways to get the message across.

If intuition is one of our greatest gifts, then developing awareness is one of our greatest responsibilities. Through awareness of Self, Spirit, and all that is around us, we open the door for direct communication and guidance from Spirit. Our task is to become aware of the energy of Spirit as it is moving through us and enter into full partnership for the realization of our soul mission. Awareness is the key. It is not something that you do. Awareness is a state of being. To be aware is to be open and participate in the magical dance going on all around and within us. To be aware is to know Self. Our understanding of Spirit and the universe evolves with our own self-evolution. The more we know ourselves, the more we know Spirit.

When we live our lives unconsciously, we begin to take on the attributes of whatever is around us, both positive and negative, being easily swayed by the forces and opinions of others. We move somewhat mindlessly through the motions of our lives, following the patterns and footsteps of parents, teachers, friends—anyone who might be there to show us the way. However, when we live mindfully, with full attention and awareness given to each and every moment in our life, we begin to glow in our own light and truth. Our intuitive gifts begin to appear and we learn to trust them. Intuition then becomes another very powerful tool for stepping into our own power and strength, and living our soul mission.

How do we develop awareness and intuition? First by paying attention. Open your awareness to everything around you and within you—everything you think, sense, feel, and experience. When you discover inner blocks, resistance, or issues that have not yet been resolved, invite the healing or resolution process to begin. It is all a part of self-discovery. And, as we have said, through coming to know Self, you come to know Spirit. As you work through your personal issues, you become a clearer channel through which Spirit can move. Then, as you hear your intuitive voice or sense its guidance and respond, you learn to trust that guidance and know that it is your truth.

You may have experienced being in a place that just "felt good"—you found that you wanted to spend time there because it made you feel peaceful, quiet, and at ease within yourself. Or you may have experienced very uncomfortable feelings in a place, and were anxious to get out of there. The same is true with people—with some people you have a very good rapport and are immediately comfortable, while with others you automatically put your guard up. This is your intuition speaking to you. Pay attention to what you feel in your environment.

This doesn't mean spending time only with people who agree with you or in places that keep you from having to grow or confront aspects of Self. A part of the journey of self-discovery is learning to discern what is challenging you to stretch and expand your thoughts and realm of experience, and what is actually stifling your growth and development. Choose to be in environments that support you being all you can be.

As we develop intuition, we often have experiences that make perfect sense to the creative and intuitive mind, but are very perplexing to the rational mind. The purely rational mind functions on only one level of awareness at once—the awareness level of the five outer senses. It can only accept and process what you can see, hear, touch, smell, and taste. When working in the intuitive mind, however, we function on many levels of conscious awareness at once, and therefore have access to a tremendous amount of information. Know your own experience. Trust it and don't be in such a hurry to find a rational explanation. As you recognize kindred spirits among your friends and acquaintances, cultivate those relationships so you have people with whom you can share your experiences.

As you develop your intuitive gifts, you will gain greater insight into life—both your personal experience, as well as life on a larger scale. At times, you may even experience profound revelations. Some people welcome these revelations and new insights, while others become afraid, not knowing what to do with the information or understanding they have just received. Intuitive understanding is a gift to all of us for the enrichment of our journey. When you gain new insight or experience great revelation, give yourself time to process it. Allow yourself to sit with it for awhile. Don't feel like you must be in a hurry to *do* anything with it. Give yourself time to just *be* with it. Your new understanding will continue to unfold, and through your patience and willingness to accept this new understanding, you will be shown your next step, and can integrate this understanding into your life.

The exercises of this book are all designed to tap into and exercise your intuitive gifts. You will find that your awareness develops and you open to deeper and deeper aspects of Self. If developing your intuitive gifts is something that you would like to explore beyond the exercises of this book, spend some time with my book *Intuitive Living: A Sacred Path*. You will find many tools there that will further enhance your soul-mission journey.

Activity: Chapter Reflection

Take a few moments to write your thoughts from this chapter on entering the silence. What in particular did you learn about yourself, your journey, and your relationship to the silence? As after the previous chapters, think of someone with whom you can have a conversation about what impressed you from your work in this chapter. Talking about it will help solidify your ideas, thoughts, and discoveries, and perhaps bring new thoughts for your pondering.

The Laws of the Universe   5

 EVERYTHING IN LIFE flows according to universal laws or principles. These laws, as they have been handed down to us, are known as the Hermetic Laws of the Universe. They are attributed to the ancient mystical (and perhaps mythical) Egyptian philosopher and teacher, Hermes Trismegistus. Religions and belief systems of the world have interpreted these laws in various ways to create the foundations of their beliefs. We don't necessarily have to know or understand these laws in order to live within them, but without a working knowledge of the laws we can never fully understand how we accomplished what we did, or why we failed in our attempts. We can facilitate success more effectively and efficiently when we understand these laws and how to apply them for conscious creation.

In this chapter, I introduce you to The Seven Laws of the Universe. Some of the laws will seem like common sense and easy to grasp, at least at the surface level. Others will be more complex. Don't be discouraged if all is not clear at first. Through our circular process, we will keep revisiting these laws throughout the book, and your understanding of how they influence daily life will grow.

The fundamental principle through which you can understand all of the laws is: Energy is. This simply means that the universe and everything in it is composed of energy. And, according to the Law of Vibration, which we will discuss later in this chapter, that energy is always vibrating or in motion. Therefore, everything is energy in motion. This book you hold in your hand is energy in motion, as well as the chair in which you sit, the house in which you live, the ground on which you walk, the food you eat, the sky you see, the air you breathe, even your body—everything is energy in motion at its fundamental level. Solid matter is energy vibrating at a very thick and slow pace, while the air is a very fine and fast vibration. Thoughts are also energy in motion. Actions are energy in motion. And habits are patterns of energy in motion.

We cannot create or destroy energy. It can only transform into something new. That means that all the energy that has ever been and will ever be exists in some form right now. Your wooden table was before that a tree and before that a seed and before that another tree. The air you breathe was in some other part of the world yesterday, and has been recycled since the Earth was formed. Your body was created by the fusion of a sperm and an egg, which were themselves the offspring of procreation and evolution since there was first life. Your habits are formed out of your thought patterns and your socialization, influenced by thought patterns that have shifted and transformed over the millennia.

What is important for you to understand about energy and your life journey is that you cannot create or destroy energy—you can only transform it. Therefore, if you wish to change your habit, you cannot destroy it. You can only transform it into another habit. If you wish to change your thought, you cannot destroy the old thought—you can only transform it into another thought.

Understanding these concepts on a mental or intellectual level is the first step toward their conscious integration into your life. However, in order to become skillful at using these laws in your conscious life-creation process, you must recognize how they are influencing your life now. Therefore, remember to take time with the "Questions to Ponder" that appear with each law. The questions take these laws directly into your daily life. It is through your considerations of the questions as much as through the discussion of the laws that you will come to understand them more fully.

UNIVERSAL LAW NUMBER 1— THE LAW OF MENTALISM: LIVING GOD

The Law of Mentalism states that the universe is mental—that everything that exists was first a thought before it manifested in the physical dimension. Out of thought comes creation. We will look at this aspect of the Law of Mentalism more fully in chapter 11 when we discuss the power of mind and thought.

At this point in our journey, however, I want to focus on the second aspect of this law, which states that everything exists within the mind of God, and the mind of God exists within everything. You could also say that everything exists within Love, and Love exists within everything. Indigenous cultures understand this pantheistic concept of God or Spirit being within everything. Therefore, they see all of creation as sacred. In our Western religious traditions, however, we have created separation in our consciousness, considering God to be an outside force that rules over us in a judging, omnipotent kind of way. The Law of Mentalism shows us a different perspective. As Wayne Dyer writes in *Wisdom of the Ages*, "God is everywhere. When you pray to God, you pray to a silent and powerful eternal presence that is a part of yourself. Commune with this presence without any idea of being separate."

This is the central idea within most mystical traditions. Although interpreted in various ways from tradition to tradition, the common thread is a desire for union or oneness with God or some great, universal principal. Quantum physics shows us a oneness among all creatures as it explains that originally we were all borne of the same creative burst of energy, we breathe the same air, exchange the same molecules, drink the same water, and exchange energy in the form of thoughts and interaction. Everything and everyone is a part of the whole. Again, the Law of Mentalism: Everything exists within the mind of God, and God exists within the mind of everything. It is only in the relatively modern (by civilization history standards) Western interpretations of this law that we have adopted a doctrine of separation—a belief that everything was created by God, but God remains separate from that creation.

John Donne's words in his *Devotions upon Emergent Occasions* reflect this unity consciousness:

> No man is an island, entire of itself; every man is a piece of the continent, a part of the main; if a clod be washed away by the sea, Europe is the less, as well as if a promontory were, as well as if a manor of thy friends or thine own were; any man's death diminishes me, because I am involved in mankind; and therefore never send to know for whom the bell tolls; it tolls for thee.

This truth shows itself in every aspect of our lives. Even though your foot may never touch your heart, if your heart is in trouble, your foot will suffer. If you get an infection in one organ of your body, your entire body can soon be affected because that organ is not able to function fully and support the body. Any aspect of your life that is out of balance soon affects all other aspects of your life in a negative way. The whole Self cannot thrive when any of its aspects are compromised. And so it is in our global community. When one suffers, all suffer on some level. There is no separation in the larger reality of life. Everything is one.

Understanding this concept of God in all and all in God brings great compassion, understanding, love, and acceptance to your conscious awareness. Living in unity consciousness, you recognize your similarities with others rather than your differences, and move toward a world peace consciousness. Living the Law of Mentalism involves seeing God or Spirit in everyone and everything, and suspending judgments of others. Living this law means letting go of divisive labels, and meeting others face-to-face, soul-to-soul, heart-to-heart. You will be amazed at how your paradigms shift just by committing to living the Law of Mentalism.

Mentalism also tells us that God is everywhere and everywhere is in God. Therefore, there is no place that God is not, and no place that is not God. This includes each of us. When we understand that concept and open to the flow of Love, we can step into our power as aspects of the divine creation. Then our every act is God acting and God being acted upon. Every word is God speaking and God being spoken to, every thought is God thinking and God being thought of. Again, true to form. The 1st-century Greek philosopher Epictetus said, "You are a distinct portion of the essence of God in yourself. Why, then, are you ignorant of your noble birth? Why do you not consider whence you came? Why do you not remember when you are eating, who you are who eat; and whom you feed: do you not know that it is the divine you feed; the divine you exercise? You carry a God about with you."

Many people struggle with the issue of deserving to have all they dream of. The Law of Mentalism as reflected in Epictetus' words clears up the issue immediately. If you are the human manifestation of an aspect of God, does not every part of God deserve the very best? We are not talking about entitlement or frivolous spending and extravagant living because "I deserve it." We are talking about allowing yourself the absolute highest quality of balanced, full, conscious, abundant life because you are here in service of the God within.

But there is yet another way to address the issue of deserving, and that is the universal life purpose. We all come into this lifetime with three principle assignments: to know who we are from a soul perspective; to discover and live our soul mission; to learn the lessons that are presented to us during the process of discovering who we are and living our soul mission.

Knowing who you are means exploring every aspect of your being— leaving no stone unturned. Through this exploration, you come not only to know Self, but you grow in your knowledge and understanding of God, since you are in God and God is in you.

To live your soul mission means that every aspect of your life is in harmony and alignment with that mission. Then every thought, word, and deed is a representation of your divine essence, and is a gift to the world. Through living your soul mission, you make your unique mark on the world, consciously creating a legacy for the generations to follow.

The third assignment, learning your lessons, means accepting the opportunity for learning and growth in each experience. Every interaction with the world around you offers a gift. Our assignment is to recognize the gift or lesson, receive and integrate it into our awareness, and further expand our sense of Self.

If we focus our lives around these three assignments, it is no longer a matter of deserving to have our dreams but rather our responsibility to manifest them. When you embrace these assignments, it becomes your responsibility to be all you can be in order to accomplish all you are here to do. You are no longer manifesting dreams for the pleasure and satisfaction of your ego, but rather fulfilling your soul mission in service to Love.

Questions to Ponder: The Law of Mentalism

How does God or Love live in me? Do I open to the flow of Love within me, or do I resist it?

What am I here in this life to do? What is my purpose? What would I like to give to the world?

Do I believe that I deserve unconditionally the full and complete manifestation of who I am?

Do I believe that I deserve the life that I will have once I have manifested all of who I am?

Listen to the voices of your current beliefs and thoughts. Then ask Spirit for guidance about what shifts are necessary in your thought and life in order to move to a mindset of deserving, and how to reach your true Self.

In order to help you understand the Law of Mentalism in your life, play with the following activity for a week or so and keep a record in your journal every day of what you experience in your thoughts and beliefs.

Activity: The Divine in Every Person

For one week, make a conscious practice of seeing the unfolding of an aspect of God (or Spirit or Love) in each person you meet, regardless of the encounter. Let go of your judgments about what is "normal" or appropriate, and allow each situation to stand on its own, offering its particular gift. You will probably have experiences in which the divine is fully expressed and felt, and others in which fear, anger, or some other reactionary feeling blocks the possibility of divine expression. They are all part of the daily human experience.

At the end of each day, reflect on your experiences and encounters and see what each has to teach you about the essence of divinity, and how divinity moves in your midst.

Because we are all aspects of God, no one, at their soul essence, is better than or less than another. We are all on equal footing as aspects of the divine. At a soul level, no one can have power over you, nor can you have power over anyone else. Soul does not know titles or social or economic status. Soul only knows meeting another soul, and honoring the journey taken together.

UNIVERSAL LAW NUMBER 2—THE LAW OF CORRESPONDENCE: INNER AND OUTER UNIVERSES

The Law of Correspondence states "As above, so below. As below, so above." Anything that exists on one level of reality or consciousness also exists or is reflected on all levels. As a very simple example, think about your home. Your home exists in the physical plane as a solid structure. When you are in it, it is a part of your immediate, seen reality. However, it also exists in your mind as a thought or image. On this mental plane, you might perceive your home differently than you do in its physical reality. You might remember a chair or a picture to be in one place, when actually it is in another. Both realities—the immediate physical and the mental—exist.

The house also exists in your emotional reality, which may offer yet another view. When everything is in harmony within your home, it feels to you like a peaceful place. But when there is discord among family members, home may feel like a challenging place. The emotional reality of the home changes, yet the physical reality, the structure itself, remains the same.

If you have lived in your home for a long time, you have many memories related to it. Each memory represents a different plane of reality, for each one holds a different perception or view of your home. Some will be happy and joyful, while others might be sad or painful. Again, each is its own level of reality. You may also have a future view of your home, as you make plans for improvements or renovations. Or you may have a vision of your home with a new partner or an expanded family. This is yet another level of reality—one that you are creating in your mind so that it can, in time, manifest in physical form. All of these levels of reality exist concurrently and within one another, but we are conditioned in our human awareness to perceive only one level at a time.

A greatly expanded view of "As above, so below; as below, so above," means that we each hold the entire universe within us—each one of us represents the universe in microcosm. The universe, in turn, represents each of us in macrocosm. Pythagoras said that we have an understanding of all the laws of the universe within us. In *In Search of the Miraculous*, P. D. Ouspensky quoted the spiritual teacher, Gurdjieff, as saying "The study of the world and the study of man will assist one another. In studying the world and its laws a man studies himself, and in studying himself he studies the world. In this sense every symbol teaches us something about ourselves."

Remember Spirit's teaching about entering the silence to explore your inner universe in chapter 4: "When you can fly freely in your inner world, your outer world will become the perfect mirror of your inner freedom." We can only experience as much freedom in the outer world as we experience in our inner selves.

In order to have an experience of the Law of Correspondence in its larger context, take some time for the following meditation exercise.

Meditation: The Inner Universe

Take a few moments to go to your Point of Stillness. Then imagine yourself high on a mountain, in an open meadow, on a crystal-clear night. The moon has not yet risen and there is no other light. You are alone with the brilliant night sky. There are billions of stars—you can even see the Milky Way clearly.

You have come prepared for stargazing tonight, so spread your blanket on the soft but firm ground and gaze out into the star-studded sky. Travel in your imagination out past the Milky Way to the far reaches of the universe and beyond. Explore it fully. You can travel from one part of the universe to another in an instant, just by your thought.

Now imagine that this vast, boundless universe also exists or is mirrored within you. Imagine that your body is hollow, and within that hollow space exists a vast universe of you that is a reflection of the outer universe. Imagine free, open space in every part of your body. If you find resistance in any part of your body, gently breathe into that area and open it to spaciousness and vastness. Take your time and open to a sense of spaciousness in your shoulders, in your neck, your arms, wrists, and hands. Feel the vast openness in your chest and upper back, your abdomen and lower back, your lower torso, and pelvic region. Open the space in your legs, knees, ankles, and feet. And finally, open into the spaciousness of your head. Experience the vastness of your mind.

Spend some time in your inner space and experience the freedom that is yours. Then, when you are ready, let the boundaries of your physical body vanish and your inner universe expand into a completely boundary-free realm. You can now begin to experience and know that your inner universe, just as the outer universe, contains all that is and all that ever will be.

You are all of creation in microcosm. And so is everyone and everything else. Here is the Law of Correspondence. Each person accesses different aspects of the inner universe, and that is a part of what makes each of us unique. By opening your conscious mind to the awareness of all of creation, you open yourself to the full potential of Self.

As you come back to outer conscious awareness, keep one part of your awareness focused on this expansive feeling, and know that this larger reality is also yours to live within.

In chapter 1 we talked about life lessons, those lessons that keep coming up throughout our lives. The Law of Correspondence gives more clarity to this concept. Because there are many layers to everything, each life lesson also has many layers. Think of a particular recurring lesson in your life as an example. The first time you experienced that lesson, let's say you were at Level I. Imagine that Level I had ten steps through which you had to pass before you could progress to Level II. However, when you reached Level II, you had to start at Step 1 again on this new level. Here is the circular nature of life lessons, and the Law of Correspondence. When you have passed through all ten steps of Level II, you will advance to Step 1 of Level III. Each time you may feel like you are starting over again with this lesson, yet if you open your awareness, you see that you have come to the lesson from a new level of consciousness. On each new level, you will learn about a different aspect of the lesson, and therefore, about yourself. So even though the linear self might say, "I've been here before," and may experience frustration, the circular self can say, "I've been here before and learned from the experience. This time around I can approach this lesson differently."

The design of our graded educational system also illustrates the "multilevel" concept of the Law of Correspondence. A child begins elementary school in the first grade and continues through the eighth grade. Then she graduates to high school, but must begin again as a freshman, grade one of this new level. After four years of high school, she graduates to college. However, as she enters college, she is once again a freshman, starting at the beginning, but on a completely new level of education. Upon graduating from college, she embarks on her professional path by taking an "entry level" position within her field. She "starts over" once again. And so it continues throughout her life. Each time she advances to another level of development, there are ways in which it seems that she is starting over.

The Law of Correspondence also offers the gift of perspective. In order to observe an object completely, we must look at it from all sides, from the top, turn it over to see the bottom, feel its texture, listen to it, perhaps even taste and smell it. The same is true with life. Each person has their own view of life, and even that view will change as they grow and gain life experience. In any situation or circumstance, we can choose to change our perspective at any time. We can choose to walk to another side, to step into another's shoes, or give ourselves some distance for a more objective view. The situation has remained the same, but our perspective on it has changed. As we develop greater awareness, we can shift quickly between many perspectives and see the whole picture at once. The opportunity within the Law of Correspondence is to develop our awareness so we can see the many possibilities.

I love Oriental rugs. When you look at a very good, hand-tied rug, at first you see a beautiful carpet of rich colors and unique design. However, if you choose to go to another level of observation, you will notice that as you stand at one end of the rug, you see the lighter, brighter shades of its colors. From the other end of the rug, you see the darker, warmer shades. This is part of the detailed craftsmanship of the rug. As you spread the rug on your floor, you can choose whether you want to be greeted by the lighter, brighter shades of the rug as you enter the room, or the darker, warmer side. The view of the rug and how you perceive its colors may be radically different from one end to the other.

Yet there is still another level of observation. If you walk very slowly around the perimeter of the rug, pausing to observe the rug at each step, you will notice that your perception of the colors and patterns in the rug change slightly with each step you take. The colors and design, of course, do not change, but your perception of them does. Each step offers you a new vantage point, a new perspective.

The Oriental rug offers a great metaphor for life, and for the Law of Correspondence. The colors and design are there in the rug all the time. However, you must constantly move from one position to another, one perspective to another, in order to see all the many shades of color and every detail of the design. Every possibility of life is there in every moment, but we must constantly move between layers of awareness and reality in order to recognize and access the possibilities.

In order to experience several layers of consciousness right now, take time for the following meditation.

Meditation: Exploring Many Layers of Reality

Choose a current issue or concern in your life in which you are having difficulty finding clarity or understanding. Then enter into meditation through the same process as when you go to your Point of Stillness (see p. 49). However, this time, within your first layer of awareness, pause and ask for guidance on your issue or concern. Expect to receive a response, but hold no expectation about what the response will be. Be open to any possibility, and reflect in the guidance you receive.

When you feel complete in that layer, allow the floor to open, and gently float down to the next deeper, quieter level. Ask for guidance again on the same issue. Again, expect to receive a response, but hold no expectation about what the response will be. You may receive a new perspective or access a higher level of wisdom at this layer. Take time to reflect on the guidance you receive.

Continue this process of floating down to deeper levels and asking for and receiving guidance until you feel complete. As you return to outer consciousness, maintain an awareness of each of your layers of guidance and how they were different.

You may want to repeat this exercise over the next few days or weeks in order to continue gaining clarity and understanding about your concern.

"As above, so below. As below, so above." When we fully understand that whatever we can imagine on the mental plane also exists in some form in the physical plane, a whole new world of creation is opened to us. Walt Disney said, "If you can dream it, you can achieve it." Whatever you can develop fully within your imagination, you can also create in physical reality if you remain focused and are willing to take the necessary steps. The Law of Correspondence helps us see that anything really is possible.

Metaphysical sciences such as astrology and numerology can also be explained through the Law of Correspondence. Similarly, this Law helps us grasp the concepts of "seen" and "unseen" worlds. Our inner universe, by its very nature, is unseen. The outer universe, however, contains elements of both the seen and the unseen. Just because we can't see it, feel it, touch it, taste it, or smell it, it does not mean that it doesn't exist. As the part of the iceberg that we see is only its tip, what we can experience with our five outer senses barely scratches the surface of all that exists in the greater sense of reality.

Think about the unseen forces in our lives, such as electricity, radio waves, and microwaves, that 150 years ago would have seemed pure fantasy. Today, not only have we accepted and incorporated the reality of these unseen energies into our daily lives and become more dependent on them, we have built whole technologies upon them and altered our daily lives accordingly. If we accept these unseen forces as coexisting with our physical reality, why not allow our perspective of reality to include the mystical forces of the universe? The Law of Correspondence helps us comprehend the existence of unseen reality.

There are an infinite number of planes of reality. We are constantly moving among some of them in our minds. In everyday life, our thoughts vacillate between past, present, and future. We fantasize about possibilities while standing in the present moment and remembering how it has been. The degree to which we have developed our awareness determines the depth and breadth of levels of reality through which we travel. In a narrow view of life, you will only be aware of a narrow spectrum of realities—perhaps the current physical plane, your conscious memory, and your future plans. You will be limited to the seen reality or what the rational mind can process. However, if you expand your view to also encompass the larger unseen spiritual/intuitive dimension that lies beyond outer conscious awareness, you open the door to vast new worlds. This is the boundless realm of soul. It is here that we experience full-spectrum living.

Ego is a part of the seen reality, and is most comfortable living in rational-mind consciousness. Western culture encourages living by ego-perception, which is limited in experience by what the outer senses can grasp and comprehend. Soul, on the other hand, is a part of the unseen reality—that vast, timeless and boundless dimension that is so illusive to the rational mind. It is only by stepping into the all-inclusive intuitive mind of Soul that we begin to experience the unseen reality. It may come at first as a fleeting moment of clarity, understanding, or perception of another possibility. We've all had these "Aha!" moments when we've suddenly experienced a flash of insight. We have broken out of the box of rational thought, and experienced, if only for an instant, the powerful presence of the intuitive mind.

Many people speak of having "mystical experiences" at least once in their lives—experiences that were very real and tangible to them in the moment, yet could not be explained by the rational mind. In my Intuitive Living classes, I suggest to the students from the beginning that they will have experiences that they cannot rationally explain, and I ask that they refrain from trying. It is important to allow each level of reality to exist by its own rules. We cannot define or explain things from the unseen world by the rules of the seen world. Accepting the unseen world as simply another level of reality that functions interdependently with the seen world is an important part of the journey of soul mission, self-realization, and full-spectrum living.

Ideas and thoughts are part of the unseen reality. It is here that creation and manifestation begin. Everything that exists in physical form was initially a thought in the unseen world, whether it was a plan for putting a man on the moon or a vision of how you want to redecorate your living room. Here, again, is the Law of Mentalism—that everything begins as a mental concept. Creation is a process of taking an idea from the unseen reality into the seen, from the spiritual realm into the physical realm. Through the Law of Correspondence, we understand that the idea will progress through various stages of development on its way to physical-plane manifestation. Just because it hasn't reached physical form doesn't mean that it isn't real. The more the idea is fed and nurtured in the imagination, the more powerful it becomes. As you share it with others and they support you, the idea continues to evolve because it is now vibrating in others' conscious thoughts as well as yours. The energy keeps building, and the idea finally begins to take physical form.

The Law of Mentalism tells us that we are human manifestations of the divine. It tells us that all is one, in that everything exists within the mind of Spirit, and Spirit exists within the mind of everything. The Law of Correspondence tells us that everything exists at every level of reality. Therefore, the person you wish to become already exists within you. Personal transformation means moving to a greater understanding of our divine selves—learning to move back and forth between the physical and spiritual realms, between an ego perspective and soul perspective, and, ultimately, to see all perspectives at the same time. These are the most complex of all the Laws, and very important to grasp as the foundation upon which all of creation exists. The more we grow in understanding of these first two laws, and integrate that understanding into our daily lives, the more we enter into full-spectrum living.

Questions to Ponder: The Law of Correspondence

What are the recurring lessons in my life?

Am I patient with myself as I work through them?

How is my experience changing each time the lesson comes up?

Am I gaining new perspective and insight each time, or am I stuck?

Where in my life could I benefit from different perspectives?

How can I make a shift to view the situation differently?

Am I able to step back and see the "big picture?"

What is my comfort level with both the seen and unseen worlds?

Can I accept the unseen world as being just as "real" as the seen world?

Soul and Ego

Western traditions teach that ego and soul are separate. Western religion might call ego "the secular self" and soul "the sacred self," seeing ego only as self-serving and therefore "bad," while soul is "good." The Law of Correspondence, however, helps us to see that ego and soul are actually one. They are simply different aspects of you, opposite ends of a spectrum. If we look at the bigger picture to see the many layers of reality at once, we see that ego and soul, as well as the Higher Self, all exist within the same large framework.

Higher Self—the aspect of your being that is pure spirit. The Higher Self creates soul and ego so that it might experience itself in physical form, and learn the lessons required for its growth and development.

Soul—the spiritual component of the Higher Self incarnated in a physical body

Ego—the physical component of the Higher Self incarnated in a physical body

Let's step aside for just a moment to define some terms. First is "Higher Self," the aspect of your being that is pure Spirit. When you are born into physical life, the Higher Self remains in Spirit. Within Higher Self exists all of your being. It creates soul and ego so that it might experience itself in physical form and learn the lessons required for its growth and development. "Soul" is the spiritual component of the Higher Self incarnated in a physical body, and is at one end of the spectrum. "Ego" is the physical component of the Higher Self for that particular lifetime, and is at the other end.

Through the Law of Correspondence, we understand that there are an infinite number of layers of reality, and that everything exists in some form on every layer. We have the ability to move freely between layers. Living in higher awareness simply means that we have learned to access many layers of reality at once. Soul is at a very high vibratory rate or level of consciousness, remaining very close to the highest spiritual essence of the individual, the Higher Self. Ego, on the other hand, is a much lower vibratory frequency, representing the material and physical realities of life. When we live in the limited consciousness of the seen reality, we are being guided by ego. When we are open to the boundless possibilities of the unseen reality, we live from the energy and guidance of soul. You might envision the ego-soul spectrum as looking like a giant cone laying on its side. Ego is at the narrow end of the cone, experiencing only a limited realm of possibilities, while soul occupies the larger end that opens out into infinite possibility.

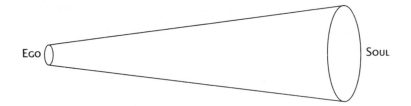

As another example, imagine that you are standing in a room in your house. From the ego's perspective, you can see everything in the room, the view out the window, and perhaps into a little bit of the next room through the open door. In other words, you can take in whatever can be perceived by the outer senses. This is a very limited view of the world. All you know is what you perceive in your limited outer sensory awareness. Soul perspective, on the other hand, is as if you were standing on the edge of the universe, peering into all that exists, all that has ever been, all that will ever be. You see not only yourself standing in the room, but also your entire life journey, inner and outer, that led you to this house and this moment. You can sense where your journey will take you from here, every detail of your life, and the reasons for everything that you have experienced. What an infinitely larger view of life!

Ego awareness holds on tightly—it can only see the options in its immediate, outer senses of reality. It lives within a consciousness based on survival and control, and only knows life from a moment-to-moment, physical limitation standpoint. However, it is also a strong grounding force, our connection to the physical dimension. It is essential for physical existence, yet limited in its perspective.

Soul awareness is constantly setting itself free. It lives within a thriving, free-flight consciousness, embracing what we think of as surrender, giving life over to the flow of Love. But soul doesn't consider it surrender at all, for soul is already in the flow of Love. Therefore, free flight seems perfectly natural to soul. There is nothing to surrender to, because soul already is freedom. It is ego that ultimately must surrender in order for soul and ego to fulfill their great partnership potential as different aspects of the whole.

Ego and soul exist as opposite ends of the physical-spiritual spectrum. Both are essential for full-spectrum living. They are of equal importance. Ego is not bad and soul good. They both have a purpose and a function. Either without the other is a trap.

Questions to Ponder: Soul and Ego

Do I live each day from the broad universal perspective and awareness of soul, or from the narrower perspective of ego?

Do I find that I have both the vision and tools with which to manifest my vision, or do I feel that I have one without the other—a great sense of life vision but no tools, or great tools but no vision?

Do I base my decisions only on the moment and what I might want for immediate gratification (ego approach), or do I try to see the larger ramifications and possibilities that will present themselves because of my decisions (soul approach)?

UNIVERSAL LAW NUMBER 3—THE LAW OF VIBRATION: EVERYTHING IN MOTION

The Law of Vibration states that everything in the universe is in a constant state of vibration. We spoke about this at the beginning of this chapter when we talked about the fundamental law that Energy is. One of the highest and most potent forms of energy is thought. Thought is electrical energy, vibrating at a very fast frequency. You may have heard it said that thoughts are things. Every thought creates a vibration, which travels out into the universe and begins to take a form.

Remember we said that energy can neither be created nor destroyed. Therefore, that thought was borne of another energy form, and will exist in some form or another forever. This fact means that we have tremendous responsibility for monitoring and disciplining our thoughts. Our thoughts form energy fields that travel from our mind into our world. A passing thought will receive little energy, but if the thought begins to develop and you give it attention, it begins to carry power. The more attention it is given, the more it begins to affect or shape our world and our relationship to it.

The Law of Attraction— "Birds of a Feather Flock Together"

This brings us to the Law of Attraction, one of the two subsidiary laws to the Law of Vibration. The Law of Attraction tells us that like attracts like—that we will draw to us energies similar to our own, as well as similar to whatever we focus on in our thoughts. Vibrations of similar frequencies attract one another, those of different frequencies repel one another. This is why we attract to us the things we focus on, think about, and give energy to. What you think about you will tend to bring about. When you think positive thoughts, you attract positive people and circumstances to you. When you think negative thoughts, you attract negative people and circumstances. Like attracts like. Whatever you seek is exactly what you will find. You set up the expectation in your mind, and your mind will respond. The energy goes out into the universe as a thought-form or command, and you will draw the object of your thought to you.

There is a field of energy vibration called the aura that surrounds all objects and human beings. Our body's vibration creates the aura, and our thoughts and how we process life experiences govern it. It is universal. Everyone has this energy field; it is not bestowed upon a special few.

The energy field vibrates at a faster rate around those individuals who function on high levels of conscious awareness. For those who are less aware and who move through life on "automatic pilot," the energy field vibrates at a slower rate. Again, like attracts like—we attract to us whatever we ourselves project.

The Law of Change—Change Is the Constant

The second subsidiary law, the Law of Change, tells us that since everything is energy, and energy is in a constant state of motion, everything is constantly changing. Ultimately, change is all there is. Nothing ever stays the same. This is a challenging concept for the person with limited awareness. We all know people whose security lies in everything staying the same. Change engenders fear, because it opens the door to the unknown. People will stay in bad situations just because it feels easier or safer to them than changing—they feel that at least they know what is going to happen, even if it is bad. If they make change, they enter a world outside of their realm of experience.

For those with highly-developed awareness and a broader sense of all that life can offer, riding the waves of change is much less threatening. They are more secure in themselves and have more trust that somehow the universe will take care of them. To them, change may even be exciting, because there is always something new—a new opportunity, a new challenge, a new gift from life.

Futurist Eric Hoffer said, "In times of change, the learners will inherit the earth, while the learned find themselves beautifully equipped to deal with a world that no longer exists." The learners are those who remain engaged in and excited about the ever-evolving journey of life. The learned, on the other hand, studied what they needed to know in school or learned it from parents and mentors, and would be much happier if life would stop evolving! They are much more comfortable with stability than with change. There are fewer challenges that way, but also fewer opportunities.

Questions to Ponder: The Law of Vibration

What kinds of people and experiences am I attracting into my life? Am I attracting what I desire?

How do I feel about change? Am I comfortable with riding the wave of change, or do I prefer for things to stay the same, creating as few waves as possible?

Are there shifts I need to make in my life around the Law of Vibration? If so, how can I make those shifts?

UNIVERSAL LAW NUMBER 4—THE LAW OF POLARITY: THE ANSWER IS IN THE QUESTION

It is perhaps easier to grasp the Law of Polarity by first looking at its subsidiary law, the Law of Relativity. The Law of Relativity states that nothing can exist alone. It can only exist in relationship to its opposite. Up and down, wrong and right, simple and difficult only exist in relationship to one another. We cannot recognize joy if we have never known sadness, courage if we have never known fear, light if we have never experienced darkness.

Furthermore, there are never only two possibilities. The Law of Polarity tells us that everything exists on a spectrum, and that there are an infinite number of points between the opposite ends. Darkness is a degree of less light, fear is a degree of less courage, sadness is a degree of less joy. Nothing is purely black or white. There are thousands of shades of gray in between. Therefore, the Law of Polarity shows us that when we have a decision to make in our lives, we must not be caught up thinking there are only two possibilities. There are always more options if we look deeply enough or change our perspective.

Since everything exists on a spectrum, opposites exist within each other. Therefore, within any situation exists all possibilities of how that situation could play itself out. This means that within every problem lies its solution, within every failure lies its success. We can only recognize success when we have experienced failure. It is through failures that we develop the skill and knowledge to bring us to success. Babe Ruth held the world record for the most home runs, but rarely is it mentioned that he also held the world record for the most strikeouts! We learn to make wise choices through the experience we gain by making poor choices. Ultimately, there is no such thing as a failure or a poor choice. There are just results. You just learned another way not to do it, realized another choice that will not take you there. In time, you will find the way that will take you there.

The Law of Polarity can be taken another step to realize that all the possibilities and wisdom we need for our lives is already inside us. Through the Law of Correspondence, we know that we just have to get to the level of consciousness where that wisdom is fully developed. To finally believe and trust that the journey begins inside, and all the maps and tools we need for the trip are within us, will be a major paradigm shift for much of Western society.

The Law of Polarity helps us further understand the ego-soul continuum that we discussed under the Law of Correspondence. The choice is never between soul or ego. The magical dance of life is a constant balance and flow on the ego-soul spectrum. Soul may be the captain of the ship, but there are times when soul must step aside to let ego do its job of carrying out the physical aspect of the mission. At other times, ego must step aside from its limited perspective to let soul be the guide.

In the same way that you explore Self on every level, explore your life situations on their many levels to see where there is room for growth or shift. See your life circumstances from every possible perspective. Then you will see solutions within problems, gifts within challenges, opportunities within conflicts. Great riches lie within every life experience. Our challenge is to recognize them and get the most out of them.

Where in my life am I stuck in a situation or a problem? Where does the solution or resolution lie within the situation?

Where do I get caught in thinking there are a limited number of possibilities in my life? How can I open my mind to the reality that there are an infinite number of possibilities?

UNIVERSAL LAW NUMBER 5—THE LAW OF RHYTHM: ALL OF LIFE IS A DANCE

The Law of Rhythm explains that all of life exists within an order, a flow, or a pattern. We see the Law of Rhythm in nature with the phases of the moon, the flow of the tides, the rising and setting sun, and the cycle of the seasons. Our bodies and emotions also have rhythms and flows. Everything in creation has its own rhythm and pattern. It is all a part of the order of the universe.

Science expresses this through the principle, "For every action there is an equal and opposite reaction." A pendulum illustrates this law as it moves in a steady rhythm from one pole to the other. However far it swings in one direction, it will swing in the opposite direction. The farther back you are able to pull the string on a bow and arrow, the farther forward the arrow will fly. The deeper you allow yourself to experience sadness, the more profound will be your experience of joy. Full-spectrum living means letting your inner pendulum swing wide and free, and in fact, encouraging that wide swing.

Keeping your emotions and life experiences in check can create a false sense of "being in control" of your life—a false sense of safety or predictability. But somewhere inside you the emotional pendulum is still swinging wide. When you do not allow yourself to feel and express your feelings, in time the pendulum will break through your carefully-crafted reality and force you to see the larger picture. Your soul seeks freedom, and will issue wake-up calls when it is suppressed. The wake-up calls may be subtle at first, such as a challenging conversation or a narrow escape from an accident. If we pay attention and set the pendulum free once again, allowing ourselves full expression, the soul is at peace. However, when we don't notice the subtle calls, they are more direct the next time around. Perhaps they come in the form of an illness or the loss of a job—something that gets your attention and calls you to pay attention to your soul's needs and desires. The soul will find a way to be heard. Life is much easier when we live in an open dialogue with soul, and allow ourselves to feel and experience life fully. When you limit the pendulum swing within your experience, life remains limited in its possibilities. Let life bring you all that it has to offer.

Catch Your Personal Jet Stream

The Law of Vibration states that everything is energy in motion. The Law of Rhythm carries that concept to its next step, stating that every person, place, and situation has its own energy, pulse, rhythm, and flow. You, therefore, have your unique energy, pulse, rhythm, and flow. When you really tune in to your energy system, you discover that you have different rhythms and flows at different levels of your conscious awareness. The outer levels of your awareness will tend to move at a rhythm and pulse similar to that of your outer environment. However, when you go to your Point of Stillness, you find your true soul rhythm and pulse. This rhythm and pulse of your soul is like your own personal "jet stream" or wave of energy that, when you remain tuned to it, can propel you through your life. This is your true, fundamental rhythm. When you tune in to your jet stream and ride that wave of energy, you come into complete alignment and harmony within self. All of you comes into balance. The more you are able to remain tuned in to your jet stream, the less you are affected by your outer environment. Regardless of the energies, rhythms, and pulses of others, you are able to maintain your steady, sure sense of self, as long as you ride your inner jet stream.

This aspect of the Law of Rhythm is important for cocreation and manifestation with Spirit. When you are riding your personal jet stream, you are riding the wave of Love that flows through you. You are sitting in your divine essence, giving life to yourself as a human manifestation of an aspect of God. Then you and Spirit are one. And that's when the magic happens! Synchronicity and miracles.

Riding your personal jet stream also allows you the greatest forms of cocreation with others. When riding your stream, sitting in your soul, you can more easily feel the soul rhythm and pulse of your cocreative partner, and let your rhythms begin to dance together. This doesn't even have to be such a conscious thing. The more you sit in your divine essence, the more you will instinctively recognize the divine essence in others, and the dance will begin.

Take time for this meditation to help you discover your personal jet stream.

Meditation: Personal Jet Stream

Go to your Point of Stillness, allowing yourself as much time as you need to go down through the many layers of awareness. Once you have reached the Point of Stillness, tune in, almost as you would a radio dial, to your inner pulse and rhythm. It may be very subtle at first, feeling like a heartbeat or a hum. Don't be in a hurry. Just relax into it. If you don't tune in to it right away, don't worry. Each day when you go to your Point of Stillness, listen and feel. Let go of preconceived notions of how you should experience your jet stream, and let it show itself to you.

When you do experience it, again allow yourself the time to sit in it—to ride it for awhile. Give yourself time to get used to this newly discovered feeling. It will feel great! In fact, you may not want to leave your meditation! And you don't have to. As you get accustomed to this feeling, you can bring it back out into your daily activity. Be aware of your personal jet stream and ride it in every moment. Make riding your jet stream simply the way you live your life.

The Law of Vibration taught us that everything is always changing. The Law of Rhythm goes on to say that everything is always either growing and expanding or dying and withering away. Therefore, any part of your life that is not growing and expanding is dying and withering away. There is no such thing as standing absolutely still. There is no such thing as no change.

Questions to Ponder: The Law of Rhythm

How do I experience the Law of Rhythm in my life? What are the recurring cycles, both physically and emotionally?

Do I allow myself full-spectrum living by letting the pendulum swing wide and free, or do I keep my emotions and life experience held in check? Are there shifts I need to make?

What in my life is growing and expanding? What is dying and withering away? How are they related? Are these patterns in harmony with the life I wish to create?

UNIVERSAL LAW NUMBER 6—THE LAW OF CAUSE AND EFFECT: "AS YOU SOW, SO SHALL YOU REAP"

This is a law with which most of us are already familiar. The Law of Cause and Effect states that every cause has a resulting effect, and every effect becomes the cause of another effect. Therefore, as they say, "There is nothing new under the sun." Nothing starts a new chain of events. The universe is a perpetual cycle.

There are many ways of expressing this law: "What you sow, so shall you reap," "It must be karma," "What goes around, comes around," "As you give, so shall you receive." What is important for us on our journey together is to examine the effects in our lives and what the causes are. We must become consciously aware of all of our choices, because they will all become causes of results down the road. If our thoughts create our lives, how do we need to change our thoughts (cause) to get a different effect? And what outside forces do we allow to cause effects in our lives?

Questions to Ponder: The Law of Cause and Effect

How is the Law of Cause and Effect working in my life? Am I setting up causes in order to get the effects I desire, or am I sabotaging myself by choosing causes that can't really yield the supposed desired effects?

How am I allowing my life to be the effect of outside causes?

Where do I need to take back my life so that I am proactively involved in cause and effect, creating a chain of cause-effect-cause-effect that serves me?

Universal Law Number 7—The Law of Gender: Yin/Yang and Everything in Its Own Time

The last of the Hermetic Laws is the Law of Gender, which has two parts. The first part states that within everything there is yin and yang, feminine and masculine energies. Both are necessary for full manifestation to occur. We speak here not just of the physical attributes of masculine and feminine, but of the ways those energies express themselves in life. There must be a balance of strong assertive action (masculine) with reflection, contemplation, and gentle flow (feminine) in any creative process.

The second part of the Law of Gender states that everything comes in its own time, that there is a natural gestation period for all things. We have discussed that when you imagine something, it immediately exists on some level of reality. Therefore, if we remain focused on the vision and take the appropriate action steps necessary to bring it into the physical reality, it is only a matter of time until the vision manifests.

With time and many successful manifestations, we reach a place of faith and trust that it will happen in its own time. With faith and trust, we are able to let go of the sense of urgency with a manifestation project. There is no sense of hurry. Hurry, on some deeper level, is a manifestation of fear that it won't happen, so we try to hurry it along to insure that it will. When you live the Law of Mentalism and know that you are in God and God is in you, you trust that all is in divine order. With the proper balance of masculine and feminine energies, and allowing the necessary gestation period, manifestation will occur.

Questions to Ponder: The Law of Gender

In my life, do I have a balance between strong, assertive action, and reflection, contemplation, and gentle flow?

Do I have faith and trust that my vision will manifest, or do I try to manipulate results quickly out of fear that it will never happen? If I do not trust that it will happen, how can I change my attitude and grow into faith and trust?

The Laws of the Universe form a solid foundation upon which to build our lives. They work together in a synergy that can bring extraordinary results. Our task is to become masters at understanding and applying these laws, utilizing them for manifesting a life that we desire and that is in harmony with our soul mission. Once we have done that, anything is possible. Since everything in the universe is connected through energy vibration, the vibration of our soul mission will begin to unfold, bringing all the pieces together at just the right time, in the right place, with the right people. A synergy is created among all of the pieces, and magic and miracles happen. It seems that everything just falls into place. The universe has brought us everything we need.

There is a tremendous amount of information to absorb in this chapter. Take your time to read portions several times, digest the information, and make it a part of you. As at the close of previous chapters, take time to write before you move on.

Activity: Chapter Reflection

Reflect on what you have learned in this chapter about the Laws of the Universe. Write about each law in your own words so that you begin to have a personal understanding of each law. Think of someone with whom you can have a conversation about the Universal Laws and how they influence your life. Talking about them will help solidify your ideas, thoughts, and discoveries, and perhaps bring new thoughts for your pondering.

The Laws of the Universe

Law	Essence	Principle
The Law of Mentalism	Living God	Everything exists within the mind of God or Spirit, and the mind of God or Spirit exists within everything.
The Law of Correspondence	Inner and outer universes	As above, so below. As below, so above.
The Law of Vibration	Everything in motion	Everything in the universe is in a constant state of vibration.
The Law of Attraction	"Birds of a feather flock together"	Vibrations of similar frequencies attract one another.
The Law of Change	Change is the constant	Everything in the universe is in a constant state of change.
The Law of Polarity	The answer is in the question	Everything exists on a spectrum and there is an infinite number of points or possibilities between the opposite ends of the spectrum. Within any situation lies all its possibilities. The problem can't exist without its solution also being present.
The Law of Rhythm	All of life is a dance	All of life exists within an order, a flow, or a pattern.
The Law of Cause and Effect	"As you sow, so shall you reap."	Every cause has a resulting effect; every effect becomes the cause of another effect.
The Law of Gender	Yin/Yang and Everything in its own time	Within everything exists both masculine and feminine essence. Everything comes in its own time and has its own natural gestation period.

THE HUMAN ENERGY SYSTEM:

CHAKRAS

6

IN OUR WESTERN TRADITION, we tend to think of the brain as the mind. However, Eastern traditions help us understand that the mind actually exists as a vibrating field of energy that flows around the body and through every cell. The brain is simply the computer that keeps the body functioning. The brain is the command center, but the energy field and the cells of the body are where the real action is, and therefore, where memory and wisdom are stored.

The human energy system is governed by seven energy centers in the body known as "chakras." *Chakra* is a Sanskrit word meaning "wheel of light." It is important to note, however, that these energy centers are not just a part of one particular belief system. If you were to study the mystical foundations of the world's religions, you would find that these energy centers were known to mystics of all traditions. In her book, *The Interior Castle*, St. Teresa of Avila, a 16th-century Spanish Christian mystic, referred to them as the seven inner mansions of the spiritual journey. In the ancient Jewish mystical tradition of the Kabbalah, we find these energies in the Tree of Life. In the African religion, Yoruba, they are known as the Seven African Powers. Indigenous cultures all over the world refer to these energy centers in various ways in their traditions. The chakra energy system is an ancient tool that transcends any particular belief system. It is the way the energy of the universe flows through each of us.

This chapter is an overview of the chakra system and the spiritual/emotional attributes of each chakra. It will help you to begin using the chakras as another tool for understanding and accessing inner wisdom as you take your soul mission journey. The goal here is not to lead you through in-depth chakra exploration—for that, I would refer you to *Intuitive Living: A Sacred Path*, where you will find extensive descriptions, explanations, and experiential exercises for each chakra. For our purpose, we are using the chakras as tools for understanding aspects of your being that are serving your soul mission, as well as those that are blocking the full manifestation of you. We will look for the paradigms that have settled in each of your chakras, recognize where shifts are needed, and then facilitate those shifts. Then as we proceed through the book and refer to particular chakra energies and issues, you will have an understanding of these concepts.

All feelings, emotions, and thoughts are registered immediately in the body on some level. The greater the flow of energy through the chakra system, the higher your level of awareness, and, therefore, the more conscious you are of your feelings, emotions, and thoughts. A weak flow of energy results in a low level of awareness, and therefore you are not conscious of your full experience. Your life will go by largely unnoticed by the most important person—you.

Through the chakras, we exchange energy with the world around us. In very simple terms, you can think of the human energy system as having two principle aspects: mental/intellectual and physical/emotional. The mental/intellectual aspect exists primarily from the third chakra (solar plexus) up, while the physical/emotional aspect primarily lives in the first two chakras. In many of our Western cultures, we are socialized to live through the mental/intellectual chakras and stay away from the physical/emotional ones. Yet if the body-mind is all-encompassing, when we ignore the physical/emotional aspect of our being, we have cut off a major part of the self—a part that is essential for making any concrete and lasting change.

Because we register all experience in the cells, the body can be a great indicator of our overall state of being—are we happy, sad, confused, excited, joyous, stressed, anxious? Body awareness is a very important part of intuitive development, because the body is the physical home of our senses, both inner and outer. Pay attention to what you feel in your body in a tactile, physical sense, as well as on an emotional level.

THE FIRST CHAKRA—THE ROOT CHAKRA

The root chakra is located at the bottom of the torso, at the perineum, between the genitals and the anus. It is the seat of life-force energy and your grounding force. The root chakra energy is similar to that of a rocket, in that with a rocket, the greater the force down to the ground, the higher the rocket will fly.

In our personal energy system, the greater our grounding in the physical, seen reality, the higher we can fly in the spiritual, unseen dimension. The grounding force runs from the root chakra down the back of the legs through the sciatic nerve and into the earth. The life-force energy, or kundalini, travels from the root chakra up the spine and out the top of the head.

We must constantly balance the grounding force and the kundalini energy. If we have only the grounding force, we become rigid in our thinking, inflexible in life. On the other hand, if we have only the kundalini force, we lose our connection to physical reality and float around in our thoughts and ideas, never being able to bring anything into physical reality. When both of these forces are in balance in the root chakra,

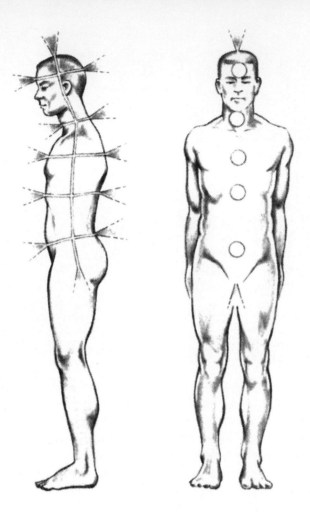

the grounding force serves as an anchor, a sure footing, a solid rock on which to stand, while the kundalini serves to lift your awareness and energy to the tremendous heights that are yours to master. The grounding force gives you the ability to harness and discipline the powerful and unbridled kundalini.

As the home of your life-force, this chakra should also be the center of gravity in your body. When you feel the center of gravity this low in your body, you are much more in touch with the true life-force that enters your body through the root chakra. One of the challenges we face in our fast-paced world, however, is to truly feed our lives from this life-force rather than from our fast pace. When you are wrapped up in activity, it is easy to mistake the nervous energy or hyperactivity of busyness for true life-force. This takes your life out of balance, and cuts you off from the power and strength of the universal flow of energy.

As you get to know the root chakra and its relationship to your daily life, be sure that you are living in your body and not in your activity—that you are fully present in your physical being. Let your activities be fed by your true life-force, not by frenetic busyness and tension. It is easy to become addicted to activity energy and be fooled into thinking you are accomplishing a lot. Unfortunately, the reality is that you are only maintaining the craziness, not feeding your creative energy.

The root chakra is your connection to all that the physical and material world represents. It is where you find your survival instincts, your issues of physical safety and security, your primal instincts, and your basic attitudes about your body. It is the seat of the masculine aspect of your being, and for men, is related to the physical aspects of sexuality.

In the root chakra, we find our fundamental feelings about abundance. Do you feel that there is plenty for all—of anything and everything? Or are you stuck in a poverty consciousness that says it is all you can do just to survive? Do you feel secure exploring new places, or do you feel safe only within your comfort zone? Do you allow others to enter your space, or are you reluctant to let anyone get too close?

The root chakra contains the seeds of potential within you. It is the beginning of full-spectrum living. All that you can be is planted in the root chakra. Therefore, if you do not open to this energy center and keep it alive and thriving, you cannot become all that you have the potential to be because you can't get to the seeds. The root chakra is the wellspring from which all your life flows. Its full aliveness is not only critical to your physical well-being, but also to your complete manifestation of divinity in human form. Although we tend to think of it as the most base, primal, physical energy center in the body, I invite you to consider it as perhaps the most sacred, for it holds the divine seed of You. This seed can bear many fruits throughout all of your days if you open to all of its possibilities.

For each chakra, I have included an exercise that is a combination of meditation and activity. The meditation will lead you into that particular energy center to experience it on a physical, emotional, and spiritual level. The exercise then continues with a series of questions that will help guide you in your understanding of how this chakra influences your life.

You will also notice that I suggest you focus on a particular color in each chakra. These colors are based on the light spectrum mirrored in the rainbow, and are the colors whose vibrational frequencies correspond to the vibrational frequency of that particular energy center. The colors are:

Root chakra—red

Sacral chakra—orange

Solar plexus chakra—yellow

Heart chakra—green

Throat chakra—light blue

Brow chakra—indigo (deep blue)

Crown chakra—violet

Meditation: The Root Chakra

Set your journal within easy reach of where you will ultimately sit to do this exercise. Then stand up straight and bend at the waist as if you are going to touch your toes. Let your arms dangle freely and breathe deeply. You will feel the breath automatically go to the bottom of your body, filling your pelvic basket and expanding your lower back and upper buttocks. Take several long, slow, full breaths in this position. Then, slowly straighten to a fully upright position, but continue breathing as deeply as when you were bent over. Practice this deep breath a few more times before moving to a sitting position.

Sit in a chair with your legs uncrossed or on the floor with your legs folded under you. Keep your back straight. Close your eyes and continue breathing into the bottom of your body as you did when standing. Feel your breath go all the way down through your root chakra and into your chair or the floor. Continue breathing in this way for a while. You may want to visualize the color red, the color associated with the root chakra, breathing in red energy. Feel this lower part of your body come alive. You may feel a warmth or tingling or some other symptom that energy is moving there. You may also experience resistance. If you do, be patient and gentle with yourself and ease your way into your root chakra with your breath. If there is a great deal of resistance, it may take you several sessions of focusing just on your breath to make your way in. Give yourself whatever time you need to be able to breathe freely down through your root chakra.

Once you are comfortable breathing this deeply and feeling the energy flowing freely in your root chakra, become aware of this chakra as the source of your life-force energy and your center of gravity. Here is the true source of life-force within your body. Have you been accessing this true life-force prior to now, feeling your physical center of gravity this low in your body? Or have you mistaken activity and busyness for your life-force? Be sure that you are truly living in your body and not in your activity.

Consider the following questions. Write your thoughts, feelings, and responses to the questions in your journal.

Who am I at this time in my life? How do I identify myself?

Am I able to stay focused in my sense of Self, or do I easily lose myself in the whirlwind of life around me?

How do I feel about my body? Am I pleased with it, or do I often wish it was different? If I wish it was different, what changes can I make, both inner and outer, in order to be at peace with my body and feel good about it as the physical home for my soul?

How do I feel about growing older and the physical changes that occur? Do I look at them as a natural part of the life process or fight against these changes?

Do I experience a balance of grounding force with kundalini in my life? Do I easily get stuck in a current reality and can't seem to move, or, on the other hand, seem to float through life without a real grasp of reality? If I am out of balance, what shifts do I need to make?

On the spectrum line between poverty and unlimited abundance, where do I fall in my attitude toward what life offers? Am I surviving or thriving in my life? Am I just getting by, always concerned about the next paycheck or paying my bills and meeting basic survival needs, or am I thriving in a consciousness of plenty, always having much more than I need in my life, never being concerned about meeting my needs?

Do I feel free to let my life be an adventure, stepping beyond comfortable and safe boundaries? Or do I prefer to stay in familiar surroundings where nothing will threaten my carefully-constructed world? Do I fear for physical well-being when I am in unfamiliar surroundings or with people I don't know?

Am I in touch with my sacred potential—the potential of all I can be and all I can share with the world in this life? From my current perspective, what is my potential?

What are my gifts to share with the world? Do I feel free within myself to share them? If not, what needs to shift? How can I free myself?

How can I more fully realize my potential? How can I enter more fully into full-spectrum living?

The Second Chakra—The Sacral Chakra

The sacral chakra is located in the pelvic region just below the navel. It is the center of creativity and emotional life. It is the seat of the feminine expression of your being, and therefore regulates the emotional aspects of sexuality for men, and both physical and emotional aspects of sexuality for women.

Because the sacral chakra is the center of emotional life, it also plays a big role in our social interaction. Regardless of the relationship that will ultimately be established, we first meet one another in the second chakra. Here is where the initial "chemistry" happens that draws you to another person or place, or says, "Get me out of here!" As a relationship takes shape, it moves on up the chakra ladder and many layers of connection are formed.

One of the ways to know how you are doing in the second chakra is to notice how you feel in social interaction. Are you comfortable meeting new people, and sharing emotional intimacy with your close friends and family? Or do you feel guarded, not wanting to extend yourself to others or allowing others to get too close?

The root chakra is very much about "me"—what I need right now in this moment. In the sacral chakra, the focus begins to be on "we." We start to realize that there are others with whom we might want to relate. This brings us into the feminine, nurturing, and creative energy of the sacral chakra. The root chakra energy is assertive, action-oriented, masculine. The first two chakras together balance the life-force energy for the inner dance of masculine and feminine.

Creativity and sexuality, in their more highly developed forms, are about "we," not about "me." More freedom in one will usually lead to more freedom in the other, as well. The primal creative spark comes out of a desire to express. When we are open and free in this chakra, both creativity and sexuality flow easily, and we are able to create in partnership with others as well as on our own. When there is a block in this energy center, creativity and sexuality will be stifled at some level. Moving forward with creative projects or manifesting your desires in life will be a struggle.

Another aspect of the feminine energy is intuition. Intuition actually begins in the root chakra as we get in touch with the physical messages of the body. However, in the second chakra, we begin to experience empathy, an awareness of others' feelings. It is through the sacral and solar plexus chakras that we experience clairsentience, or clear knowing. Balance in the second chakra creates a more fluent connection to your inner knowing.

Meditation: The Sacral Chakra

Set your journal within easy reach—but not in your lap—and then sit in a chair with your legs uncrossed or on the floor with your legs folded under you. Keep your back straight. Close your eyes and breathe into the pelvic region of your body. Feel your breath go all the way down into your sacral chakra. You may want to visualize and breathe in the color orange, the color associated with the sacral chakra. Feel this part of your body come alive. You may feel a warmth or tingling or some other symptom that energy is moving there. You may also experience resistance. If you do, be patient and gentle with yourself and ease your way into the sacral chakra with your breath. If there is a great deal of resistance, allow yourself several sessions of just breathing to make your way in. Take whatever time you need to be able to breathe freely down into your sacral chakra.

Once you are comfortable breathing into this chakra, consider the following questions. Write your thoughts, feelings, and responses to the questions in your journal.

How do I feel meeting new people? Is it easy for me? Do I usually feel comfortable right away, or does it take a long time for me to "settle in" with someone new or in a new group?

How willing am I to share emotional intimacy with close friends and family? With whom is this sharing easy? With whom is it difficult? What do I feel from them that makes it easy or difficult? What do I feel from me?

Do my creative juices flow freely?

Am I comfortable with my sexuality and its role and expression in my life? If not, what shifts do I need to make?

Do I allow myself to listen to my intuition?

Am I comfortable with the fact that within me dwell aspects of both the masculine and the feminine? Have I developed each to its full potential? If not, what shifts do I need to make?

THE THIRD CHAKRA—THE SOLAR PLEXUS CHAKRA

The solar plexus chakra is located just under the base of the sternum in the arch of the rib cage. Because it is the center for self-confidence and assuredness, personal power and strength, control, mental life, emotional safety, and individuality, it is in this chakra that we spend most of our time. It is here that we begin to claim our independence, march to our own inner drumbeat, and claim our personal power.

The solar plexus is about healing. Again, we speak of healing as coming to wholeness, not just getting well when you've been sick. In chapter 3, we discussed inhabiting all of your being. This work can be associated with the solar plexus chakra. This energy center is about discovering and being willing to inhabit all of who you are—both the parts you like and the parts you don't like.

In chapter 4, I shared Stephen Levine's description of healing as "entering with intention and awareness that which we have avoided and run away from." He went on to say, "Healing is the growth that each person seeks. Healing is what happens when we come to our edge, to the unexplored territory of mind and body." What a powerful directive for our lives! Here in the solar plexus we come up to the edge of our known reality, acknowledge that there are worlds beyond, and summon the courage to step off into the unknown possibilities. It is here that we develop our will.

The journey through the solar plexus to the heart is the journey from living life directed by ego to living from soul. It is in the solar plexus that we take charge of our lives and begin to create proactively rather than reactively. We take active steps to claim our lives as our own rather than be pawns in someone else's creation.

It is in the solar plexus that we first start to become aware of our "calling" in life, our soul mission. The seed of that mission is planted in the root chakra, fed and watered in the sacral chakra, and begins to blossom and make itself known in the solar plexus. At that point, we can either choose to claim it and let it guide us forward in our lives, or we can resist it. The choice is ours. Claiming it will certainly have its challenges and lessons, but it will still be easier than a lifetime of resistance to who we really are and what we are here to do. Resistance is an uphill battle all the way. The journey through the solar plexus to the heart involves surrendering to soul mission—letting go of our resistance and committing to our true path.

Intuition continues to develop in the solar plexus as the "fire in the belly"—that "gut feeling" that is such a strong indicator of which choice you should make or how things could turn out. This is also the fire that begins to burn off all that is not true to our nature. It is the purification fire, for the journey through the solar plexus to the heart is a kind of rite of passage or initiation. It is the fire that lifts us out of the physical bonds of being and allows us to begin the dance with Spirit. As we reach the heart chakra, the gates to the higher worlds of awareness and possibility open wide, and we experience a great metamorphosis—the emergence of the true Self. The inner spiritual warrior is born.

All of this is part of the journey to healing and wholeness. Ralph Blum wrote in *The Book of Runes*, "Seeking after Wholeness is the Spiritual Warrior's quest. And yet what you are striving to become in actuality is what you, by nature, already are. You must become conscious of your essence and bring it into form, express it in a creative way."

The Law of Correspondence showed us that our full potential already exists fully developed on one level of consciousness. Our journey is to discover those seeds of potential deep inside and cultivate them so they can grow to maturity. In the solar plexus, the seeds of potential that were planted in the root chakra now begin to reveal themselves. The drums start to beat, the excitement begins to build, the stakes are raised a little higher, and the clarion call of the soul is heard!

Meditation: The Solar Plexus Chakra

As with the first two chakra meditations, set your journal within easy reach but not in your lap, and then sit in a chair with your legs uncrossed or on the floor with your legs folded under you. Keep your back straight. Close your eyes and breathe into the solar plexus region of your body, the arch in the rib cage just below the sternum. Feel your breath fill the solar plexus. You may want to visualize and breathe in the color yellow, the color associated with this chakra. Feel this part of your body come alive. You may feel a warmth or tingling or some other symptom that energy is moving there. As with the other chakras, you may also experience resistance. If you do, be patient and gentle with yourself and ease your way into your solar plexus with your breath. If there is a great deal of resistance, allow yourself several sessions of just breathing to make your way in. Take whatever time you need to be able to breathe freely into your solar plexus.

Once you are comfortable breathing into this chakra, consider the following questions. Write your thoughts, feelings, and responses to the questions in your journal.

Do I have a clear sense of my role in the world—how I fit in? Have I heard my "calling" in life? Do I feel like I belong here?

How does Stephen Levine's definition of healing ("entering with intention and awareness that which I have avoided and run away from") speak to me in my life? Are there things that I avoid or run away from? Do I recognize where my "edge" is? ("Healing is what happens when we come to our edge, to the unexplored territory of mind and body.")

Do I live primarily from ego or from soul?

How do I experience the "fire in my belly?"

Is there a purification fire raging within me? If so, what is being burned off? What is emerging as the true me?

THE FOURTH CHAKRA—THE HEART CHAKRA

The heart chakra is located in the center of the chest. It is the center of unconditional love. The transition from the solar plexus to the heart represents passing through the gates to the higher worlds. For in the heart chakra, the spiritual energies of the upper three chakras meet the physical energies of the first three, and we start to experience our wholeness as individuals and our oneness with all of creation. The heart is the ultimate uniting force, the alchemical cauldron of transformation, healing, and understanding.

As we make the journey from solar plexus to heart, we learn that unconditional Love is our essence. When both the solar plexus and heart chakras are open and free, we experience our supreme power as the constant flow of Love through our beingness.

The heart chakra is the physical manifestation of the Law of Rhythm in our bodies. Whereas in the solar plexus you found your independence, recognizing who you are as an individual, in moving through the heart chakra, you find your interdependence with the world. Here, in the heart, we understand cycles, relationships, and the fact that we all need one another on some level. The more complex our society becomes, the more interdependent we become. I don't know anyone today who can, all on their own, find all the right seeds and water sources to then grow all their own food, find all the necessary materials and tools without the aid of a store or anyone else to then build their own house, and take care of all their health and wellness needs, including medications and elixirs. And that's just for basic survival. We have become an interdependent global culture. The heart chakra helps us understand that when we can embrace all beings in acceptance for who they are and how we might serve and be served by one another, we will all lead happier and more fulfilling lives.

Intuition continues its development in the heart as we reach soul essence. The heart chakra is the seat of the soul. When we sit in soul, we are able to meet others in their souls. This is the highest level of physical-plane communication: human soul to human soul. We understand our oneness with all of creation from a heart and soul perspective, and our compassion and love for others develops more fully.

The heart chakra is an energy center of expansion, contraction, and integration. Just as the heart muscle expands and contracts, the heart chakra expands to take in new experiences and concepts, and then contracts to integrate that experience or concept into our lives.

In the solar plexus, we find the first recognition of soul mission. In the heart chakra, that recognition becomes further defined as we expand our awareness to see more clearly how to live that mission. Then we draw that clarity of understanding back inside to integrate it into our daily lives.

In the heart, we move into a place where "there are no words." In the solar plexus, many shifts and discoveries occur, and we talk about them, examine them, evaluate them, analyze them. But in the heart, we become very quiet. It is all about experience and feeling. Therefore, the less I say and the more you experience, the better.

There are three exercises for the heart chakra, the first two experiential in nature, while the third includes questions for reflection. You will need a partner for the first two, so if you are reading this book alone, find an adventurous companion to join you. The experience you share will surely enrich your relationship.

Activity: Soul Gazing

Sit face-to-face with your partner in chairs or on the floor, cross-legged and close together, but not touching. Begin with your eyes closed and breathe into the center of your chest, the heart chakra. Take some time to allow your breath to settle there and center yourself. When you are both ready, open your eyes and peer into each other's eyes. Simply be with one another, feeling your hearts open to each other as well as to yourself. Do not speak—just be. Stay in the exercise for as long as you wish. But if you experience resistance, try to stay in the exercise for at least five minutes. When you feel complete for now in your soul gaze with one another, take some time to talk about what you experienced together. If you have a lot to talk about, that's fine. But it is also fine if you are filled with feeling and have very few words.

Activity: Mutual Support and Unity

Invite your partner to join you once more. Sit on the floor back-to-back, and lean against each other so that you are supporting one another. (If you have a physical challenge that makes being on the floor difficult, you may stand back-to-back and lean against one another instead.) Once again, close your eyes and do not speak. Breathe into your heart center and allow your heart to open and commune with the heart of your partner. The back side of the heart chakra is your connection to others as supports for your life. Here your wills are aligned with one another. Allow a feeling of mutual support and love to flow between you. Again, stay in the exercise for as long as you wish. But if you experience resistance, try to stay with it for at least five minutes. When you feel complete for now, take some time to talk about what you experienced together. Once again, if you have a lot to talk about, that's fine. But it is also fine if you are filled with feeling and have very few words.

Meditation: The Heart Chakra

As with the first three chakra meditations, set your journal within easy reach but not in your lap, and then position yourself for your meditation. Close your eyes and breathe into the center of your chest. Feel the breath fill your heart. You may want to breathe in the color green, the color associated with this chakra. Feel the center of your chest come alive. You may feel a warmth or tingling or some other symptom that energy is moving there. If you experience resistance, once again give yourself the time necessary to be able to breathe freely into your heart center.

Once you are comfortable breathing into your heart, consider the following questions.

What does unconditional love mean to me?

What did I learn most about myself in doing the first two exercises? Do I meet people from my soul (heart) or from my ego (personality)? Are there changes I could make in my interactions with people in order to meet them soul-to-soul? Am I willing to make the shift?

Choose several people from different parts your life and consider the following question about your relationship with each of them: *How do I experience interdependence with* [name] *in my life?*

THE FIFTH CHAKRA — THE THROAT CHAKRA

The throat chakra is located at the base of the neck. This is the center where you live your truth—express who you are—your creative self. It is here that you fully accept the Truth of your being and live that Truth. In the solar plexus, you recognize what that Truth is. In the heart, you integrate it into all of your being, and in the throat you carry it out into the world. I call the throat chakra "the adult chakra," because it's where you claim full responsibility for everything in your life and let go of seeking something or someone else to blame. You step fully into Self.

In the first chapter, Spirit offered a powerful teaching about spiritual warrior energy in the 21st century (see p. 20). You may want to go back and read that teaching again, because it is here in the throat chakra that your inner spiritual warrior moves into action. Truth becomes a mighty sword that cuts through all illusion and embraces full reality on every level of consciousness. As we move on up the ladder through the last two chakras, we understand more fully that reality may be different on various levels of consciousness, but that it all fits together into the total package that makes up our being.

The throat chakra is also about death—death of the parts of you that no longer serve you, death of illusion, death of roles that you have played or costumes or uniforms you have worn that are no longer in harmony with your truth. Here we honor that spiritual warrior commitment to living truth, "no matter what." In the solar plexus, we recognize our principles, in the heart we integrate them into every part of our lives, and in the throat we stand up for them and live them.

In the throat chakra, we let go of the past. We fully acknowledge both our joyous and painful memories, and see how they fit into the total picture of our lives. We integrate them into our experience, and say, "Yes, all of that happened, but that was then and this is now. Time to get on with my life." In the throat chakra comes the final release of whatever may be holding us back from the past. We take full responsibility for everything that ever happened to us, realizing that on some level of consciousness, we drew that experience in so that we might learn, grow, and move to another level of understanding.

This is a huge concept to grasp, but when you open to this perspective, taking responsibility can be incredibly liberating and empowering. When you fully accept that you created or attracted every experience, then you can also claim the power to create a different experience. We are not talking about blame or "whose fault it is." We move way beyond that level of awareness to a place where we recognize that, for some reason we may never fully understand, our Higher Self called in that experience as a part of our soul's journey. At this level of awareness, nothing that happens is anyone's "fault." Instead, all parties involved chose on some level of awareness to be a part of that particular situation and play their respective roles so that everyone involved could experience their individual lesson. One of my teachers used to say, "nothing happens to you—everything happens through you." All of our experiences involve or have an impact on others. This is another example of interdependence. In some way, our Higher Self chose for us to be a part of these experiences. Our Higher Self is a part of us, and therefore, we chose the experience.

You cannot change someone else's creation. That is their life. But you can change yours! Accepting full responsibility for your life is one of the most self-empowering steps you can take in the road to full-spectrum living. You will experience freedom of the soul as you have never known it before, because you have recognized and embraced its full power!

Clairaudience, literally "clear hearing," refers to intuitive hearing, and begins to develop in the throat chakra. As you begin to live your truth and fully claim your creative power, you begin to hear the voice of your intuition much more clearly. When you are ready and willing to share your spiritual gifts through how you live your life, the gifts flow.

When the throat chakra is fully open and developed, we move full throttle into the upper two chakras. The kundalini energy that has been traveling up through the chakras gets a major boost in the throat. It is as if this chakra is the root chakra for the upper energy centers. In the heart chakra, the gates to the higher worlds opened wide for your triumphal entrance. Now, by fully embracing your truth and living your soul mission, the road through the higher worlds becomes clear.

The throat chakra is ultimately about freedom—the freedom to be who you are in all of your glory. At the same time, you recognize that the glory is really Love pouring through you, and that you are simply the caretaker for Love's journey as it manifests through you. You accept your soul mission and your gifts and talents, and offer them without hesitation to the world.

Activity: Rediscovering Your Truth and Freedom

Take several sheets of blank paper, and in the center of one sheet, write the word TRUTH, just as you did in chapter 2 with the word

FREEDOM. Draw a circle around it. Then, as if free associating, write on this page every word that comes into your mind from the word TRUTH. Just cover the page with words. When you come to a stopping point and you seem to have no more words for TRUTH, take a clean sheet and write in the middle the last word that you wrote on the first page. Then continue free associating, writing every word that comes to mind. Continue this process until you feel that you are coming up to a personal issue or revelation. At that point, go to yet another fresh page and write in paragraph form anything that is coming to you.

In chapter 2 you did a thought clustering exercise on the word FREEDOM. You have just done it here with the word TRUTH. Do the clustering exercise with the word FREEDOM again now and see how your experience is different, how your perspectives have changed.

Meditation: The Throat Chakra

As you have been doing for the chakra meditations, set your journal within easy reach but not in your lap, and then sit for your meditation. Close your eyes and breathe into your throat chakra at the base of your neck. Feel your breath fill this area. You may want to visualize and breathe in the color light blue, the color associated with this chakra. Feel your throat open, and allow yourself the possibility of freedom as you have never known it before. You may feel a warmth or tingling or some other symptom that energy is moving there. If you experience resistance, once again give yourself the time necessary to be able to breathe freely into your throat chakra.

Once you are comfortable breathing into this chakra, continue with the following questions.

Who is the spiritual warrior in me? What is my uncompromising truth?

Where in my life am I still living in illusion? Where have I not yet been willing to cut through to the absolute truth of the situation? Am I willing to cut through now? What is the truth?

For what experiences of my past do I now need to claim full responsibility for so that I can release them and create something new?

THE SIXTH CHAKRA—THE BROW CHAKRA

The last two chakras are very important for our soul-mission journey. By the time we have worked our way through the first five, we go soaring into the gifts of the sixth and seventh. Like the heart chakra, they are much more experiential in nature. They are of such high vibrational frequencies, that focus on them moves us way beyond the verbal dimension into the spiritual.

The brow chakra is located behind the eyes and between the ears, in the middle of the head. It is the center for light, imagination, perception, clairvoyance, visualization, and projection. It is essential to your journey because it is here in the brow chakra that you first make a picture of your life vision. You then project that picture out into the world, and the energy of the picture begins the process of transmuting into physical reality. Therefore, this chakra is key for the manifestation process.

The brow chakra is also important in relieving anxiety. Anxiety is caused by feeling trapped—by not being able to see any other possibility than where you are. By breathing into and opening the brow chakra, you are able to perceive other possibilities, and understand your situation on many levels of consciousness. Then you understand that you are not trapped at all, but must now exercise your free choice to create another reality.

Here we have reached a much higher level in the development of our intuition. We now begin to "see" with our inner vision and perceive energies in a completely new way. At issue for many people is trusting the perceptions that they receive through the brow chakra. We think of it as the "psychic" chakra, but it is much more than psychic. It is the inner window to the soul. Psychic energy is but a small part of the much larger spiritual dimension that is soul.

The brow chakra is vision. Take some time to ponder this energy center, its involvement in and influence on your soul-mission journey.

Meditation: The Brow Chakra

As you have been doing for the chakra meditations, set your journal within easy reach, but not in your lap, and then sit for your meditation. Close your eyes and breathe into your brow chakra—behind your eyes and between your ears in the middle of your head. Feel your breath fill this area. You may want to visualize and breathe in the color indigo (deep blue), the color associated with this chakra. Feel your brow open and light stream through. You may feel a warmth, tingling, or some other symptom that energy is moving there. If you experience resistance, give yourself the time necessary to be able to breathe freely into your brow chakra.

Once you are comfortable breathing into this chakra, consider the following questions:

Do I have an active fantasy life? Do I allow myself to dream about what could be, about the life I would like to live?

Do I allow myself to perceive with my inner or intuitive senses? If so, what have been some of my experiences? If not, have I been resistant to using and trusting the vast realm of information and guidance available to me through my inner senses? Why? Am I willing to let go of my resistance?

THE SEVENTH CHAKRA — THE CROWN CHAKRA

The crown chakra is located in the crown of the head, at the place we know as the "soft spot" on a baby's head. This is the center of spirituality—your relationship to Spirit and to the divine within Self. When this chakra is open, you experience a sense of peace and serenity, and your oneness with all of creation from a purely spiritual point of view. The crown chakra is the portal through which Spirit enters to speak and bring you guidance, direction, and understanding. When this energy center is closed, it is very difficult for you to comprehend anything spiritually related. Through an open crown chakra, Spirit inspires and gives life to your intuitive gifts. Your soul mission comes into full alignment with the greater spiritual and universal flows.

Meditation: The Crown Chakra

As you have been doing for the chakra meditations, set your journal within easy reach, but not in your lap, and then sit for your meditation. Close your eyes and breathe into the crown of your head. Feel your breath fill this area. You may want to visualize and breathe in the color violet, the color associated with this chakra. Feel the top of your head open and Spirit enter in. You may feel a warmth, tingling, or some other symptom that energy is moving there. Invite Spirit to communicate with you. Let go of preconceived notions of what form the communication should take. Just let come what comes. You may hear a voice, you may see pictures, you may experience feelings, you may just suddenly "know" something communicated through thought transference. Whatever way it comes is the right way. If it helps you to write, then write. If you want to just be in the experience of communion with Spirit, then do that. There are no rules here. This is your personal connection with Spirit. Let it be whatever it is.

If you experience resistance or if nothing comes at all, be patient and gentle with yourself. You may just need silence and peace right now. Further guidance will come later. Just keep breathing into the crown chakra and give yourself time and permission for the experience to be whatever it is.

The chakras represent levels of conscious awareness. Although we might think of the journey through the chakras as climbing up a ladder from one level of consciousness to another, the journey is really more of a curve. The progression through the first three chakras, while certainly advancing in awareness, still remains within a physical-dimension consciousness. When we enter the heart, the curve begins to move upward more rapidly as development accelerates by awakening to the spiritual dimension. By the time we have passed through the throat and are in the brow chakra, the curve is going almost straight up, as we have stepped onto a "fast track" of development.

In the root chakra, we experience the animalistic level of awareness, which focuses totally on survival. Here we make the quick decision of "do I stay and fight for my life, or do I run for safety?" Self-preservation is the only consideration or concern. In the second chakra, we move to a mass consciousness of following the crowd. Here we establish relationships at the most basic levels out of a desire to connect emotionally and be accepted. The solar plexus chakra lifts us to an aspiration consciousness where we aspire for a better life, to be more than we are. In the solar plexus, we make a choice to further invest in growth and development, or to fall back into the safe and nonthreatening consciousness of the second chakra. We discover our inner spiritual warrior and choose to either become individuals with our own thoughts and opinions, or to remain in the group consciousness and have no opinions of our own.

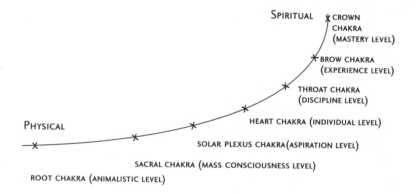

As we advance from the solar plexus consciousness to the heart chakra, we begin to expand beyond ego awareness toward an awareness of soul. We begin to honor who we really are in our hearts—the essence of our being that is behind the outer ego personality. We begin to develop an awareness of the spiritual dimension and take the first steps toward integrating our physical life into our growing spiritual awareness.

In the throat chakra, we step fully into the spiritual dimension. This chakra brings us into self-discipline. Here we gain the ability to give ourselves a command and follow it. We develop the spiritual warrior essence in our being, and become disciplined not only to further clarify our truth, but to live it. At this point of the journey, we realize that there is no turning back—that we will never return to our former, less aware selves. We have come this far, and now must complete the journey. The brow chakra then lifts us into a much higher level of awareness of our experience. The process of learning becomes a more expansive experience as our intuitive and perceptive gifts mature in powerful ways. Growth and development on all levels and in all aspects of our lives greatly accelerates. Finally, the crown chakra brings an awareness of mastery. By the time we reach the crown in our development process, we have truly moved into a new consciousness and a new life.

We can find these seven levels of conscious awareness at both the individual and societal levels. When we look back over human history, we can observe how civilizations passed through these stages of development. We can look at different parts of our world today and see various societies and cultures in various stages of their journeys. An understanding of these seven levels and the seven chakras helps us grasp the great arc of life, and can engender compassion for ourselves and others as we all make our way on our individual and societal paths. By identifying where we and others are in their development process, we have a context within which to understand actions taken and choices made, and therefore are able to release harsh judgment on others and ourselves.

The chakras are powerful tools for creation and manifestation. The process begins in the crown chakra with a thought or idea that begins to develop in our imagination. We then bring that idea down into the brow chakra, where it begins to take form as a vision. From there the vision is pulled down into the throat chakra where it is given a name and a voice. In the brow chakra, the idea was still pure light and thought energy—a very fine vibration that is beyond the range of our outer senses or physical form. As it moves to the throat chakra, it is transformed into sound energy, a slower vibrational frequency that our outer senses can begin to perceive.

As the idea is pulled down into the heart, it connects with our heart passion and emotion. We get excited about it and begin to imagine how this idea could really play out in our lives. As our emotions get involved, the vibration gets even slower and more available to our conscious awareness and senses. The idea moves out of the purely spiritual, conceptual dimension into the physical, tangible realm of physical reality as it is pulled on down into the solar plexus.

In the solar plexus, we begin making plans, setting goals, and taking action, slowing down the vibrational frequency to the point where the idea is taking on physical attributes. Many pieces start to come together, and physical form begins to appear. As it comes on down into the sacral chakra, our powerful creative force kicks in and the form becomes even more fully developed. At this point, the form enters a "birth canal" and travels on down to the root chakra where it becomes fully realized in the physical world.

As an example of how this process works, imagine that you want to start a new business selling organic vegetables. Your initial idea is born in the crown chakra, where your imagination is inspired by Spirit. Your great desire to create this new business grabs the idea and pulls it down into the brow chakra where you start to create a visual image of what your business will look like, and how your life will be when you are running this business. As your energy builds toward the idea, your desire pulls it on down into the throat chakra where you begin talking to other people about it, and perhaps give your new business a name.

As your excitement builds, your desire pulls the idea on down into your heart chakra where you begin to imagine all the people you can help by providing them with your organic vegetables. You also begin to see how this business will be integrated into your life. As the idea takes on more concrete form, your desire pulls it on down into the solar plexus chakra where you create a plan of action and put it into motion.

As action steps are taken, your full creative juices of the sacral chakra begin to flow, and you start making all the necessary personal and business connections to make your new business happen. Soon everything is in place and the new organic vegetable business passes through the birth canal into the root chakra and is born!

By design, we are creative beings. We are designed to recognize our potential, create a vision of how that potential can take form, and then work in partnership with Spirit to manifest it. That's the journey of this book. In Part II, you will identify your soul mission, your fundamental calling and potential. Then you will, in effect, pull that mission down from the crown chakra into the brow and create a vision for your life. Parts III and IV then guide you in the journey toward living your mission and vision.

The Law of Correspondence tells us that our bodies—our cellular minds—hold all the wisdom of the universe. During this lifetime, we are the universe, manifested in a very particular form for our journey this time around. Our bodies hold the keys to unlock all the mysteries of life. Our task is to go deep inside to the core of our being and recognize those keys—keys that we may then realize have been available to us all along, but we were not aware enough to see. Or, perhaps the keys were buried in the depths of the subconscious and we had to uncover them through the discovery process.

This journey is so much about discovery. An old adage says that in order to find the answers you have to ask the right questions. It is our job to keep asking questions and make the expedition into the deepest realms of self where we become one with God, Spirit, and Universe. Then everything flows.

Activity: Chapter Reflection

Reflect on what you have learned in this chapter about the chakras. Write about each chakra in your own words so that you begin to have a personal understanding of how each influences your life. Think of someone with whom you can have a conversation about the chakras and their role in personal development. Talking about them will help solidify your ideas, thoughts, and discoveries, and perhaps bring new thoughts for your pondering.

The Seven Chakras

Chakra	Location	Color	Attributes
Root	Under the bottom of the torso, at the perineum	Red	Life-force energy, survival instincts, fight or flight syndrome, physical sensation, root of masculine energy
Sacral	Just below the navel, in the pelvic region	Orange	Emotional life and feelings, sexuality, creativity, root of feminine energy
Solar plexus	Just below the base of the sternum, in the arch of the rib cage	Yellow	Mental life, intellectual activity, judgement, personal power and strength, manipulation and control, security
Heart	Center of the chest	Green	Love for humanity, unconditional love, dreams
Throat	Base of the neck	Light blue	Expression of creativity and truth, letting go of aspects of your personality and life that no longer serve you; claiming your freedom
Brow	In the middle of the head, behind the eyes and between the ears	Indigo	Clairvoyance, visualization, imagination, access to your future
Crown	Crown of the head	Violet	Opening to higher consciousness, integration of spirituality into life

Part II

IDENTIFYING MISSION,
CREATING VISION

Soul Mission

IN OUR INITIAL DISCUSSION of the Law of Mentalism (see p. 58) we talked about the principal assignments for everyone's life. The first assignment is to know who you are. The second is to discover and live your soul mission. The last is to learn the lessons that are presented to you as you engage in your self-discovery process and live your mission. The first assignment has been a large part of our journey together thus far. The second and third make up the journey of the rest of this book. There is a mission at work in everyone's life. You may be very aware of your personal soul mission, or it may still be hidden in your subconscious. But the mission is there. The next two chapters are devoted to uncovering your soul mission, writing your soul mission statement, and then creating your life vision.

Let's begin by looking at the difference between a soul mission, a life vision, and a goal. Your soul mission is your reason for being, your life purpose. It's your calling in life—who you feel called to be, what you feel called to do. Mission is an energy that flows through you—a drive, voice, or passion that you cannot ignore. Your mission is not an activity, but rather your fundamental reason for doing that activity. It's what you know in your heart you must live if you are to experience inner peace and harmony.

Life vision is how you see yourself living out your mission—how you choose to respond to your calling. It's the picture of how your life looks and feels, the career path you choose, the people with whom you live and work, your activities, where you live and travel—every detail of what you desire as you create a life that is in perfect harmony with your soul mission. Vision is the big picture view of your life. It's not just what you want for this year or even the next five years, but what you want for your lifetime. What you want for this year can be goals or steps toward your ultimate vision. Mission gives your life purpose; vision gives it shape and direction. Mission is your calling; vision is your creation. Together they make up the big picture upon which your attention must remain focused.

Goals are stepping stones toward the manifestation of your vision. Once the vision is clear in your mind, you begin to work out the steps that you need to take in order for the vision to become your physical reality. For instance, if your soul mission is to open doors for global business and finance, your life vision might include owning homes in North Carolina, Scandinavia, and on the coast of Spain. A goal supporting both your mission and vision might be to establish business connections in each of those places in the next two years as a first step toward residency there and expanding your international business involvement. Goals are short-term, vision is long-term.

Again, the process is circular. You begin by identifying the mission that you feel your soul calls you to live. Out of that mission, you create a long-term vision for your life. As you think about how to manifest that vision, you create goals. Goals break down into projects. Those projects facilitate the accomplishment of your goals. The accomplished goals take you closer to the manifestation of your vision. We move from soul mission to life vision to goals to projects to achievement, and then back to soul mission as the cycle continues. As you manifest your vision, you gain more clarity about the soul mission you are called to live. This new clarity helps you further refine your vision, out of which come new goals and projects. And the circle continues for your entire life.

Full-spectrum living means a life that is always engaged in full-consciousness experience—observing, learning, growing, questioning, seeking, expanding—ever evolving in its sense of Self, ever marveling at the oneness of all of creation and the amazing dance in which we all get to participate.

Very few people ever clearly identify and state their soul mission, create a vision, set goals, and accomplish those goals, living to their full potential. Most people simply take on the soul mission and life vision of their parents, teachers, or friends. It may seem easier that way—to go along with the crowd, play by the crowd's rules, and do what is expected.

But this is "life by default." Because these people didn't undertake deep self-exploration, or never seriously considered the idea of having a mission and big dreams, they live the life that others want for them—other people's dreams. That is not full-spectrum living.

Your soul mission is your unique, individual purpose for being. It is about fulfilling the needs of your soul as it continues its development and offers its gifts to the world. It is not simply accepting the life your family, religious organization, or community wants you to live. As you consider how your life and the lives of those around you relate to one another, look for the uniqueness of each person—the possibilities inherent in life when each person knows who they are here to be. Let go of trying to put yourself or anyone else into a preexisting mold.

This soul mission expedition is about recognizing your reason for being. In exploring your soul mission, you may indeed find that it lies very comfortably within your present family, religious, and community structures and beliefs, and that you are called to follow a familiar pathway. But you may also find that you have a different calling, and have to find your own path. Honor and respect others' choices and beliefs, and recognize that you must walk a different path. If you betray yourself and your soul's mission, inner conflict is inevitable.

Clarity about your soul mission and life vision gives you a reason for being and doing. Any activity is much easier to undertake and follow through to completion when you know why you are doing it—what purpose it will serve. In order to experience fulfillment on a regular basis, you must know what it is within you that wishes to be fed. You must know what it is that your heart and soul thrive on. Then you have a reason and motivation.

Soul mission is the path your Higher Self chose for your soul's learning, growth, and development in the physical plane. Your task is to identify your soul mission and choose the career path, lifestyle, and activities through which you will live it. This becomes your life vision. Identifying your mission and creating your vision is an evolving process. The more you get to know Self and recognize what it is that feeds, inspires, and excites you—where your passions lie—the more clearly you can identify your personal soul mission.

Meditation: Fulfillment and Legacy

Make yourself comfortable and go to your Point of Stillness. Then imagine that you are in your seventies or eighties and are happy and healthy. A huge party is being thrown in your honor and people from all parts and times of your life have come to celebrate *you!* One by one, people come to speak with you and thank you for what you have meant to them. What are they saying?

Continuing in your meditation, consider the following questions, writing your responses in your journal.

If I knew that this would be the last year of my life, what would I do? What would be my priorities?

Are these priorities the same as my priorities now? If not, why am I waiting to live my priorities? Are there changes I can commit to making now in order to begin living my priorities today?

When I am no longer here, what do I want people to remember about me?

In light of how I want to be remembered, are there things I need to shift in my life today?

Writing a soul mission statement is the first step toward creating life vision and manifesting your dreams. It empowers you to create a future that you truly desire based on what you care the most passionately about.

Laurie Beth Jones, author of *The Path: Creating Your Mission Statement for Work and For Life*, wrote, "Having a clearly articulated mission statement gives one a template of purpose that can be used to initiate, evaluate, and refine all of one's activities." She goes on to say, "A personal mission statement acts as both a harness and a sword—harnessing you to what is true about your life, and cutting away all that is false." When you have a concrete mission statement by which you live your life, you have a criterion against which to measure every decision, choice, and action. Rather than being caught up in the whirlwind of considerations, your first questions in any decision-making process become, "Does this support who I am, my mission, and my vision for my life? Will this be in harmony with my purpose for being, and further the accomplishment of my mission, or will this go against who I am and what is important to me?" There may be other criteria that ultimately you must consider, but these should be the first. When you address these fundamental questions as the first step in the decision-making process, you are honoring yourself and your mission. You are setting up the situation to be in harmony with who you are at your essence.

Even though identifying and stating soul mission leads to great empowerment, inspiration, and excitement toward life, the actual process of identifying it and putting it on paper can bring up tremendous resistance and struggle. The whole idea of a life-long purpose or reason for being, and committing to living out that purpose can be overwhelming. It is perfectly normal to experience these feelings. As we talk about this, notice what you are feeling, both physically and emotionally. As resistance comes up, just breathe, and allow yourself to proceed one step at a time.

We are conditioned to identify ourselves by what we do, rather than who we are, or by our relationships rather than who we are within those relationships. The challenge comes when we realize that we've been living in a kind of safety zone of activity and relationship, giving our attention and energy to all the things on our "list," the daily routine of life and just keeping up with all that life seems to entail. "Seems" is the operative word here, because our relationship and response to everything in our life can sometimes get caught up in our perception of the moment and of the situation—what we perceive in that moment to be the top priority. When that happens, our priorities constantly shift, because they are being shaped by the needs of the moment in our outer drama of life rather than by true soul essence.

The thought that a single soul mission can shape our priorities can be both appealing and terrifying. We immediately think of all the "responsibilities" of our lives, and question how we could possibly honor those responsibilities if our thoughts are not focused on meeting every need and requirement of those responsibilities. We tend to get caught up in a "mission of the moment," and never get to the fundamental essence of our life journey. Furthermore, the mission of the moment is often changing based on the moment-to-moment situation. This leads to living in conflict and frustration because we realize on some level that we are not being true to Self, yet don't know how to break the pattern, to get out of the vicious circle of reacting to the needs of the hour.

No matter what challenges our life seems to offer us, we usually find a way to "cope." Our coping mechanisms lead us to the false sense of "being on top of things"—of really being in control of our lives. We feel a sense of power and accomplishment in the management of day-to-day details. The idea of identifying and living soul mission, however, flies in the face of our coping way of life. The farther away we are from living soul mission, the more threatening it can be to claim it. On some level, we know that once we identify and commit to living our mission, our life will be forever changed. Change means the unknown, and therefore we resist. We perceive that life will be less challenging if we just stay on the treadmill that we know, and just try to keep up.

Recognizing and claiming soul mission brings the fear that "if I recognize it, I have to do something about it. If I ignore it, maybe it will go away, and I can just keep doing what I'm doing. It's not really that bad— I've managed all these years. I'm sure I can keep going. I know how it works." Coming to the truth of your being can challenge every aspect of your current life reality. And it can liberate you to a life of freedom, peace, reward, and fulfillment.

Living our mission calls us out of the false safety and real chaos of the activities of life into the truth of our being. Once we consciously choose to create a life built on soul mission and not on moment-to-moment situations or crisis management, we find harmony and peace within our being. This harmony and peace comes from feeling that we are "on purpose" all the time. We are consciously directing our lives and our responses to each situation.

There are some very clear things that your soul mission is not. Your mission is not your "to do" list. That is the list of things that must be done in order to accomplish a particular goal. If your "to do" list includes things that cannot possibly be done within a day, they need to be rethought as goals or projects, which become steps toward the accomplishment of your mission. Then you break down the goal into much smaller projects that can easily be accomplished on your "to do" list.

Your soul mission is also not your job or your career, or any role you may play within family, relationship, or community. Any of those things may be vehicles for the accomplishment of your mission, but they are not your mission, just as they are not your identity. Mission is much larger than any individual activity or role could be.

Intention is the key when it comes to living your soul mission. Jobs or roles that we assume by default often keep us from our soul mission. They become distractions and keep us from devoting time, energy, and focus to our true purpose. Declaring your soul mission helps you stay on track.

Soul mission is also not something that only famous or influential people have. Everyone has a mission. Everyone's presence and purpose is important. Simply by how we choose to live our lives, we each have an impact on those around us, whether it is just on our immediate circle or on the community or world at large. Every thought, word, and deed has an impact on some level. Therefore, we have a responsibility to identify our soul mission and live it, fulfilling our purpose for the benefit of all.

There is a good chance that you are already living your soul mission on some level. One of the ways of identifying soul mission is to look back over your life to find the times when you have felt the most fulfilled, the happiest, and the most inspired. As you remember those times and situations, look beneath the activity itself to find the fundamental energy at work, the common thread through all of those activities. For example, my soul mission is to help people set themselves free. It took me several years to clearly identify it. For a long time I thought that my mission was to create sacred space in which people would feel safe to more fully discover themselves. But then I realized that creating sacred space was just one component of the larger mission of helping people set themselves free. I looked back at my life and all of my various career activities—professional singer, voice teacher, church musician, minister, composer, counselor, publisher, life coach, author—and realized that, at a fundamental level, each has been about helping people in some way find inner freedom.

Living soul mission does not necessarily mean changing career paths, relationships, religious affiliation, or communities. Living soul mission can be as simple as a shift in awareness. The more you focus on your soul mission as the primary consideration for everything you do, the more your soul mission informs your life, and you experience harmony and peace within your being.

At this point, you may still have no idea what your soul mission is or where to begin looking for it. Identifying soul mission is a process of recognizing when in your life you have felt the most alive, the most fulfilled, the most fed by Spirit. Then you look beneath the activity of that moment to identify what was really fulfilling to you on a soul level. For example, watching people's faces light up in new discoveries about their soul journeys while in a workshop or coaching session is incredibly rewarding to me. But the conversation or workshop is not what is actually feeding my soul. What feeds my soul is that, through our work, they have just taken another step toward freedom. A friend of mine who is an actor finds being on stage exhilarating. His soul mission is to recharge human hearts. What makes his experience exhilarating is not just that he is a successful actor doing something he loves, but that he has the opportunity to recharge many hearts at once!

In the last exercise, you experienced people coming to thank you for what you have meant to them and for the influence you have had on their lives. You explored what you wish to be your legacy when your life is complete. Your insights from that work are strong indications of your soul mission because they help you see what is more important to you than anything else. Soul mission is your top priority in living. It is your greatest life lesson and your greatest gift to the world. It's what keeps calling you. Your job is to get quiet enough to hear.

When you are living your soul mission, everything in your being knows that this is what you are supposed to be doing. You feel excited about it, and find yourself wanting to do things that foster and sustain your mission. Choices about what to do come more easily as your desire to live your soul mission gets stronger. You will notice a growing commitment to being true to your soul mission even in the face of great challenge. There is also a quality of "I just have to do it." You realize that in order to be at peace within yourself you must remain true to your soul mission.

Where soul mission is concerned, money is not a consideration. You know that you must live your soul mission no matter what, because, although taking care of basic needs is a requirement for life, you realize that taking care of your soul's needs is also a requirement. When you truly honor soul mission and commit to your life vision, money will take care of itself. It will flow and provide you with all you need and desire. You will be living in harmony and alignment with the universal flow of abundance.

When you are living your soul mission, you find that you don't burn out. The flame of soul mission is never extinguished. It keeps feeding you and giving you energy to carry on. Basic rest, rejuvenation, nutrition, exercise, and recreation are, of course, necessary, but when you are working with soul mission, you have an eternal inner fire.

Synchronicity becomes the norm in a life aligned with soul mission. The right people walk in the door, the needed contacts are made, the necessary resources appear, and your intuitive guidance is easily accessed. You recognize that there are no coincidences, and are grateful for each piece of the puzzle as it falls into place. When you are living soul mission, you are allowing soul to guide your steps, and therefore you connect to everyone else at a soul level. Amazing collaborations occur because you are working together on such a high level of awareness. You draw to you those people and situations that will take you to the next step. "Networking" just seems to happen all the time. The universe makes the connections for you. All you have to do is follow through, talk to the people, and engage in the situations when they show up.

When you are living soul mission, you don't worry about how long things take. You have such a sense of rightness in the process that you don't hurry the result; you absolutely trust that all will unfold, everything will fall into place, and you will have taken another step toward the fulfillment of your mission. You will feel no need to concern yourself about what you will receive in return for your giving, because when you're living soul mission, you have an innate understanding that "what goes around, comes around." All will be repaid in time, so that as you give, it will in time flow back to you.

There are several characteristics of a dynamic soul mission statement. First, it should be inspiring. If your soul mission does not inspire you, chances are it's not your true mission. Your true soul mission is compelling, undeniable, and insistent. Soul mission keeps knocking until you answer. Simply identifying it becomes inspiration.

Your soul mission is the gift you bring to others, as well as the essence of your path. It encompasses all aspects of your life, not just your career or personal life. A life that is in perfect harmony with soul means that every aspect of that life is aligned with its soul mission.

Your mission statement should be big enough to encompass your entire lifetime. This is your life purpose, not your year or decade purpose. Your soul mission must be big enough to inspire and motivate you for a lifetime.

All of this may seem somewhat daunting at first, but the following exercise will bring it down into simpler terms. It will help you identify and write a first draft of your personal soul mission statement. Take as much time as you need to complete the exercise, even if you work with it for several days. You will address a number of questions, each of which will help you clarify your mission. Then, at the end of the exercise, you will write your soul mission statement. This is your first draft. Throughout the book, and then throughout your life, you may continue to refine your statement. It will evolve as you evolve in self-understanding and truth.

Meditation Activity:
Writing Your Soul Mission Statement

Go to your Point of Stillness. Then consider the following questions, writing your responses in your journal:

As I reflect back over my life, what has fed and nurtured me more than anything else? When is it that I feel the most highly energized?

When in my life do I most feel Spirit moving through me, inspiring me and guiding me in each step?

Now put down your pen and notebook. Take a moment to be sure you are still in your Point of Stillness. Then, imagine that you are suspended in space, thousands of miles above the Earth. Imagine the Earth without you ever having been there—as if you had never been born. What is missing from the Earth because you were not there to provide it? What is your unique gift that the world will never receive because you are not there? Then return to your journal and write.

Once again, take a moment to settle into your Point of Stillness. Then consider these questions: What just feels right to do? What do I find great enthusiasm for—enthusiasm that is undiminished, no matter what challenges arise? What do I just "have to do?" What do I lose myself in, never watching the clock or considering what anyone else thinks?

Write your responses to these questions.

You are now ready to write your soul mission statement. Go back to your Point of Stillness and ask Spirit to guide you as you declare your soul mission. Just as when you first wrote your Declaration of Intention, this is a work in progress. Write as much as you need to write in order to explore fully your soul mission. It will continue to evolve over time. This is your first draft.

Once you have written your soul mission statement, condense it into one sentence or phrase, so that when you are asked what your life is about, you can state it clearly and succinctly. Look over what you have written and find the key words or phrases. You will probably find that all you have written can really be encapsulated in one sentence. That single sentence does not have to explain your mission in detail. It must simply capture the essence of your soul mission and be an umbrella statement that is big enough to include its greater meaning. It is a statement that, when you speak it, you know and feel the full impact of what it represents to you.

Congratulations! You now have your first draft of a soul mission statement. If you have done any writing in the past, you know that the first draft is the most challenging step. As you continue your journey, your statement will evolve out of your continued self-understanding. As you revise and refine, do not change what you have written here. Instead, write a new statement, so that you have a record of your growth.

Just as your recognition of your soul mission evolves over time, so does living your soul mission. Your soul mission is your primary life lesson. If you feel that you are already fully living your soul mission every moment of every day, then you may not have gotten to the core of your mission yet. You may have only identified a component of your mission that you have now mastered. Don't confuse having mastered an aspect of your soul mission with having mastered the totality of it. Your soul mission is the primary lesson you work your whole life to master. So give yourself some slack and know that you will probably not be living your soul mission in every moment yet. But that's the long-term goal. With commitment and consciousness, by the end of your life, you will be living a larger portion of your days in full alignment with your soul mission.

Now that you have written a clear soul mission statement, you can begin creating your life from a completely new level of understanding and purpose. In the next chapter, you will explore what you really want your life to look like, and create a dynamic and vibrant vision for your future!

Life Vision 8

 In Proverbs 29: 18, it is written: "Where there is no vision, the people perish." Vision is the first step toward building the future we desire, the life through which we can experience fulfillment and a sense of accomplishment. Vision gives us hope, direction, and a path to follow. In times of crisis, it is vision of another possibility that helps us through. And in everyday living, it is vision that keeps us on track, engaged in the creation of a positive, purposeful, and rewarding life.

We constantly create visions without even realizing it. We think in pictures and project those pictures into our world. We have a vision of what we want to eat, of the places we will go, of the people we will see, of how we want a project to unfold. What we think and project is what manifests. When we allow ourselves to focus on adversity and challenge, then challenge and adversity will manifest at many turns. If, however, we project harmony, understanding, and cooperative creation onto our world, then our relationships, interactions, and circumstances will have a flow and an ease about them. What we think about comes about. The vision we hold in our hearts and minds becomes our world.

As we move into the manifestation portion of this book, the first step must be to create a vision of what you want your life to look like. Where do you want to be five, ten, twenty years from now? Who or what kinds of people do you want around you? Where do you want to live? What will be the source of your income? Where do you see yourself spiritually? What kinds of relationships will be present in your life? What particular skills have you developed, both professionally and personally? How do you want others to think about and remember you? Do you want to travel? Do you want to be able to donate large sums of money or time? How do you see yourself involved in a community of people?

In this chapter, you will create your life vision, and begin planting seeds for the life you desire. If you already have a vision for your life, then this chapter will help you continue to refine that vision, and realize more ways through which you can nurture it. If you are just starting to think about what your vision might be, you will find tools to help you clarify what you really want, let go of limited thinking, and create a life vision that is in alignment with your soul mission.

The Law of Mentalism taught us that everything begins as a thought. That means that the picture of your current life in some way reflects your current thoughts—conscious, subconscious, or both. Taken another step, this means that if you keep thinking what you have always thought, you will probably keep doing what you've always done and getting what you've always gotten. If your life is totally on track, everything is unfolding in powerful and dynamic ways toward the full manifestation of your vision, and you feel that you are really living your soul mission, then congratulations! Keep thinking what you are thinking. It's working. However, if things are progressing nicely, but you know there could be more, or if you are just plain stuck, perhaps it is time to ask some direct questions and not stop until you have some direct and clear answers.

What do you want in your life? What would you do with it if you had what you want? Are you clear about what you want and why you want it? Many people think that they want a lot more than they really do, but end up settling for much less than what they truly want. How do you find the balance? How do you create the vision of what you really and truly want, and then manifest that vision?

Fantasy is the first step of any creative process. Fantasy is simply free-flowing, creative thought. It is inspiration—the state of being in Spirit. We have said that your mind exists within the mind of Spirit, and Spirit exists within your mind. Therefore, we could say that the highest form of thought is Spirit in action. The highest form of imagination is Spirit in creation. When you free yourself from preconceived notions of what you "should" be thinking, or what is "possible," then your fantasy can take flight.

When I first began my life-coaching practice and asked clients to fantasize about the life they would have if absolutely anything were possible, I was surprised at how many of them didn't know how to respond. Many said in amazement, "No one ever asked me that before," or "Gee, I never thought about that." Sometimes we get so used to being in a particular "box" that we don't even recognize that there is an entire world of possibilities out there beyond our current perspective. However, if we never allow our minds to expand beyond our current realities, how will we ever know what might really be possible? In *The Seven Stages of Money Maturity*, George Kinder wrote, "To become who we most truly are, we must be free first to dream, then to translate that dream into the practicalities that might allow it to be accomplished."

It doesn't matter whether or not what you fantasize is possible when you dream. Dreaming is about "getting out of the box"—imagining another world. Remember the Law of Polarity—every possibility exists within any situation. If you deeply explore your dream, you will find the path that can make it happen.

The next three exercises, inspired by those used by authors and success coaches, Bob Proctor and James Ray, will help you climb out of your box, set your imagination free, and identify your true desires and priorities.

Meditation Activity: Climbing Out of Your Box

Money may or may not be high on your list of priorities in creating the vision of your life, but since money often seems to determine what we can and cannot do and have, we use it here as a point of departure.

Go to your Point of Stillness. Then bring into your mind the amount of money that is your annual income. Imagine that you've just turned your annual income into a monthly income. We are not talking about a one-time occurrence. This is permanent. Every month you will now receive what was previously your annual income. And each month that amount will grow! How would your life change? What would you do differently? Allow this idea to play in your mind. Let your fantasy run wild. Then go to your journal and describe your life in this totally new scenario.

How did it feel to do this exercise? How did it feel to fantasize on this new picture of your life? When we allow ourselves fantasy, we suddenly have many more possibilities available to us. We find that we have many more choices than we may have originally realized when we were trapped in a limited vision of what was possible. With these many choices, we can create a much more expansive vision for our lives.

It is easy to get caught in only dreaming about what you know is possible. This creates two problems. First, you have set your sights way too low, and, therefore, are not reaching for your full potential. Second, if your dream falls short of or is not what you really want, you will have no excitement about it—no passion. Passion is essential for the manifestation of dreams. Your soul wants to experience its greatness in this physical lifetime. It will not invest itself in anything less than full potential. So let's go to what you really want. It doesn't matter how possible you think it is right now. If you can dream it, you can manifest it. You just have to make the dream really clear and detailed, alive and full of passion. In this second exercise you can move from what you know is possible within your current circumstance and belief, to what you really want.

Activity: Know, Think, Want

Get together several blank sheets of paper. At the top of the first page, write "What I *know* I Can Be, Do, and Have." Then, based on present circumstance, paradigms, and conditioning, write on this page everything that you absolutely know you can be, do, and have. Remember that what you write here represents only what you know is possible within your current belief system and circumstance. Take time to do this before moving on.

Now that you have written what you *know* you can be, do, and have, at the top of a fresh page, write "What I *think* I Can Be, Do, and Have." Begin to let your mind dream a little, expanding to what you think might be possible if you stretch some, still given your present circumstances, paradigms, and conditioning.

Finally, at the top of another fresh page, write "What I *want* to Be, Do, and Have." As you write this page, open into completely free fantasy—no restrictions from your present circumstances, beliefs, or conditioning. Anything is possible. Given absolutely no restrictions, what would you want?

Now that you have stated what you want, the next step is to categorize your dreams into who/what you want to be, what you want to do, and what you want to have. Then you can prioritize your desires so that you can identify which are the most important.

Activity: Prioritizing Desires

Once again, you will need a pen and several sheets of paper. At the top of the first page write "Who and What I Want To Be." Then take at least five minutes to make a list in response to that statement. Remember that anything is possible. Include every aspect of your life—personal, professional, emotional, spiritual. Who and what do you want to be?

Once you have completed the first page, take another sheet, and write at the top "What I Want To Do." Again, write for at least five minutes, listing everything you want to do in your life, personally, professionally, emotionally, and spiritually.

Finally, take a third page and write at the top "What I Want To Have." Once more, write for at least five minutes, describing everything you want to have in your life, personally, professionally, emotionally, and spiritually.

Now that you have listed your desires, go back to the first page and count the number of items you wrote. Divide the list evenly into three priority columns: Priority A, Priority B, and Priority C, with A being the top-priority items, B being second in priority, and C being third. Once you have divided your desires into three columns, number them in order of priority within each column. The desire that appears in the A1 position is your top priority for who and what you want to be. This does not mean that the other desires listed are not important. If they were not important, you would not have written them down. This process simply helps you identify what is absolutely the most important to you.

Follow the same procedure for the "Do" and "Have" pages to identify your top priority in those two categories.

Through this exercise, you now have a clearer picture of what you really want in your life, and where various desires fall in your hierarchy of priorities. This does not mean that you focus only on your three A1 desires and forget the rest. But you have a good sense of what is more or less important to you in the grand scheme of things.

After these three exercises, you should have a clearer vision of what you want your life to look like—who you want to be, what you want to do, and what you want to have. It is now time to write a first draft of your life vision statement. I say "first draft," because any vision is a living and vibrating energy, and, therefore, will always be evolving. You will no doubt refine your vision many times in the course of your life, but you must make an initial statement.

You will need to consider many elements in creating your vision. First, include a great deal of detail. Whereas your mission statement ultimately needed condensation into one sentence or phrase, your vision statement can be as long and detailed as you wish; the more details, the better. The mind thinks in pictures, but it also is capable of conceiving sounds, fragrances, textures, and tastes. The more all of your senses are involved in creating your life vision, the more it becomes anchored and real in your mind.

Your vision should also include the kind of people you want in your life. Who do you want to be working with? What kinds of gifts, skills, and personality traits do they have? How about personal relationships? What does your life look like in that area? What kind of activities do you want to be involved in with these people, both personally and professionally?

What does your day-to-day life look like? Where do you spend your time? What activities fill your day? What do you wear? What is the source of your income? How much money do you make in a typical month or year? Where do you live? Describe your home and family life. What kind(s) of car(s) do you drive? What is your health status? Include all of these considerations in your vision.

Finally, your vision should in some way be a vehicle for living out your soul mission. It should be in complete harmony with your reason for being. Otherwise, you will experience inner conflict.

Perhaps parents or mentors have cautioned you "not to put all of your eggs in one basket." This is an important consideration in creating your life vision. Plant multiple seeds that can grow into the vision that you hold so dear. Every gardener knows that not every seed that he or she plants actually grows to maturity, nor does every plant thrive in every environment. You might not accomplish *every* goal that you set, and not every project will pan out as you had planned.

There are many factors at work in the manifestation of any vision, and the bigger the vision, the more pieces there are to fall into place for full manifestation. Therefore, set the process in motion on many fronts. Know that among all the possibilities, projects, and pursuits, some will grow and develop, showing you a clear path toward your vision. Others will be dead ends. It doesn't mean that you shouldn't have taken that path. You will have learned a tremendous amount about who you are and what your path *is not*, which may be necessary in helping you recognize even more clearly what your path *is*.

As time goes on, you will probably find that your eggs fall into just two or three baskets—that you narrow your focus to the few projects and goals that are proving themselves as powerful means to manifesting your vision. Go with what is working. If you have been true to Self in planting each seed in your garden, then whatever seeds grow and mature will lead you toward your vision and fully living your soul mission. Therefore, the many aspects of your life should be in peace and harmony with one another.

I cannot stress enough the importance of this exercise. I remember so clearly what happened when I first wrote my life vision statement.

Within days it seemed as if my life started coming alive in new ways. My coaching client load began to increase significantly, new opportunities to teach and speak began to come in as never before, my personal relationships shifted to a new level of emotional connection, and I took another step toward more financial freedom. It was like my life had just been given a new jump-start, and it was very exciting.

Each time I teach visioning in a workshop or intensive retreat, I get letters and e-mails from participants during the following weeks and months telling me how their life was transformed by identifying their mission and clearly stating their vision. And each time I update or revise my vision as I get clearer about my desires, there is another burst to a new level of energy and manifestation.

Give yourself whatever time it takes to do the following exercise, and most importantly, have a great time doing it. This is your chance to declare the life you truly desire into being. Follow the guidelines in the exercise, and go for it!

Meditation Activity: Writing Your Life Vision Statement

Place your journal and pen nearby, and then go to your Point of Stillness. Once there, visualize, big-picture view, the life that you want to have. As you begin to get clear pictures, go to your journal and write your vision, following these guidelines:

This is your creation. From this moment, you get to design your life as you want it to be.

Write in as detailed a manner as possible as you describe your vision. Be specific and comprehensive, making it real and tangible.

Let your fantasy fly freely.

Write in the present tense. Write your vision as if it is here now. Call your life into being! Know that what you desire already exists (Law of Correspondence) and start to live your vision now!

Fill your statement with passion. Be excited about it and write in descriptive and passionate terms. Your soul is not interested in a mediocre existence. Your soul wants to know its greatness!

Write what you do want, not what you don't want.

Be sure that all areas of your life are represented in your vision. You may even want to write your vision in categories, such as: Professional Life, Finances, Health, Family and Friends, Intimacy and Romance, Personal Development and Spirituality, Recreation and Fun, Physical Surroundings.

Be in the picture as you write about it, don't just watch yourself in it. Visualize from the perspective of being inside yourself looking out at your world, within your new life. Be yourself within the vision. For instance, instead of seeing yourself sitting in the driver's seat of your new car, experience yourself driving the car. Look out at the dashboard and over the hood from behind the wheel. Feel the excitement of driving this car that you've dreamed about. Let your visualization be experiential.

Again, write as much as you can. Let your imagination flow and your fantasy soar. Write the life you desire into being. Then continue with this exercise.

Now that you have written your life vision statement in great detail, you have created a clear picture of the life you want to live. By making this statement, you have sent a message to the universe that this is what you want and intend to manifest. There is just one last step in this vision statement process. Using the statement you have just written, go back and write your statement once more, leaving room within the details for Spirit to work. Spirit may actually have more in mind for you than you can yet imagine. So, for instance, instead of writing that you live on ten acres atop a mountain in a three-story stone house with a marble entry foyer, five bedrooms, seven bathrooms, a swimming pool, and a hot tub, with a spectacular view and complete privacy, consider this: You might write that you live in a mountaintop home that is your dream design. It is beautifully appointed, equipped with every luxury and amenity you could desire, plenty of space for each family member to have privacy and pursue their particular interests, and room for as many guests as you desire. Let go of some of the specifics that might still, grand as they may seem, limit your possibilities. Leave room in your vision for Spirit to show you even more possibilities. You will further understand how this can work in Part IV as we work with the Manifestation Wheel.

The Law of Correspondence has taught us that things exist on many levels of reality. That means that once you have created a vision, it now exists fully developed on one level of reality. We have said many times, "If you can dream it, you can achieve it." That seems just too simple, doesn't it? In fact, it's not as simple as that. One of my teachers used to say the three basic requirements for manifestation were desire, belief, and expectancy. She said you could manifest anything if you truly desired it, totally believed it could and would happen, and fully expected it to happen. I would say that there are four basic requirements:

1. To really want it;

2. To discipline your thoughts to remain focused and not be distracted or talked out of it;

3. To bring your dream into full alignment with your soul mission;

4. To follow through with growing into the person you need to be in order to manifest that vision.

The Manifestation Wheel in Part IV provides a structure through which to meet those requirements. Then, anything is possible.

Once you have created your vision, don't worry about how far-fetched it might be. Just begin to set goals and take action in what seems to be the first step. Focus your thought on who you need to be in order to do what needs to be done so that what you want to have (your vision) can fully manifest. In Part III, we will explore your paradigms, learn the workings of conscious and subconscious thought, and take stock of where you are right now in your life, so that in Part IV the full manifestation process can begin.

Part III

Paradigms, Mind, and Thought

PARADIGMS:

HIDDEN KEYS TO CREATION

9

IN CHAPTER 1, we defined paradigms as belief systems or structures which, consciously or unconsciously, shape every aspect of our lives. Recall James Ray's definition of "paradigm": "the sum total of our beliefs, values, identity, expectations, attitudes, habits, decisions, opinions, and thought patterns—about ourselves, others, and how life works . . . the filter through which we interpret what we see and experience." Although our paradigms shape the personal world we choose to create and our relationship to it, these fundamental belief systems often remain hidden to our outer awareness. In this chapter, we will delve further into how paradigms are formed, how they influence our lives, and how we can change them.

From birth through our early twenties, we spend much of our lives thinking and doing what we are told or shown by parents, teachers, religions, society, authority figures, and our peers. Anyone with whom we spend a great deal of time during those formative years plays a part in shaping our fundamental beliefs. Without making conscious choices, we take on beliefs and behavior or action patterns for basic life skills and principles. These patterns come to us in the forms of religious beliefs, ethical and moral standards, prejudices, and opinions.

In early childhood, the greatest influences on a child's development and paradigm formation are parents, or those who fill the parental role, and those with whom the child spends the most time. In today's society, child-care workers or other "surrogate" parents often spend more time with the child than do the parents. Once the child enters school, other children and teachers become significant influences in paradigm formation. Children have a deep desire to be liked and accepted, and will often do whatever they feel is necessary to gain acceptance and recognition. They will do what they see other children do in order to "fit in." At this age, children form fundamental beliefs around how to be liked and accepted, what gets them immediate recognition and approval, and what they feel that they can or cannot do well.

As children continue in school, they pick up very quickly on the "unspoken rules" of life—a set of expectations, behaviors, and attitudes that many seem to live by, but are never actually verbalized. One of those unspoken rules is conformity. Our education process places very little emphasis on individuation and creativity. Everything is standardized. The curriculum serves the masses, not the individual; it contains little room for the creative and imaginative child who doesn't easily fit the "standard."

Child and creative education advocates have been working for years to change the system, and they have made progress. However, we still have a long way to go toward allowing each individual child to discover his or her own worth and process, and to design an educational system that fosters creativity, individuality, and facilitating the child's discovery of who they are and their place in the world.

Because conformity gets so much unspoken attention, children receive little instruction about making decisions and choices. The decisions become whatever seems to be expected to meet the standard. The choices seem predetermined by the path that the child finds him- or herself on, or that the child's peers are taking. By the time the child becomes a young adult in his or her mid-twenties, when it is time to make concrete decisions and choices about relationships, career paths, and how he or she wants to live, the person doesn't know how to choose. Sometimes, in fact, knowing where to start is seemingly impossible. Therefore, once again, someone else's lead becomes the path to follow— the path of least resistance or that seems well trod.

We can shift these patterns at any time in our adult lives. Whether you are in your early twenties, just starting out on your own, or you are well into your adult years, you can choose to create your own life. It is never too late to change. You can choose to claim your life whenever you are ready. To conform to the standard means disappearing into the crowd and making no significant contribution to yourself or to society. Claiming your life doesn't mean you must stand up and wave a flag so that everyone sees you. It just means that you honor the flag that waves deep within your soul, and let your soul, not the path that the standard shows you, guide your life.

Often we are not aware of our paradigms or of influences around us. Robert Hargrove, author of *Masterful Coaching*, illustrates this with the metaphor, "People are like a goldfish in water. Just as the water is invisible to goldfish, people's thinking, practices, and environment are for the most part invisible to them. They are often so wrapped up in the routine of what they are doing that they may not be aware of the things they are doing that lead to unintended results." Our own level of conscious awareness determines how much we allow others to shape our paradigms and how proactive we are in creating our own belief systems. When we do not probe our thoughts and beliefs deeply enough to be secure in who we are and what we think, we unconsciously allow others to think for us. We live within a mass consciousness that makes the rules and sets the standards for all. Many people consider living within the mass consciousness quite acceptable. They don't have to think or feel for themselves, or worry about what is or is not appropriate. The group mind takes care of that for them. Or they may defer to one very dominant person in their life to whom they look to know what and how they should feel, think, and do. Again, this may not be a conscious process, but it happens all the time. We are influenced greatly by those with whom we choose to spend our time. Nature abhors a vacuum. Where there is empty space, whatever is around it will automatically fill it. The same is true in our minds. If we do not know what we think and feel, there is empty space that will be filled by the thoughts, feelings, and opinions of those around us.

Paradigms are deep-rooted emotional conditioning, and are often well hidden from our conscious awareness. They anchor themselves in our cellular memory. Our early development environment may have given us positive, empowering paradigms, or limiting, rigid beliefs. For most of us, our formative years brought some combination of the two. If we want to shift paradigms, we must be willing to examine everything we have been taught. Some of what has been handed down to us resonates within as truth. Other inherited beliefs, after examination, do not. Those who came before us passed on truth as best they knew it. However, truth is relative to each person, and evolves in depth and understanding from generation to generation. Many ancient and pure teachings have been distorted through hundreds or thousands of years of interpretation. We have the opportunity to clear away as much distortion as possible for the generations to come. And then we pass on the torch to future generations who will continue this evolution in understanding, clearing away some of our distortions.

You have probably already identified certain paradigms in your life through our work thus far. However, if you are still unclear about your fundamental paradigms, think about something you know you need to change in your life. It can be anything—a belief, a circumstance, or a conflict that needs resolution. Then make a clear statement about how you want it to change, what you want the new belief or circumstance to be, how you would like to see the conflict resolved. For example, let's say that you want to be more comfortable in public speaking. Declare the statement, "I love speaking before large groups of people, and do it very successfully on a regular basis." As soon as you make the statement, your paradigms that have blocked you from this success will begin showing themselves. You will hear the "inner critic" telling you why it is not possible, or you will be filled with doubts and all the reasons why you don't believe being a successful public speaker is possible for you. The inner critic and your doubts are showing you your self-limiting paradigms. Making a clear statement of what you want in your life is like bait for the limiting paradigms. The stronger you make the statement, the more attractive the bait. Therefore, the more detailed you make your desire, the more the paradigms that hold you back from realizing it will surface.

The following exercise will help you identify some of your paradigms and their origins. Allow yourself an hour or more of uninterrupted time so that you can get the full benefit of this process.

Meditation Activity:
Identifying Paradigms and Their Origins

Place your journal close by so that you will have it when you are ready to write. Go to your Point of Stillness and consider the following questions. Write in your journal about each one, letting the voices of your soul, Higher Self, and Spirit speak. Don't worry about who is speaking when. Just write. The wisdom will flow. Where the guidance comes from is not important. Truth is truth.

> What are some things in my life that I would like to change or do better?
>
> What positive statements can I make to call those changes into my life?
>
> What inner critic voices or doubts come to the surface when I state what I want?
>
> What paradigms are being revealed to me?

Make a list of the people who have had the greatest influence on how you think about yourself, about others, about success, about love and power, and about life. Then take each name individually and do a clustering exercise with each one, just as you did in chapter 2 with "freedom," "success," "power," and "love." Write each person's name in the middle of a blank sheet of paper, and then as if free-associating, write every word that comes to mind on this page. Even if you feel like you already know how someone has influenced you, do the exercise with that person's name anyway. Deeper insights may emerge.

When you have come to the end of your list, take a fresh page and write in the center the last word that you wrote on the first page. Draw a circle around it, and continue free associating with that word, writing every word that comes to mind. Continue this process for each name on your list of people, starting as many new pages as necessary, until you begin to feel that you are coming to an understanding about how that particular individual contributed to your paradigms. At that point, go to yet another fresh page and write in paragraph form anything that is coming to you. Ask the question, "What beliefs, attitudes or perspectives, and thought patterns have they passed on to me?"

Having looked at the ways specific people have influenced your paradigms, now let's examine society, educational systems, and religious traditions and their impact on your current beliefs. Use the clustering process again with the following:

The name of your home town

The name of your elementary school

The name of your junior high school

The name of your high school

The name of your college

The name of your graduate school

The name of your religious institution(s) from birth to age twenty-five

Finally, consider whether these beliefs, attitudes, and thought patterns from individuals and institutions are supporting you in your life and in your success. Are there things that need to change within you and your relationship to these beliefs, attitudes, and thought patterns? If so, write about those changes.

Don't worry if you end up with a long list of needed changes. Just choose one and work with it. Everything else will begin to shift as you work on that one. Continue working with this exercise over the next week or so. Let it keep playing in your conscious awareness, and you will continue to receive insight and understanding.

So how do we change our paradigms? Changing paradigms involves altering your deep-rooted emotional conditioning. Remember that energy can neither be created nor destroyed; it can only be transmuted into another form. Emotions and feelings are energy. Emotional conditioning is simply habitual energy patterns. Thoughts and beliefs are also energy. Therefore, we can't get rid of them. To change the conditioning of our thoughts and beliefs, we must transmute the old programming to a new belief. That means if we want new thought patterns, we have to constantly and consistently put new thoughts into our minds. When we consciously concentrate on and hold these new thoughts in our minds, we will create new conditioned responses, and therefore powerful new paradigms. Everything in life begins with a thought. If you want to make a change in your life, you must first change your thoughts.

In *Science of Success,* James Ray offers a great metaphor for changing thought patterns. Imagine a glass of cranberry juice and a very large pitcher of clear, sparkling spring water. The juice represents your old thought patterns, while the water represents your new thoughts. If you begin to pour water into the glass of juice, the juice begins to dilute. You get excited as you see your attitudes, thoughts, and feelings begin to change. But as you keep pouring, the glass overflows and the juice begins to run all over the table. Unfortunately, here is where you might stop pouring, thinking, "Oh this can't be right. I'm making a mess of everything. I'd better stop before this goes too far." And so you stop, having only watered down the juice to a lighter shade of cranberry. If, on the other hand, you keep pouring, eventually all of the cranberry juice has overflowed and you are left with a glass of clear, sparkling water.

Just as the cranberry juice is transformed into clear water, so it can be with your thoughts. If you stop half way and return to your old thought patterns, ultimately nothing will have changed. You must be willing to let things get messy if that is what is necessary for the transformational process. If you just keep pouring, giving energy only to the new thought, the old paradigm will fade and the new one will take hold. Once it has taken hold, you must keep nurturing it and supporting it so that it grows strong enough to remain firm in the face of doubt.

Consistency is the key here. Without consistency, former habit takes control again, and the new paradigm will elude you. Discipline is required to keep putting the new thought pattern into your conscious mind. Through discipline, you create the new paradigm, which sets you free to reshape your life, giving you more control over what your life looks like. Paradigms are created by repeated and consistent thoughts, not passing thoughts. Any thought that is given enough attention and focus will form a paradigm. What you think about comes about.

Changing your paradigms may mean entering into uncomfortable territory. You've never done it this way before. The old way was comfortable, not because it was right for you, but because it is what you knew. It was familiar. "Familiar" and "comfortable" can be dangerous. They lead to stagnation. Focus on your new thought.

Significant change in your life can also threaten others or make them uncomfortable. They may have a lot invested in you staying just the way you are. Whether it is a parent who wants you to be a certain way, a boss who prefers that you just do as you're told and not think for yourself, or a friend or partner who doesn't want anything or anyone to challenge their carefully crafted and protected way of life, they will try to keep you as you are. They may tell you that you are "different now," that they "don't know you anymore," or that what you are doing is "risky and dangerous. You could fail. It will never work. Better to come back into the safety of what you know and not take any chances."

Living soul mission means a life of dynamic thought, feeling, and action. When something is dynamic, it is energy in motion, a force with direction and intention, ever changing, ever evolving. When others try to stop you from moving forward in your life, stop to ask yourself, "Are these people whose lives I wish to emulate?" If not, know what is right for you and stick to your guns! If you truly want to make a difference in this world, leaving it a better place for having been here, you will probably not do things the way everyone else has. Sometimes you must take the risk of not fitting in, not feeling accepted, in order to truly make a difference. Many of those who have made the most profound changes in our world were bucking the system all the way.

Engaging in full-spectrum living depends on your willingness to create and think new thoughts, to discipline yourself to allow into your consciousness only the thoughts you desire. It may be that someone before you has laid the groundwork for your journey so that you can follow an already established path. However, the path for your life could also be into new and uncharted territory. You must be willing to face the new frontier of possibilities and blaze a trail that can lead you to the fullness of you and all that you desire. Whether you are following an established pathway or cutting through the dense thicket, commitment to your truth is essential.

It is difficult to commit to something that is not aligned with soul purpose and mission. The attempt to commit will be met with tremendous inner conflict. However, when you are living your truth and on task for soul mission, commitment is easy, because you are doing what you love. You have no desire to be doing anything different with your life. What you have committed yourself to is your glorious, fulfilling, rewarding life.

The following exercise will help you begin the process of creating your new paradigms. Give yourself as much time as you need. Allow your creative juices to flow, as well as your total and complete honesty with Self. After all, you are embarking on the creation of the rest of your life.

Activity: Creating New Paradigms

Go back to the end of the previous exercise (page 145). Review the list of changes that you wrote about in response to that question, and choose one change that you wish to make now. What is the paradigm shift you must make in order to effect that change in your life? Using the following guidelines, write your new paradigm.

Your new paradigm may be huge and expansive or it may be something that others would deem small. It doesn't matter. This is your creation. From this moment on, you get to design your beliefs as you want them to be.

Be as specific, detailed, and comprehensive as possible in stating your new paradigm.

Let go of all limitation of thought. In other words, climb out of your box! This may be the biggest challenge for you. All of our thoughts and beliefs are shaped by the boxes in which we live.

Always use the present tense. Call your new paradigms into being. Call your life into being. Know that what you desire is here now (Law of Correspondence), and live every moment within your new paradigm.

Get excited about your new paradigm. Feelings and emotions are your ticket to the subconscious mind, and the subconscious mind is where your real power lies. When you get excited about something, you have motivation. Your soul is not interested in a mediocre existence. Your soul wants nothing less than manifestation of full potential!

State very clearly what you do want, not what you don't want. Your mind does not distinguish between a positive and a negative command. It only knows the subject upon which you are focusing and thinking. What you think about, comes about.

Visualize your new paradigm. Create every detail of what your life is like in this new paradigm and be in it, don't just observe it.

Again, take your time and write as much as you need to write to create your new paradigm.

Once you have written your paradigm following all of the guidelines listed above, condense it into a single sentence—a workable sentence that you can use as an affirmation. Write that sentence down. Be sure that your statement brings your paradigm into clarity and gives it a concrete form for your life, right now, today. Doing this work doesn't mean anything if it stays in the abstract.

If you have someone with whom you can share this new paradigm, and who will support you in making the shift, then share it with them. This will help you further clarify it, claim it, and call it into being. If there is no one with whom you can comfortably share your new paradigm, then simply sit in your silence and offer it as a powerful declaration of freedom to the universe.

Anything that you can imagine, you can create. The more global the magnitude of the paradigm, the more important it is to develop a clear picture of what that paradigm looks like in your daily life. Specificity is very important for the development of your passion around the paradigm. The words of the paradigm statement must trigger a clear manifestation picture.

Congratulations! You have now officially begun your personal paradigm transformation. The process has been happening "behind the scenes" since you picked up this book for the first time, and probably long before that. Thoughts have been stirred and ideas sparked. But now you begin to bring it into a tangible form. In the next chapter, we begin our exploration of how thought creates our lives, and how to use the conscious mind as a dynamic tool for manifestation.

Activity: Chapter Reflection

Reflect on what you have learned in this chapter about paradigms. Write about paradigms in your own words so that you begin to have a personal understanding of how they shape your life. Then think of someone with whom you can have a conversation about the paradigms and their role in your manifestation journey. Talking about them will help solidify your ideas, thoughts, and discoveries, and perhaps help you identify more of your personal paradigms.

THE UNIVERSAL TRINITY

10

OF CREATION: CONCEPT, FORM, ACTION

THE LAW OF MENTALISM states that the universe is mental. This means that everything exists first as a thought or idea. All of creation was first a thought within the mind of Spirit. It goes on to say that everything exists within the mind of Spirit, and Spirit exists within the mind of everything. This means that as creation takes form, it contains within it the mind of Spirit.

If everything exists within the mind of Spirit, and Spirit exists within the mind of everything, then our mind is within the mind of Spirit, and Spirit is within our mind. When we open fully to this concept, our mind becomes Spirit in action.

This is simultaneously a very empowering and humbling thought—it's empowering to realize the magnitude of possibility within our mind, and humbling because of both the great opportunity and responsibility we have to open our minds to our full potential. Full potential will manifest very differently for each person, for we each have our own soul mission through which the mind of Spirit is moving. With soul mission as the backdrop, we begin to paint the picture of our life. Soul mission is our divine purpose for being. The picture we paint is our choice of how we wish to fulfill that mission.

All of creation unfolds from thought. Thought begins to take shape and develop into form. The form then assumes a function or has an effect on the world, be it subtle or monumental. I call this unfolding the universal trinity of creation: concept, form, action. The Law says that Spirit is within us and we are within Spirit. As we create, we have the choice of whether or not we open our awareness to Spirit's presence, inviting Spirit to inform our creation—to flow through us, inspire, and guide us through every step of the creative process. This is what we mean by cocreative partnership with Spirit. This is how we open our minds to be Spirit in action.

The universal trinity is at work in every part of our life, and on every level of creation. In daily life, it appears as thinking, being, doing. Thinking is concept, being is form, and doing is action. Every part of life begins as a thought. Our thought creates who we are. Who we are leads to what we do.

Within us, the trinity unfolds as:

> Concept—Spirit's idea of how It wants to appear, what It wants to do, how It wants to interact with the rest of creation;
>
> Form—Spirit takes on physical form through each of us;
>
> Action—how Spirit flows through us in thought, word, and deed.

The trinity unfolds from the divine into physical creation, and then into interaction within creation. It transforms from a very high and fast energy vibration to a slower and more dense energy form. Any act of creation has within it the unfolding of this universal trinity. We can choose to open to the full awareness of this trinity and enter into a dynamic, cocreative partnership with Spirit. This means that we fully participate in partnership with Spirit in each step of the process of creation—from the first spark of the idea all the way to complete manifestation. Or, we can not choose this awareness, and therefore never know the splendor of the creative presence of Spirit in our lives. All awareness begins in the mind. How we open to the magnificent spiritual essence of the mind, to Spirit in action, determines our ability to access the full bounty of both the seen and unseen riches of life.

Dreams, imagination, and inspiration are the beginning of your cocreative partnership with Spirit. Inspiration is the result of being "in Spirit." That word also implies that when you are inspired, the object of your inspiration already exists in a "spirit" form, or in the unseen reality. When we open our mind to be Spirit in action, then our imagination becomes the activity of Spirit in action. This is cocreative partnership.

As you focus on your idea, it begins to take on a life of its own. Energy builds around it, and the universal trinity, through the Law of Correspondence, continues to unfold on multiple levels of reality. A powerful dynamic is created as concept, form, and action manifest in new ways. Spirit works through the idea or the form to show you the steps toward action and result.

All the laws of the universe are present within the universal trinity. The Law of Mentalism forms the cornerstone of the trinity by stating that the universe is mental—that everything begins as a thought or concept before it can evolve into form and action.

We have said that the universal trinity can be seen in everything. This is the Law of Correspondence at work. Whether we are talking about the formation of galaxies, stars, and planets, or the preparation of a meal, the trinity is present. The process begins with the idea that food must be prepared (concept), continues with planning the menu and ingredients (form), and concludes with preparing and eating the food (action).

The Law of Vibration, stating that energy is always in motion, ever changing and transforming, is the fundamental method through which the universal trinity evolves. By nature, the initial concept or idea cannot remain static. It will constantly vibrate and transform. Because of the Law of Attraction, it will draw to itself the vibrations necessary for the full development of the concept. Without vibration, there could be no creation or evolution, no form or action.

The Law of Polarity tells us that everything necessary to bring an idea to full development and manifestation already exists within the idea itself. If we look at the idea deeply enough and from every perspective, it will show us the form it is to take, how to create that form, what its function will be, and how it will execute that function. For example, let's say you want to build a house. You have a picture of the house in your mind (concept). However, you aren't sure how to go about building it, what materials are necessary, what form of construction is required. So you explore your inner vision of the house and begin peeling away layers. You strip away the façade of the house, the walls, the infrastructure, and the framing, observing at each level, until you get to the foundation. At each level, you learn more about how to build your house. All of these levels exist within your original vision of the house. They can show you how to begin. From there a plan is drawn (form) and the building process begins (action). All the possibilities and options available to you can be found within your initial idea. You just have to go through the layers to find them.

The Law of Rhythm shows us that inherent in the universal trinity there is a system for creation, an order in which things must be accomplished. In building your house, you can't begin construction if you don't know what you are going to build. There must first be a concept and a plan. You must choose what color you want the walls before you can paint. Even though the creation process may appear at times to be random or chaotic, there is always an order at work.

The flow of concept to form to action is the Law of Cause and Effect at work. The initial cause is the concept or idea that leads to a form (effect). Form in turn becomes cause and leads to action or effect. Effect cannot exist without cause, action cannot exist without form, form cannot exist without concept.

Finally, within any creative process there is a gestation period. This is the Law of Gender. You may have a time schedule in mind, but any act of creation will have its own inherent schedule. The cake will not bake faster than the necessary chemical reactions can occur. A business can only be built as fast as a product can be developed or clientele established. By the same token, as momentum builds, things may happen faster than you expected. In this case, all was in place, the ideas were clear, everything was ready to go. The idea's time had come.

Living soul mission is the universal trinity operating in full swing. Living soul mission means opening our mind and thought to full awareness of soul essence and Spirit guidance, letting that awareness shape who we are, and in turn informing how we present ourselves and our actions to the world. Who we are in the world is then a perfect mirror of our divine nature. Living soul mission is living Spirit in action.

These are powerful concepts. As you grasp them, you will understand your own creative process much more fully. In the next chapter, we will explore how this universal trinity manifests in our personal lives as thinking, being, and doing. We will look at the conscious and subconscious minds, thought, perception and attitude, imagination, results, and habits. This will help you get a clearer picture of how you are creating your life, how the universal trinity is operating within you, and how you might want to employ the universal trinity differently if you feel that the picture of your life needs some adjustments.

Activity: Chapter Reflection

Reflect on what you have learned in this chapter about the process of creation. Write about this process in your own words so that you begin to have a personal understanding of how creation occurs. Then think of someone with whom you can have a conversation about the universal trinity. Talking about them will help solidify your ideas, thoughts, and discoveries.

THE POWER

OF MIND AND THOUGHT

THE BUDDHA SAID, "We are what we think. All that we are arises with our thoughts. With our thoughts we make the world." A simple way to grasp the power and influence of your thoughts is to light a candle in a dark room. The light from the candle immediately shines out to dispel the darkness. The longer the candle burns, the brighter the room seems to get. The candle light is energy that is pouring out into the room. So it is with your thoughts. Thought is a very high and fast form of energy vibration, similar to light. The vibration of your thoughts fills a room the same way as the vibration of light.

Another illustration of how energy permeates a space is the burning of incense. If you light a stick of incense, the smoke immediately begins to rise in a wispy, delicate dance. As the smoke rises higher it dissipates into the room. At this point, you might think that its effect is gone— you can no longer see it. But very soon you begin to notice the sweet fragrance that has permeated the air. Soon the fragrance is no longer confined to one room, but has permeated the entire house. The same is true with your thoughts. The energy of your thought dances out into space and forms a vibrational matrix. This matrix is the web of your thoughts, and becomes your personal world. Anyone who enters your personal world is influenced by this web, just as you are influenced by the thought webs of others. In this chapter, we will explore thought and the conscious and subconscious minds, and their impact on attitude, perspective, and habits.

In the last chapter, we established that everything first exists in the mind. As we have said before, many people think of the mind as the brain. The brain, however, is simply the computer that keeps your body machine functioning. The brain is just one small part of the larger, intuitive mind that flows throughout the body. The larger mind flows through all the cells of your being. It is energy in motion.

In our Western world, we live in a rational/empirical society that asks for concrete proof of everything. We are conditioned to rely only on the rational mind and empirical understanding. We are a "seeing-is-believing" culture. However, the rational mind is just one small part of the larger intuitive mind. As conscious awareness develops in our society, more people are paying closer attention to the stirrings deep inside, the voices of intuition, and acknowledging the possibilities of an unseen reality. Through the larger intuitive mind, we can live in an expanded consciousness. We can get in touch with our bodies, with Spirit, with the rhythms of the Earth, and the flow of the universe. In chapter 2, Spirit spoke of human and divine orientations to living (see page 28). The human orientation corresponds to a rational approach, while the divine orientation corresponds to an intuitive approach. The divine or intuitive orientation to living recognizes the role of the unseen in everything.

The Conscious and Subconscious Minds

The mind is divided into two parts, the conscious mind and the subconscious mind. The conscious mind is the part over which we have conscious control. It could be considered the outer mind, in that it is the part of the mind where we are clearly aware of our thoughts. It is also where rational thought takes place. We can easily perceive what is going on in the conscious mind. We can choose our thoughts, and discipline them to create new thought patterns and paradigms.

The subconscious mind is the inner mind, the great expansive mind of which the conscious mind is just one small part. It expresses itself through feelings and responses or reactions. It has no walls or boundaries. The conscious mind controls how much of the subconscious mind we bring to full awareness. We access the subconscious mind by choosing to go beneath the surface of the conscious mind—to enter into the vast, unseen realities.

CONSCIOUS MIND

SUBCONSCIOUS MIND

The subconscious mind functions in every cell of your body. It is the larger, intuitive mind, and could also be called the body-mind that we discussed in chapter 6. It is constantly moving and shifting, constantly taking in information, processing it, forming feelings, and taking action based on that information. However, the subconscious mind has no ability to censor or discern which information it takes in. Whatever the conscious mind focuses on or gives attention to is what the subconscious mind absorbs. Furthermore, when there is no conscious filtering of input from the environment, the subconscious absorbs the prevailing feelings, opinions, and beliefs of the surrounding people and situations. The subconscious will immediately begin to take action or develop more fully whatever thought it is given.

Therefore, our level of conscious awareness is very important. The conscious mind is the filter for the subconscious mind. When we have a low level of conscious awareness, we are not very discerning about the thoughts to which we give energy, and, therefore, what goes into our subconscious minds. As a result, our lives are shaped by our environment and the thoughts, opinions, and beliefs of those around us. When we choose to develop our awareness, however, and are discerning about the thoughts to which we give energy and allow into our subconscious minds, we take back control of our lives. We discipline our thoughts, feelings, and opinions toward positive creation. This is vitally important in the process of identifying soul journey. If there is no conscious filter for input to the subconscious mind, we can't know which thoughts and feelings are ours and which are someone else's. We are so bombarded by others' thoughts, feelings, and beliefs that we can't get anywhere near our own soul.

The subconscious mind cannot tell the difference between material reality and fantasy. Since it has no filtering mechanism, it can only assume that any thought that the conscious mind focuses on is what it wants. Its job is to respond to the input of the conscious mind. It will immediately absorb that input and set things into motion for its full manifestation. Whatever the conscious mind engages itself with, the subconscious mind will immediately begin to manifest in your world. It will work to bring the focus of that thought into physical-plane reality. Therefore, if you want to be in touch with soul mission and live that mission through every aspect of your life, you must choose your conscious thoughts very carefully. You must discipline your thoughts to create a picture or an image of the life you desire. What you think about comes about. If you live in fear, whatever it is that you fear is sure to manifest because that is the focus of your thought. If you focus on peace and serenity, that is what you will manifest.

James Ray compares the conscious mind to a gardener and the subconscious mind to the garden. The gardener can choose which seeds to plant in the garden. If she wants carrots, she must plant carrots, not broccoli. She must plant the seeds of whatever she desires in her life, because the garden will grow whatever she plants.

We must choose carefully which seeds or thoughts we wish to plant in our subconscious garden. The subconscious mind will grow those seeds and produce results that reflect very clearly the kinds of thoughts we have planted. Whatever thoughts we accept into our conscious minds and give energy to will grow in the garden of our subconscious mind, and eventually manifest in our physical reality.

This is why we must always focus our attention and thought on what we do want, not on what we don't want. The subconscious mind cannot distinguish between what you want or don't want. It only knows the subject of your thought. Therefore, when the subject of your thought is what you don't want, your subconscious mind will do everything it can to manifest that which you don't want, because that has been the subject of your thought.

Whatever we feel about something subconsciously becomes our paradigm about it, which in turn influences how we think about it, the actions we take, the choices we make, and the results we get. The result creates more conscious thoughts, which lead to more subconscious feelings. These feelings, in turn, strengthen the paradigm, leading to further action and decision, and another result. We have a circular kind of pattern again.

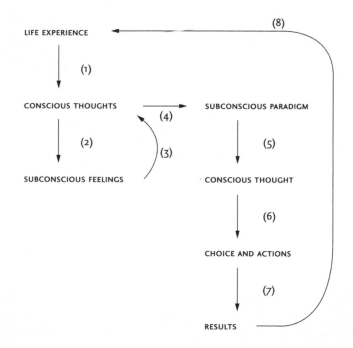

For example, a child spends all of his allowance to buy a toy. His father criticizes him for spending money foolishly and not saving for something important. The child internalizes the feeling that spending money on something for him is foolish and he will be criticized for it. Therefore, anytime that he thinks about spending money on himself, he automatically feels foolish. Without realizing it, he has created a paradigm that says that it is foolish to spend money on oneself. As he grows to adulthood, he is very reluctant to make any investment in himself because, in his eyes, that would only bring criticism.

In order to create a new paradigm, you must first choose the thoughts that will create the necessary feelings to support that paradigm, and then impress those thoughts upon the subconscious mind by giving them your constant focus and attention. As the feelings from the new thought become the new emotional pattern, a new paradigm is formed.

Thought

Thoughts are extremely fast energy vibrations. Like lightning, they move very quickly—in, out, and through our physical bodies. A thought that passes in, out, and through the conscious mind and is given little or no attention will have little or no consequence in our lives. However, when that thought is slowed down, focused on, and repeated, it creates corresponding feelings in the subconscious mind and forms a paradigm, as we just discussed. The subconscious mind is energy in constant motion, traveling through all the cells of the body. Therefore, paradigms are thoughts that have slowed down and been repeated so many times that they have charged the cells of our bodies with belief. They settle into the cells and become a much heavier and denser energy vibration. A metaphor might be water flowing through the pipes in your house. If the water flows quickly through the pipes, it leaves little residue. However, if the water runs slowly or stands for a period of time, mineral deposits are left in the pipe and the function of the pipe is affected. Thoughts are fleeting, while paradigms stay with you.

Developing the filtering mechanism of the conscious mind means learning to discern what you want to let in and what you want to let go. It is important to learn to observe thoughts and emotions without necessarily energizing them. Monitor every thought that comes in and choose which ones to give your energy and attention. This takes a lot of concentration at first if you are just developing the skill, but as you become a master of discernment, it gets much easier. In most circumstances, you will automatically pull in what you desire and toss out the rest. And when you come to a challenging situation where you are being bombarded by thoughts you do not want to energize, you will have the skills to push away that which you do not desire.

We have said that the process of change begins in the unseen realms and moves to the seen. It is true that the change must occur in the inner realms in order for it to be permanent in the outer realm. The paradigm itself lives in the subconscious mind, an unseen reality. The doorway to the subconscious mind, however, is accessed through the conscious mind. The wider we open the doorway to the world of the subconscious, the more clearly we see our subconscious emotional patterning or paradigms. Therefore, it is through the conscious mind that we must choose to look deep inside the subconscious realm and identify what needs to shift, transform, or heal. Once we have identified the paradigm, we begin working in the conscious mind to reconfigure the subconscious belief. We must create the desired thought and give it our full focus and attention for as long as it takes to make the paradigm shift. When particular paradigms are not so deeply entrenched, this may take only a few days or weeks. But for deep-seated paradigms that have been held in our cellular thought for many years, a complete shift may take months or years.

This may appear to be a daunting prospect. But once you begin the process you will see that, even for the most ingrained paradigms, shifts in perception begin right away, and you can quickly see results. However, from time to time you may feel yourself slipping back into your old patterns. This is just an indication that you have not yet completed the paradigm shift, even though you feel you have experienced change. It may take a long time before you are completely free of the old paradigm, but each time you slip back and then take the steps to reclaim your new paradigm, you are stronger and more secure in the new pattern. If you want change in your life, you must choose it in your thoughts every moment of every day until it is fully accomplished.

Thought is much more powerful than most of us ever imagined. It can work a puzzle, design a house, change attitudes, heal bodies, create miracles. And it can change your paradigms. Focus and intention are essential.

Using affirmations has become a very popular technique for transformation and manifestation. However, mindlessly-repeated affirmations will not necessarily be effective. If you simply repeat the affirmation without focus and intention, you are not changing the subconscious mind and the cellular thought. Over a long enough period of time, the affirmation may eventually sink into the cells and effect a paradigm shift. However, with intention and focus, you can charge the cells with this new thought and affect a paradigm shift much more quickly and efficiently. The process involves first having a clear thought, and then sending it down through the body, like a lightning bolt, charging the cells with the new paradigm. The new paradigm is not firmly in place until the shift has occurred in every cell of your being.

Meditation Activity: Charging Your Body with New Thought

Bring to mind the new paradigm that you wrote in the exercise on page 149 In chapter 9. Then, sit in a comfortable position, either in a chair or on the floor, with your back straight, hands resting naturally in your lap, and take deep, full breaths. Allow your breath to find its own natural, steady, even flow, so that its gentle regularity can carry you into a deep meditative state.

Begin humming quietly and gently on any pitch that feels comfortable to you. (Keep your teeth apart, and imagine saying "Ah" inside your mouth while your lips close to a hum.) Take a breath whenever you need to do so, and then return to the hum. The purpose of this is to feel the vibration of the humming move throughout your body. As you continue humming, slowly move through these next four steps:

1. Place your hands on various parts of your head and continue to feel the vibration;

2. Place your hands on various parts of your torso and feel the vibration;

3. Move your hands down to your legs and feel the vibration.

Next, beginning with the crown chakra and moving down, concentrate on opening each chakra with the hum, feeling each center vibrate with the sound. You may want to focus on the color of each chakra as you go:

Crown—violet
Brow—indigo
Throat—light blue
Heart—green
Solar plexus—yellow
Sacral—orange
Root—red

By now, your entire body is vibrating with the hum. Every chakra is open to receive a new thought vibration. If there is any part of your body in which you do not feel the vibration, simply take note of it and allow that part of your body to relax and accept the vibration.

As you continue to hum, become aware of the vibration as it extends beyond your physical body into the space around you. This vibrating space around your physical body is your aura. It is an active component of your being at all times. Continue humming, and feel the vibration of energy throughout not only your physical body, but also your aura.

Your entire energy field and body-mind are now open to receive your new paradigm. As you continue humming and feeling your body and aura vibrate, imagine lightning bolts of energy coming down through the top of your head and through your body. Attach your new paradigm to those lightning bolts and feel that new paradigm coursing through your body. Continue this for a few minutes, and then relax.

You can use this exercise for any affirmation or paradigm shift you want to bring into your life. It draws the new thought out of the mental plane of reality and into the physical. When you do this exercise every day for several weeks with a single affirmation or paradigm, you will experience a significant shift.

In chapter 4, we discussed the Buddhist practice of mindfulness (page 52) giving all of your focus and attention to one thought or task at a time. The conscious mind can focus effectively on only one thought at a time. However, the ability to do many things at once, often referred to as multitasking, has become a highly regarded skill in our culture. Multitasking creates conflict within the mind. By its nature, the mind wants to give all of its attention to one task or thought, yet we insist on making it juggle several. The result is that we become mentally exhausted in our efforts to override the mind's basic programming. By allowing ourselves to focus on one thing at a time, the mind can kick into high gear and function incredibly efficiently. Mindfulness creates balance and harmony within our lives by allowing the mind to function at its best. We accomplish tasks more quickly, and we process thoughts, feelings, and emotions more fully. The quality of mental function is much higher, and we don't get so exhausted from forcing the mind to work against its nature.

The thoughts on which you focus in the conscious mind will affect every part of your life. Therefore, choosing and disciplining your thoughts is very important. Know and state what you *want*, not what you don't want. Whatever you give attention to in your thoughts is what you will draw to you.

Attitude and Perspective

French novelist Marcel Proust said, "The real voyage of discovery consists not in seeking new landscapes, but in having new eyes." Our attitude about life in general as well as specific situations, challenges, and relationships has a powerful impact on how we view things and the results we create. Attitude is a composite of thoughts, feelings, and actions, which together create a vibrating energy pattern. The Law of Attraction tells us that like attracts like. Therefore, our attitude greatly influences what we draw into our life. Negativity attracts circumstances that reinforce and encourage a downward spiral in quality of life. Positive attitude, on the other hand, attracts support and encouragement, and creates a sense of confidence and well-being.

We have talked a lot about choice, and our freedom and power to discipline our thoughts. Disciplining thoughts gives us control over which feelings we choose to energize, and the clarity to work through feelings that we wish to transform or heal. Discipline and clarity lead to positive action that, in turn, supports confident and healthy living. Once again, we create a circle. Attitudes affect feelings, feelings influence actions, actions create results, results reinforce attitude. The attitude gets stronger, leading to more confidence in feeling, resulting in even more committed action and more concrete results.

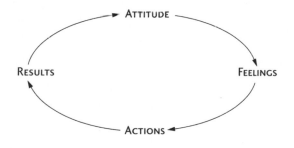

Success at anything depends much more on attitude than background, intelligence, or education. There are many stories of people who accomplished great things against overwhelming odds. Although each person's journey was different, they all agree that the most important elements in their success were positive thoughts, focus, and commitment. They refused to give in to the odds. Positive attitude is what got them through.

There are times when we are stuck in a negative attitude and we can't seem to make a shift. We know that our attitude needs to change, but from where we are standing, we can't seem to shift. When this happens, changing your perspective on the situation can be very helpful. Neale Donald Walsch writes in *Conversations with God*, "Your perspective creates your thoughts, and your thoughts create everything.... Assume a different perspective and you will have a different thought about everything. In this way you will have learned to control your thought, and, in the creation of your experience, controlled thought is everything. ... The controlling and directing of your thoughts is the highest form of prayer."

What a powerful statement! "The controlling and directing of your thoughts is the highest form of prayer." We have the gift and power of choice. When we exercise that power and discipline our thoughts, we honor Spirit who gave us the gift. The Law of Mentalism tells us that we are an aspect of the divine manifest in human form. Disciplined thought is a committed act of gratitude for the gifts we are given, and a celebration of our cocreative partnership with Spirit.

Assuming a different perspective can be as simple as taking a step to the right or left and looking at the situation from a new vantage point. Remember the Oriental rug example in chapter 5? With every step around the rug, my perception of the colors changed. Or perhaps you need to step into the other person's shoes and live their journey in your mind for a few days. You may come to a very different feeling about things then. At other times, you need to step away from the situation for a while to let thoughts and emotions become quiet. Then you can return with a fresh and clearer perspective.

Questions to Ponder: Examining Attitude and Perspective

What is my general attitude toward life? How is it shaping my daily experience?

Are there situations or aspects of my life in which my attitude needs to change? If so, what would be a more productive attitude? How can I make the shift?

Are there places in my life where I seem to be stuck or not able to find resolution? If so, how would a new perspective help? Whose viewpoint do I need to consider to help me see from a different perspective? What questions do I need to ask? Do I need to stand in a different position, either literally or figuratively, in order to perceive things differently?

Feelings

Feelings become metaphorical containers that give shape to our lives. When we experience joy, love, freedom, and other liberating feelings, the container has a loose shape with many holes that allow the air to pass through. The container is pliable and can easily be enlarged or reshaped to hold more good feelings. These positive feelings create an infinitely expansive container that encourages our boundless growth and experience.

However, when we experience fear, anger, resentment, or other restrictive feelings, the container becomes fixed and rigid. It cannot breathe. It has little or no flexibility to expand and take in another viewpoint. There can be no freedom when our feelings become a metaphorical suit of armor that clamps down hard on our bodies and restricts our movement.

Throughout our experiences, we find ourselves held in various containers of feelings. One day we are happy and satisfied, creating an open, airy container, while another day we experience stress, anxiety, or fear, creating a small and tight container. These containers of feelings become physically noticeable in our bodies. Our bodies then take on the attributes of our containers and show us our inner emotional state.

Feelings have many layers. In healing painful feelings, we must first get to the root layer. Just creating an affirmation or thinking differently about how we feel on the surface will usually not be effective in facilitating long-term healing. We must peel away the layers that cover the root feeling. Sometimes we must enter into the feeling, allowing it to completely overtake us in order to listen to its story and get to its root. Whether it is anger, resentment, anxiety, or emotional pain, the root is usually fear, and most often fear of loss. Once we get to the root feeling, then we can begin the process of healing and shifting the paradigms around that pain. We can go back to using conscious thought as the gateway to the subconscious and create new emotional patterns.

What kind of feeling container do you live in? Is your body free, flexible, and in balance? We aren't necessarily talking about being in top athletic shape, but we are talking about having physical flexibility and a sense of freedom within the body. When you are happy, you will notice that you have much more energy—a spring in your step. However, when you are angry, afraid, or under emotional stress, your body becomes tight and restricted. Symptoms of dis-ease may begin to appear or worsen. Physical activity is much more of a challenge.

Your body, as the container of your feelings, can give you great insight into your inner perspective and attitude. When you experience physical pain or discomfort, especially when there is no obvious cause, have a conversation with that part of your body. Ask what it needs to tell you. What feeling or concern are you holding there? When you notice stiffness or tension in your body, ask what it is tightening against.

The following exercise will help you identify the feeling containers around situations in your life, and get to the root issues.

Meditation: Breaking through Limiting Feelings

Take a few moments to go to your Point of Stillness. Then bring to your awareness a situation in your life that you would like to see changed or resolved. Ask Spirit to show you the container of your feelings that is keeping you from personal resolution within that situation. What does it look like? Be specific. Once you have perceived the container, bless it, and thank Spirit for giving you a deeper level of clarity about yourself in this situation. Then ask Spirit to show you how to move beyond the container to a higher perspective that will allow you to work with the situation in a positive and constructive way. Is what you are feeling at the moment the true root of your feeling in this situation, or are you experiencing a symptom of some deeper issue? Ask Spirit to help you peel away the layers to get to the root of your feeling.

Once you have reached the root, pause, and once again express gratitude for your clarity. Then begin a dialogue with your root feeling and ask what it needs to say to you. What is its fear? Write in your journal if that is helpful. Just work with Spirit and your feelings, continuing a dialogue until you reach some resolution. Ask Spirit for guidance in moving forward from this feeling. There is no set answer. Each situation will call for its own approach. And, as we learned in the Law of Polarity, there are never just two choices. There are always many shades of possibility. The Law of Polarity also tells us that within any challenge lies its solution; within any pain lies its healing. Within your feeling is the key to its transformation. Ask questions of the feeling itself. Have a dialogue with it. Work with Spirit and allow yourself to be guided. Know that the healing or resolution you need will appear. Then commit yourself to the discipline required to follow through, and do it.

Wayne Dyer wrote in *Wisdom of the Ages*, "Your kingdom is how you use your mind in the face of any and all circumstances. You are the king, the ultimate ruler. No one can make you upset without the consent of your royal mind. No one can depress you without your permission. No one can hurt your feelings without your decree." This is the goal in disciplining the conscious mind to be a highly discerning filter for the subconscious mind. We can choose what we feel, not allowing others' dramas and emotions to become ours. That doesn't mean that we aren't compassionate and supportive of others in their life challenges. But their soul journey is theirs, and yours is yours. Recognize your oneness as members of the human family, but also recognize that, at the moment, you are walking different paths. You will help others the most by staying true to your soul journey, true to your divine form, and disciplining your thoughts and feelings to keep them your own.

Habits

Habits are simply locked-in thought patterns. Habitual thought leads to habitual actions. What are the thought and action patterns in your life? What are your habits? Do they serve you or do they keep you stuck? Do you have habits you want to change?

Just as with every other change we have discussed, in order to change a habit you first have to change your thought. Just "stopping it" will not change the habit. Remember that thought is energy, and energy cannot be created or destroyed. It can only be transformed. Therefore, you can't just "stop the habit," and assume that your life will now be changed. You must get to the roots of that habit, which are your thoughts, feelings, and the resulting paradigms attached to them. When your habitual thoughts and feelings have changed, your habitual action will change. If you just stop the habitual action but do not change the habitual thought and feeling, the habitual action will simply be replaced by a different habitual action that is just as counterproductive.

Questions to Ponder: Examining Thought and Habit

Do I discipline my thoughts and actions to create habits that I desire, or do I wish that something would change, without realizing my responsibility for changing my thoughts?

Which of my habitual action patterns are serving me, moving me toward becoming all that I can be? What are the habitual thought patterns that are feeding these constructive habits?

Which of my habitual action patterns are keeping me from being all I could be? What are the habitual thought patterns that I need to shift in order to make a positive and lasting change in my habitual actions?

One of the most powerful tools we have for changing thoughts, feelings, and actions is to watch our speech habits. Along with the universal axiom, "What I think about comes about," comes, "What I say for me is true for me." Think about how many times in the course of a day you say "I am." Each time you say those two words, you declare to your cellular/subconscious mind who you believe yourself to be. Your subconscious will respond by doing its best to make you that which you have declared. Every time you say "I am," you send a potent energy vibration deep inside of you as well as out into the universe. Your words have a powerful impact on your cellular mind.

Think about the words you speak. Do you mean them—literally? Are you truly saying what in your heart you want to say? In your conversations, does your choice of words promote higher consciousness and clarity of understanding? Do they engender confidence and self-esteem in yourself and others? If you must criticize or confront, are your words inspired by love, support, and a true desire for healing?

Activity: Identifying the True "I Am"

For the next couple of weeks, pay attention to every time you use the phrases "I am" or "You are." How do you describe yourself? What do you project onto others? Discipline yourself to call into being who you truly want to be through your "I am" statements. Recognize the beauty, power, and divinity in others and affirm those things in your "You are" statements. Create an environment that supports the best in you and in those around you.

Results

In order to accomplish anything of significance, you must first *be* a person who can accomplish significant things. Much of our focus thus far has been on getting in touch with who you are at your soul essence. As you begin to recognize who you are, be that person now! Don't wait until tomorrow or next week or after you've taken care of something else. Recognize who you are on the inside and live it on the outside now. Even if you don't feel that you know how to be that person, it doesn't matter. Just live it now. One of my teachers used to say, "Fake it 'til you make it!" Figure it out as you go along. Don't sit back and wait until you have it all worked out and know every step to take, every word to speak, every thought to think. Life is too short for that. Claim it now. Step into the truth of your soul and say, "I'm not sure how all of this is going to work out, but I'm going to follow my heart and soul and be true to my divine form!"

This is not "putting on airs." This is claiming Self. This is jumping with both feet into the journey toward being all you can possibly be. This is being proactive and choosing your thoughts to control your results. This is owning the aspect of the divine manifest in human form in you! It is recognizing your uniqueness and importance in this world, acknowledging your soul mission, stepping into the role you came here to play, giving the best you can give to the world, and shining your light for all to see.

Gloria Karpinski wrote in *Barefoot on Holy Ground*, "There is no greater point of power than the one within yourself. There is no more sacred ground than where you are standing today, no more significant face in evolution than the one you are looking into, whether it's the one in the mirror, the one across the breakfast or conference table, or the one you pass on the street."

Every person is a human manifestation of an aspect of the divine. That means you and every single person you encounter. Treat every person in every interaction as the divine manifestation that they are, as pure Love. If you treat all people in this way, this becomes the vibration in which you move. Treat them as important and successful. Expect them to be full of integrity and honesty. See them in a life of abundance. This is who you are, and it is who they are. Neither of you may yet fully recognize yourselves in this way, but at your essence, you are all of those things. So act like it now. Create new results—not the same ones over and over again. The more you move in a vibration of thought that says that you and everyone in your midst is incredibly important, is absolute Love, and has a gift to share with the world that is vital to its evolution, the more you and those around you move to higher and higher levels of conscious awareness. What you think about comes about.

We progress in our journeys according to our levels of conscious awareness. One way of bringing this concept home to you is to look at whether you "respond" to things that happen in your life, or "react" to them. Response comes from a place of centeredness and awareness. You are in control of your thoughts, feelings, and emotions, and can move forward in a constructive and productive way. Reaction, on the other hand, is closer to survival instinct or a knee-jerk effect. Something happens for which you are not prepared, and because you are not centered and able to perceive what is happening from a clear place, words fly out of your mouth, you take action without thought, you grasp at any possible quick solution or fix. Response comes from greater awareness; reaction comes from less awareness. Response means making conscious choices; reaction means making unconscious choices. You can choose to be proactive in your life, developing your awareness as fully as possible, resulting in conscious choices and decisions. If you do not choose to be proactive, you will be reactive by default, making random choices and decisions that seem to keep you trapped in a vicious circle.

When you make the choice to live in a higher conscious awareness and be proactive in your life, you automatically help others around you move to higher levels of conscious awareness, not by your words or trying to teach them something, but simply by the way you live your life. Your active example has more impact on others than words ever will. Honor the higher consciousness in all those around you, and you help them grow into all they can be, as well.

The conscious mind is the most powerful tool you have for creating the life you desire, and for living your soul mission. Use it. Learn how it works through practice and experience. As you develop your abilities to listen to your soul and Spirit for guidance, become a full partner in the cocreative process by becoming a master of your thoughts. Remember the wisdom from *Conversations with God*, "The controlling and directing of your thoughts is the highest form of prayer." Become prayerful. Engage your mind to serve your soul.

Activity: Chapter Reflection

Reflect on what you have learned in this chapter about the mind and thought. Write about how the mind works in your own words so that you begin to have a personal understanding of how to use it for the manifestation of your life vision. Then think of someone with whom you can have a conversation about these concepts.

TAKING STOCK

12

OF YOUR PRESENT SITUATION

AT THIS POINT of the journey, it is time to pause and congratulate yourself for the powerful and transformative work you have done so far. You have taken the initiative to embark on a path of self-discovery and spiritual exploration. You have peeled away layers of beliefs, opinions, and identities that kept you from recognizing your essence. You have composed a Declaration of Intention, and perhaps revised that Declaration many times, in your mind if not on paper. You have entered the great silence and further developed your intuitive awareness, opening to Spirit's guidance on this often unpredictable pilgrimage to soul. You have studied the laws of the universe and gained new understanding about how life works. You have explored your body's energy system and developed a working knowledge of your chakras. You have identified your soul mission and created a life vision. You have looked at some of your paradigms, gained insight into how they shape your life, and learned how you can make changes. You have learned about the universal trinity that governs all of creation, and how to apply the power of your mind and thought to your personal life design. Having reached this point shows your commitment to being all that you can be. So, congratulations on staying the course! The work you have done has created a strong foundation that will serve you well for this last part of our journey.

Now it is time to put all of those theories and concepts into practice and integrate them into your daily life. In Part IV, we will introduce and work through the Manifestation Wheel, using it as the structure for bringing your vision into physical reality. You will set goals and learn how to accomplish them. All that you have studied to this point will be woven into the practical journey as together we set about creating your life as you want it to be.

In final preparation for the Manifestation Wheel, in this chapter we will take stock of where you are right now, getting down to the nitty-gritty of some physical realities of your life. We begin by looking at how you make decisions. Then we will explore your relationship to money and time and the ways you spend and invest them. This examination will tell you a lot about the priorities you are *living*, as opposed to those you *espouse*. Finally, we will look at your perception of who you are and take an objective look at how the rest of the world sees you.

The physical reality of your life is strongly related to the root, sacral, and solar plexus chakras. They effect your daily experience—your sense of physical well-being, your fundamental relationships with others, your perception of how you fit into the world and your role here, and your sense of self-confidence and self-assuredness in making and executing plans and decisions. In the hierarchy of the chakra system, we have said that these first three chakras function within a lower level of conscious awareness when compared to the upper chakras. However, because of the work you have done in the first part of this book, you are now able to work in these first three chakras from a much higher awareness and perspective. You now have the ability to look at issues in all of the chakras with an objective clarity—not passing judgment, but rather gaining insight and understanding through observation, and recognizing where shifts need to occur.

MAKING DECISIONS

One of the first steps is to look at your relationship to decision-making. You may have highly developed decision-making skills and employ them on a regular basis. If that is the case, read this section anyway for affirmation. If, however, decision-making is a big challenge or source of stress in your life, perhaps this discussion can help.

Unfortunately, schools don't teach decision-making skills. It is a major missing piece in our life curriculum. Many of us, though we may lead successful lives in many ways, still struggle with making decisions and following through with appropriate action. We stumble along, doing our best without any real tools for discernment. Because of our culture's stigmas around the lower parts of the body, sexuality, and self-assertiveness, many people have strong, often unconscious, resistance to tapping into the grounding and primal life-force energies of the first two chakras. When we are not grounded in these two chakras—giving us a clear and objective vision of our current reality—making decisions is even more baffling because we aren't seeing the truth of the situation as it exists right here, right now.

Clarity of intention is essential. Because we have not been taught clear decision-making skills, we often end up stating preferences instead of taking decisive action. Although most of the time we are not aware of it, we often confuse the terms "decision" and "preference." We use the word "decide" when what we are really stating is "what we would like." For instance, a friend might say, "I've decided to quit smoking soon." What they are really saying is, "I would *like* to quit smoking, but I haven't yet made the commitment to when and how." A colleague might say, "I've decided to make the most of my situation and try to be happy," yet they continue to focus on all of the negative aspects of their circumstance and wonder why they aren't feeling any better. What they are really saying is, "I'd *like* to be happy, but it is easier to just complain about all that is wrong." An actor might say, "I've decided I'm going to five auditions this week," when in actuality they only go to two because "something came up" and they never made it to the other three. What they were really saying was "I'd *like* to go to five auditions this week," because they had not made the full commitment to their career above all else, and therefore had not truly made a decision to go to all five auditions. They just had in their mind what they would like to do.

The word "decision" comes from the Latin roots *de*, meaning "from," and *caedere*, meaning "to cut." Therefore, "decision," in its root form, means "to cut from," hence the term "clear-cut decision." To decide means to cut away from any other possibility. Making a decision means committing to a particular result and cutting yourself off from any other possibility. It involves clear, firm, unflagging commitment. That is a big step. When was the last time you made a decision and cut yourself off from any other possibility?

Since the Great Depression, we have lived in a culture that says you must always have a safety net—don't leave your job before you have another one, don't leave a relationship unless you know you have some-one else in the wings, don't start a new venture unless you know where every resource is going to come from. In other words, we have lived in a culture that does not encourage taking risks. It encourages the "safe" path and has little trust in the universe. However, all of that is chang-ing in this 21st century. As financial markets become more and more uncertain, infrastructures of corporations are crumbling, and security as we have known it in generations past no longer exists, we have to find our own way. We have the opportunity, now more than ever, to listen to soul and respond to its yearning. We have the opportunity to create our own life vision, set goals to bring that vision into reality, and then commit to the process by staying focused on our vision, not allowing ourselves to be distracted by someone who says, "Where is the safety net?" We are being called to make decisions—to cut from any other possibility than that which feeds our soul.

We are not talking about fool-hardy choices, made without clearly researching things in the outer world and exploring your heart's desire in your inner world. We are not talking about stating preferences with-out any real commitment to bringing those preferences to reality. We are talking about clear-cut decisions—full and unflagging commitment to living your soul mission and manifesting your vision of who you want to be, what you want to do, and how you want your life to unfold.

Questions to Ponder: Decision-making and You

When I look back over my lifetime history of decision-making, where and when have I actually made clear-cut decisions? What was the result? If things didn't turn out the way I had planned, what did I learn? How did the experience enrich my life?

Where and when have I just stated preferences and hoped they would come about without making clear commitment? What was the result?

How can I shift my thinking to make clear-cut, definite, effective decisions?

When I have made clear-cut decisions, how have I followed through with those decisions? Do I need to make adjustments in my follow-up?

Money and Time

In *The Seven Stages of Money Maturity*, George Kinder wrote, "Money makes the dreams and aspirations of our lives possible; it brings them within our reach. Without sufficient money, we simply cannot do what we want to do—whether that means writing novels, building a thriving business that makes the world a better place, or spending more time with our children as they grow up. The notion that we can be free internally and not free financially is absurd, simply a further expression of the notion that soul work and money work exist in two separate and distinct realms. They are in fact woven together within the undivided space of our own beings."

The decisions we make, whether conscious or unconscious, point to our priorities in life. Those priorities show up in two places: our calendar and our checkbook. We may have certain perceptions of what is important to us, of where our priorities lie. We may like to think that we put our family first, our partner first, our career first, helping others first, or any number of other things that we feel should have our primary focus, and in our hearts that may be so. But our calendar and checkbook will show us the reality of what we have made priorities by where we have invested our money and our time.

These two records will show you not what you would like to value but what you have chosen to value. They will show you your decisions, not your preferences. Our society views time and money as extremely valuable commodities. You will see where you committed your time and money, and whether or not those commitments are in alignment with your heart.

Activity: Calendar and Checkbook Priorities

Take a look at your checkbook register, credit card statements, and any other expense records for the last year. Divide your expenditures into categories and total the amounts spent in each. Calculate in rough percentages how much of your total expenditures was spent in each category.

Next, look at your sources of income. Calculate in rough percentages how much of your income came from something that you really enjoy, that feeds your soul, and how much of it came from "a job."

Now look at your date book for the last year. Take time to go through each day and add up the total number of hours spent on each activity over the year. Calculate in rough percentages how much of your total time you spent on each activity.

Once you have completed the calculations above, consider the following questions. Write your responses in your journal.

Where did your your money go? Do you feel that you invested it wisely? Did you truly invest it in you and/or what you value? Did you invest in your future? Did the way you spent your money truly better your life in a way that is in harmony with what you want in life?

Where did your time go? Do you feel that you invested it wisely? Did you truly invest it in you and/or what you value? Did you invest in your future? Did the way you spent your time truly better your life in a way that is in harmony with what you want in life?

How does the money you've spent and the time commitments you've made reflect what is or is not important to you? Are there places where you have *not* spent money or time that reflect significant imbalances in your life? Are there places where you *have* spent money or time that reflect significant imbalances in your life?

Are your money and time expenditures in harmony with what you really want? Are they serving you and your desires in some way, or are they at odds with what you want in life? If not, what needs to shift? How can you make that shift?

Money pushes buttons. It's an issue that many people just don't want to deal with. To be sure, our culture can focus too much on money and material things, but turning and running the other way, ignoring these issues or pretending they are not important, is not the answer. The bottom line is that a healthy relationship to money is essential for a balanced life.

Activity: Cluster Writing on Money

Gather several sheets of paper and a pen and set them beside you. Then go to your Point of Stillness.

In the center of a blank piece of paper, write the word "money" in big letters and draw a circle around it. Then, as you have done in previous clustering exercises, write on this page every word that comes into your mind. Just cover the page with words. When you come to a stopping point and you seem to have no more words for "money," take a clean sheet and write in the center the last word that you wrote on the first page. Draw a circle around it, and continue free associating with that word, writing every word that comes to mind. Continue this process, starting as many new pages as necessary, until you begin to feel that you are coming up to a personal issue or new revelation. At that point, go to yet another fresh page and write in paragraph form anything that is coming to you.

When you have completed the first part of this exercise, go on to consider the following questions:

What did I learn from this exercise? Were there any words that surprised me?

Do I have a healthy attitude about money, or are there ways in which my attitude toward money needs to change?

Do I treat money as my comfortable friend or as a threatening adversary?

How have I used money "to save me," either by saying, "I can't afford it," in order to avoid having to invest in something that might really enrich my life and feed my soul, or by attempting to buy happiness and fulfillment?

Balance is a key to freedom. We must balance our relationship to money with everything else in our life. We must give it the attention it deserves as an essential part of healthy living. Money is a great servant and a terrible master. When we develop a healthy attitude about money and choose the role it plays in our lives, we become master over it. We then find that we always have enough, that all of our needs are met. If, on the other hand, we are not proactive in our relationship with money and let it rule our choices and decisions, it becomes master over us.

Money is not good or bad. It is just a form of energy. It is the primary instrument of exchange or barter in today's Western society. In another era, the instrument of exchange was chattel or barter for services, but now it is primarily money. In the United States, money is green, the color of the heart chakra. In other countries money is multicolored, an even fuller representation of exchange on many levels of consciousness. Let money be a symbol of exchange of heartfelt gratitude, appreciation, and love for a service rendered, whether you are spending it or being paid.

Financial debt is a challenge for many people, and contributes to imbalance in their lives. There are two kinds of debt: productive and consumptive. Productive debt is debt that serves you in some way—it is an investment in the quality of your life and feeds your soul. It helps you move toward living your soul mission in some way. Consumptive debt, on the other hand, comes from buying something just because you want it but not because you particularly need it. These things may bring you great immediate enjoyment, but at a cost. You have compromised your financial stability to some degree in order to have them. Therefore, consumptive debt becomes a financial, physical, and emotional burden. It affects many parts of your life, either directly or indirectly, as you dig your way out.

Questions to Ponder: Money—Master or Servant?

What role does money play in my life? Is it my servant or my master? Do I consciously choose how money can serve me, or do financial responsibilities in which I find myself control my decisions and freedom?

Do I carry debt? If so, why have I chosen debt

Is my debt productive or consumptive?

If you carry debt, some of it may be productive and some may be consumptive. If you have consumptive debt, reflect on the following questions:

How did I get into this place of consumptive debt?

Why have I chosen to be in debt?

What were my intentions?

What is my debt "protecting" me from? How do I use debt to be sure that I don't have to face or address something else? How does my debt keep me feeling comfortable or safe? How does it keep me from having to manifest all that I can be—from realizing my full potential?

How can I reverse this pattern and clear my debt in order to free my life-force and shift from surviving mode to thriving mode? What can be my plan of action toward freedom from debt and a financially healthy lifestyle?

If you carry productive debt, consider the following questions:

How is my debt serving me, adding to the quality of my life and feeding my soul?

Where do I need to be willing to invest money or Self more in order to accomplish what I want?

Am I willing to do what it takes to manifest what I desire, and therefore make the necessary financial and personal investments?

What is my larger financial investment plan?

In order for money to be the servant and you to be the master, you must make clear decisions about your relationship to money and the role you want it to play in your life. Make clear decisions about investments—how you want to feed your soul, provide for the life you desire, and give to others. And make clear decisions about debt. Sometimes debt is a necessary step toward realizing your dreams. But make it productive debt. Be sure that if you are choosing to go into debt, the benefits of what you are going into debt for far exceed the burdens of the debt itself. Be clear about how you spend your money. Make it work for you.

Abundance

Recall our discussion in chapter 5 (on page 60) of the Law of Mentalism and the issue of deserving abundance. If you are a human manifestation of an aspect of Spirit, then isn't it your responsibility to be all that you can be, and live in an attitude of abundance as a gift to Spirit? Isn't it your responsibility to develop a healthy and abundant attitude toward money and let it be your servant as you serve Spirit? Aren't you responsible for living in an attitude of abundance toward others, sharing your wealth, in whatever form it takes, in order to make the world a better place?

We are not talking about a specific amount of money that everyone should aspire to have or give. We are talking about an amount of money that provides for all you need and desire and for all you wish to share with others. That can be $10,000 or $10 million—it's your call. If your income does not provide for your needs and desires, then perhaps you need to address something that is out of balance.

Corporate coach Bob Proctor says a person is living a balanced life when they spend their days doing what they love, and at the same time earn the amount of money they need to provide the things they want, and the ability to live the way they choose. What a great concept—to love what you do, and have all you want. Yet most people don't even consider this a possibility. We haven't yet realized as a culture that it really is possible to love what you do for a living and have an income that provides the lifestyle you desire.

Everything is energy. Money is energy. You can choose how you want energy—money—to flow through your life; you can choose whether it will be your servant or your master. When abundance rather than scarcity becomes the focus of your thoughts and you have developed positive paradigms around income and doing what you love, your relationship to money will change.

Perception of Self

I once took a workshop in which the instructor suggested that every few months we should each take a "do not kid yourself" day. Periodically we need to step back and take stock of where we are, what is working and what is not working, where we are growing and where we are stuck. The issues we have discussed in this chapter are real "do not kid yourself" issues and we must address them as we begin to put all we have learned into practice. Otherwise, we are not being completely honest with ourselves. When we are not honest with ourselves, no amount of work will bring what we truly desire.

The Bible says "As a man thinketh within himself, so is he" (Proverbs 23:7). One of the ways in which we sometimes get stuck is in our perception of how others perceive us. Our perception of self can be shaped by how we think others see us. I once read this statement and it has stayed with me for a long time: "I am not who I think I am; I am not who you think I am; I am who I think you think I am."

Like most things in life, seeing yourself as you think others see you can be a double-edged sword. It can give you an objective view of yourself—"how am I really doing out there"—or it can keep you from moving forward because you are so concerned about what others think. Use the following exercise to gain an objective point of view and give you a clearer sense of how you present yourself to the world.

Meditation Activity: Perception of Self

Go to your Point of Stillness. Then bring into your mind three people from different parts in your life—people who you believe know you well. Imagine that I was asking each of them to tell me objectively and candidly about you, in as much detail as possible. Write in your journal what you think they would say about:

Your business, professional, occupational competency;

Your dependability;

Your punctuality;

Your integrity;

Your character;

What they think your annual income is;

How creative you are;

What kind of friend you are;

What kind of spouse/partner you are;

How well you balance your life;

Your sense of responsibility;

What your gifts and talents are;

How you have developed and shared those gifts and talents.

What did you learn from this exercise? Does what you wrote match your own perception of yourself? Does it reflect how you want to be perceived? What changes does it make you want to affect in your life? Will you commit to them? How? These are more "do not kid yourself" questions.

You may need to take some time to ponder the insights and thoughts that have come to you through this chapter. You might even want to take a few days and work with this chapter in your meditation and journaling before moving on to the powerful manifestation journey that lies ahead.

Part IV

MANIFESTING YOUR VISION, LIVING YOUR MISSION

The Manifestation Wheel   13

MANY YEARS AGO, a very important teacher in my journey, Rick Jarow, introduced me to a Lakota (Plains Indians) Medicine Wheel as a tool for manifestation. This Wheel is a model and guide for the inner journey of self-awareness and transformation that is necessary for the outer manifestation of a vision. The Wheel has eight houses, each addressing a different aspect of the personal work required for manifestation. By the time you have worked your way around the Wheel and invested time and energy in the full exploration of each house, you have done the inner work necessary to bring your vision to reality.

Adapting the principles and structure of the Medicine Wheel, I have created a Manifestation Wheel for our soul mission journey (see diagram on p. 194). The eight houses correspond to the original Medicine Wheel. I have simply phrased the concepts so that our 21st-century world can easily grasp and employ them. Your focus for the remainder of the book will be to learn how to use the Wheel as a tool for the manifestation of your life vision. We begin in this chapter with a brief overview of the eight houses.

You enter the Manifestation Wheel from the East—considered in Native American traditions as the gateway for ceremony with Spirit—beginning with the first house, "Intention." Here you clearly state what you intend to accomplish—your project. The work of this first house is to claim responsibility for the accomplishment of your project, to begin identifying the paradigm shifts that you must make, and to commit to its journey.

In the second house, "Peace," you address any issues that may cause inner conflict with your project, and make the inner and outer shifts necessary to bring your project into complete harmony with your soul. You also recognize any part of Self that is not yet accepting the idea of completing your project. Working through these issues, you come to peace with your project so that your entire being is in harmony with itself.

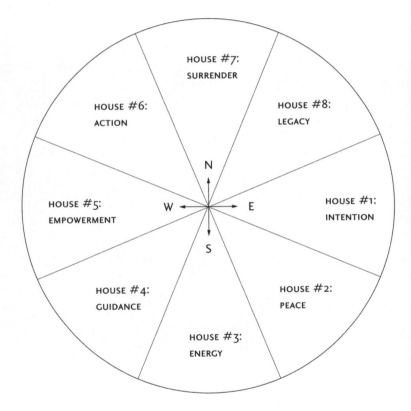

The third house is "Energy." Having clearly stated your intention and made peace with all aspects of it, you must now gather your enthusiasm, find your true motivation, and mobilize your energy for the project at hand. In this house, you thoroughly examine your project to see if you are excited or passionate about it. If not, this is a sign that something is still not in alignment with your inner being. Here you also consider other people that you must motivate and excite in order to succeed. You identify and set goals, and determine what resources are necessary to achieve your success. This is the house of the warrior. As we have said, the spiritual warrior is one who is willing to stand up for his or her truth no matter what. That can also mean sacrifice. In this third house, you explore what you are willing to sacrifice, even if only temporarily, for the accomplishment of your goal. Finally, you create an energy focus and a sense of momentum toward the full completion of your project.

The fourth house is "Guidance"—where you engage your intuitive voice for guidance and direction in your project. In this house, you ask Spirit to show you what your life will look like when your project has been accomplished. As the picture becomes clear, you then ask Spirit to show you the path that will lead you to that achievement. Once again, you may find paradigms that require shifting as Spirit shows you your path. You may also find new responsibilities that you must accept in order to manifest what Spirit is showing you as the possibilities of your future.

The fifth house is "Empowerment." In this house, you consider whether both the completion of your project and the process of getting there will be nurturing and empowering for you and for others. You make whatever adjustments in your project are necessary to see that it includes both personal and universal benefits. You examine how the process and completion of your project will directly or indirectly feed your soul, how it can feed others' souls, as well as whether any part of your project or its process could cause harm to another. In this house, you also identify the leadership skills that will be required to accomplish your goal, whether they be leadership of self or leadership of others. The ultimate question in the fifth house is, "Does this project and its process feel like a gift for everyone's benefit?"

In the sixth house, "Action," you create your plan of how you are actually going to accomplish your project, and set that plan into motion. Here you formulate a plan of action that includes the goals and resources identified in the third house, and seek the help and counsel of others who might guide or assist you in your process. In this house, you also set a time frame for the individual goals or steps toward the completion of your project.

The seventh house is "Surrender." In this house, you surrender your project to Spirit and enter a new level of cocreation. You learn more about stepping beyond the bounds of rational thought and entering into a much more dynamic creative partnership with Spirit.

Finally, in the eighth house, "Legacy," you consider whether your project will benefit not only you and your family and community, but also the greater global family in future generations. In some way, will the accomplishment of your project make life better for those who will inherit the Earth? Is the process and completion of your project in harmony with the positive evolution of our planet Earth? You align your intention with the universal flow of Love and the evolution of Earth, and see how your project fits into the bigger picture.

When you cross back to spirit at the end of this lifetime, you will leave a vibrational legacy. Your creations, thoughts, and actions will set a vibration in motion that will have impact on generations to come. This takes us back to the metaphor of the incense in chapter 11. Just as the fragrance of the incense permeates the house, so do the energy patterns of your creations, thoughts, and actions permeate the universe. Whether your project is large or small, it is still an energy system that will reach out to the universe and spread its vibration. Therefore, it is important that your intention and completed project are in harmony or alignment with what you want that legacy to be.

The Manifestation Wheel is a circular process. As you complete your work in each house, you reflect back to all of the previous houses to be sure everything remains in harmony. You may find, for example, that through working in the second house, you simply cannot come to peace with some aspect of your project. Therefore, you must go back to the first house and adjust your initial intention. Or, you may find that as Spirit shows you your future in the fourth house, there are new resources that must be developed back in the third house. As you look at your project and its impact on future generations in the eighth house, you may realize that there are changes you want to make in your initial intention statement. Harmony is essential. Where there is discord, pieces cannot fit together. Your project, your personal integrity and soul, and the universal good must all be in alignment for a fulfilling and rewarding experience. Before leaving each house, you must check in with each previous house to see how your new work has given further illumination to your project and to resolve any new conflict that might have arisen.

The journey around the Manifestation Wheel is also many circles within one. As you create goals for the achievement of your intention, you can begin a new Wheel for each goal. In the process of working through the Wheel on one particular project, you may realize that there is another project that must be completed before you can continue. So, you take your new project to its own Wheel and work your way around. At its completion, you return to your initial project and continue. You will find that with some projects you travel around the Wheel very quickly, while others take a long time. This is the nature of life. Allow the process of the Manifestation Wheel to serve you, and you will find it an invaluable friend on your journey.

I suggest you begin with something small and relatively simple for your first time around the Wheel—something that you are confident that you can accomplish, yet will stretch you in some way. You may even want to go to your Point of Stillness and seek Spirit's guidance on the most appropriate project for your first experience with the Manifestation Wheel.

Give yourself as much time as you need to work the Wheel. Do not assume you will go through all eight houses in one sitting. Depending on the complexity of your project, you may need several days, or even a week or more, to move your project around the Wheel. There is no hurry. As we said before, some projects will move around the Wheel quickly, while others will take longer. By the time you have completed the Wheel, you will have done the work necessary to accomplish your project. At that point, the Law of Gender takes over, and after the necessary gestation period has occurred, your project will be completed.

Working around the Wheel leads you through your inner work toward manifestation. Your internal manifestation then creates the space for full manifestation in the physical realm. Having gone through all eight houses does not necessarily mean that your project is now complete. What it means is that everything is now in place for you to complete the project in its own time. Your responsibility is to take care of the internal work; Spirit takes care of the external manifestation. This is what cocreative partnership is all about.

Each of the following chapters begins with the core concerns for the house you're working with. Consider the opening questions during your daily meditation time and record your answers in your journal as you go. The questions at the end of each chapter affirm what you have learned in the house and "check in" with the houses you previously worked through.

Don't be in a hurry. You may choose to spend the next several months working through the rest of this book. That's fine. But be diligent. Keep the momentum going. Even if you choose to spend a week or more in each house, read through the chapter for that house every day, and keep the exercises fresh in your mind. Each time you read and reflect, you will find new layers of awareness, discovery, and understanding.

By putting your life vision on the Wheel, you are working on a very grand scale. Along the way you will find many smaller goals and projects with which to start new Wheels. Allow the process to unfold. You are really into the fun part now. You have done a huge amount of work to get to this point. Now you get to reap the rewards of your efforts by manifesting the life of your dreams!

Manifestation House 1:
Intention

→ What is your project?

→ Are you willing to discipline your thoughts to remain clearly focused on your project until its completion?

→ Are you willing to address limiting beliefs when they arise, and commit to the necessary paradigm shifts?

→ Are you willing to listen to Spirit and your soul for guidance on how to accomplish your project, and to respond to that guidance with the appropriate actions?

In this first house of the Manifestation Wheel, you take your first steps in bringing your life vision to reality and living your soul mission. Having identified your mission and created a clear vision of the life through which you wish to live that mission, it is now time to step up to the plate, own it, and build your vision here in the physical reality. This means not only acknowledging your fundamental reason for being and the dreams you hold dear, but embracing them and committing to live them.

This first house is about committing to and accepting your responsibility in the manifestation process. Here you have five primary assignments:

1. To embrace your mission and vision and commit to living them.

2. To discipline your thoughts and begin making the necessary

paradigm shifts so that you can live your soul mission and manifest your life vision.

3. To accept where you are right now so that you can move forward, taking each necessary step along the way.

4. To listen to Spirit and your soul for guidance every step of the way.

5. To be willing to respond to that guidance with the appropriate action.

In *Martha: The Life and Work of Martha Graham*, Agnes de Mille shared these powerful words from the great dancer and choreographer: "There is a vitality, a life force, an energy, a quickening that is translated through you into action, and because there is only one of you in all of time, this expression is unique. And if you block it, it will never exist through any other medium and it will be lost. The world will not have it. It is not your business to determine how good it is nor how valuable it compares with other expressions. It is your business to keep it yours clearly and directly, to keep the channel open." She also spoke about "a queer divine dissatisfaction, a blessed unrest that keeps us marching and makes us more alive than the others."

That "blessed unrest" is your soul mission. This first house now calls you to claim it and commit to it as your life journey. This is perhaps the most important commitment you will make in your life, because it is a commitment to Self. Without a firm pledge and dedication to what you came here to do, you will not be able to give your all to anything or anyone—your words, thoughts, and actions will not be in complete harmony with your divine purpose. Making that commitment is incredibly liberating and empowering. In that moment you discover your passion for living, you know your reason for being, and you embrace the gift you have to offer to the world.

The Manifestation Wheel is a vehicle for aligning your life vision with your soul mission and with the positive evolution of humankind. Here in the first house you begin that journey. In order to fully manifest your vision, every aspect of it must ultimately come into harmony with both your soul mission and planetary evolution. Otherwise, you will experience inner conflict and never feel completely fulfilled in your experience. Here in the first house you lay the groundwork for what can be an incredible journey of transformation and learning, growth and accomplishment.

When we start out on a path toward a vision, there may be stretches that we can't see from the beginning. We will find them as we go along. We may not yet have all of the skills necessary for the manifestation of our vision, or even be able to identify what all the necessary skills might be. But the journey itself will offer us the opportunity to develop those skills. Learning and manifesting go hand-in-hand, and require a willingness to change, grow, and accept that there are things that we don't know. They require that we stretch beyond our comfort zone for personal development in every area of our lives. Learning and manifesting mean facing fears and resistance, reevaluating beliefs and behaviors, and letting go of assumptions.

Listening to Spirit and your soul, and responding to the guidance you receive is also a part of the stretching. Our culture does not yet support the idea of life being guided by intuition, but as time goes along more and more highly successful people are coming out of the intuition closet and admitting its profound role in their achievements and accomplishments. Many of the exercises in this book begin with asking you to go to your Point of Stillness. You should approach The Manifestation Wheel in the same way. Every significant decision of your life will be easier if you enter your Point of Stillness and reflect for a while on the houses of this Wheel. Then you will know your decision is based on being true to your essence.

Deepak Chopra defines luck as "preparedness meeting opportunity." Opportunities are all around us. Through an acute awareness of our surroundings and interactions, we notice them. Preparation plays a big part in that awareness. If we are prepared for opportunities, we will see them when they come up. But if we aren't prepared, the opportunities pass us by. We won't always recognize right away what the opportunity will bring or what uncharted waters we will find ourselves in, but if we aren't willing to take some chances and have faith in where we're being led, we never get beyond where we are.

A part of being prepared for opportunities is making clear decisions. If you want to have a lot of money, you must first decide to have a lot of money. If you want to have more time with the important people in your life, you must first decide to have that time. If you want to help many people, or to travel extensively, you must first decide. Put the Laws of Vibration and Attraction to work for you! Make clear decisions with definite intention, and discipline your thoughts to hold only the picture of your fully manifested vision. Do not allow a picture of even a half-baked vision. Be true to your desire. You will draw to you all that you need.

Manifestation of any vision means setting goals, figuring out how to accomplish those goals, and then following through with action and reflection until the vision is accomplished. Just holding a vision and wishing that it would manifest will not do it—at least not yet. There are those who are masters of thought and manifestation and can immediately bring to reality whatever their minds focus on—from vision straight to manifestation. They have become masters in application of the universal laws and the universal trinity of creation (chapter 10). Most of us, however, are not yet there. We must go through a step-by-step process. In time, as we become masters of the process, manifestation will occur faster and faster.

Once you have made the commitment to your vision and have that vision firmly placed in your mind, then it is time to focus on the present moment. What do you need to do now in order to set the manifestation process in motion? And even more importantly, who do you need to be now, in order to do what is necessary to manifest your desires?

In the Japanese culture, the word *kokoro* refers to perfecting one's inner nature. They believe that in order to be great at anything, you must first perfect a way of being that is consistent with the greatness you desire—that you must find your calm and peaceful center and learn to live there. In our Western culture, we don't give enough attention to the importance of a person's way of being. Instead, we give attention to knowledge, skill, or technique. We ask, "How do I do it?" or "What is the next step?" when perhaps we should first be asking, "How do I 'be' in order to accomplish that?" We need to explore the inner spirit necessary to achieve the desired goal, as well as the techniques and skills. This is how Eastern and indigenous cultures hand down wisdom and tradition, so that the tradition's integrity remains intact. When we pass along a skill or knowledge, it is important that we also pass along the fundamental essence of "being" that is in harmony with that knowledge.

This is an important lesson that I learned from my voice teacher. She always said to me, "You teach the whole person, not the singer." She talked to me about the personal development necessary to be a great artist—the importance of opening your heart to the music and to the audience. This has become one of the most important things I try to pass on to my own singing students. Performing artists have the opportunity to share great healing and love through their work. But in order to do that, they must recognize and honor themselves as Love.

I teach this to my spiritual students, as well. Who they are, at their essence, is pure Love. When they can live each moment from their heart of Love, and stand in the full power of their Truth, others will hear their message more clearly—regardless of its content. We all have different gifts and talents—singing, painting, teaching, business, caretaking, parenting, helping—but the essence of each talent is Love. It is only when we develop our own inner awareness of ourselves as Love that we can fully share our talent.

We have said that creation is a process of moving from the unseen world to the seen. Real change and growth in our lives comes from the inside out. Having "things" will not make you into the person you desire to be. But being the person you desire to be opens the doors for you to have everything that goes along with that beingness. And being the person you desire to be brings you back to the present moment. Bill Moyers, in the 1996 PBS television series, *Visionaries*, said that people are visionaries "not because they see into the future, but because they see into the moment." In this first house of the Manifestation Wheel, we are called to see into each present moment and be who we need to be—to be all of who we are—in order to start the manifestation process on a road that is sure to bring many gifts.

Once you begin having successes, if you want to continue that success, you must understand how you got there. Then you repeat that pattern. You might think that we are talking about the action steps that led to your success, but actions play only a small part. Even more important than your actions are your thoughts—recognizing the thought pattern that led you to success, and then making that thought pattern your habit. I think of it like dancing. First, you have to learn the steps. Once you have learned them, as you keep doing them over and over again, you get better and better, and you get freer and freer. In your freedom, you start creating new and wonderful variations on those steps. This takes us back to the interrelated nature of discipline, freedom, and control that we discussed in chapter 1. You discipline yourself to develop your dancing technique—that technique gives you the freedom to experiment. Soon you find that within the freedom that your technique has given you, you now have the control over your body to execute any new step.

This is the magical dance of creation with Spirit. It all begins with focused thought. When you focus your thought and use the power of the mind, anything is possible. You move into greater and greater realms of freedom. Through that freedom, you realize you can guide and shape your life in any way you desire.

In chapter 12, we looked at the present circumstances of your life and asked some hard questions. Fully accepting the honest answers to those questions is also an important aspect of the first house. You can't get from point A to point B if you don't truly know where point A is. Here in this first house it is vitally important that you be honest with yourself about where you are, accept it, and embrace it. Once you have taken that step you can set out on the trail toward your vision, plot your course, and accomplish it. However, you must first find the trailhead.

In order to move forward, we must be willing to fully accept where we are right now. We don't have to like it. In fact, if we don't like it, there is even more motivation to do the work necessary to achieve our dreams. Not liking where you are in life can be a very powerful motivating force. But not accepting where you are can keep you from ever achieving even a part of your dreams. Each step in the manifestation journey is important because it prepares you for what is to come. When you skip steps in your impatience and eagerness to achieve, you usually find that, at some point, you have to go back to pick up the missing pieces.

When you become clear about your soul mission and create a dynamic life vision, you'll probably feel great excitement and enthusiasm. These feelings fuel your journey, but you need to guard them carefully. Some family members, friends, or colleagues may not appreciate your mission or grasp your vision. Your newfound commitment to being true to your soul essence in the choices you make in life may feel threatening to them. All this is to say that you may not get support for your journey from every corner. Therefore, choose carefully what you share with others. When you are speaking with someone who you know will "get it," who will support you and be excited for you, share all you want. But when you are not sure how someone will react, keep your thoughts and plans to yourself. Share your mission and vision in the corners that you know will bring the support and encouragement you need.

Just as your emotional environment is important to the manifestation of your vision, so is your physical environment. Spend time in places that are conducive to your sense of peace and growth—places that, by their nature, allow and encourage you to go deep inside and know the beauty of your soul. Choose your environment, and be sure that it nurtures your creativity and essence.

Finally, as you begin your journey around this Manifestation Wheel, aim high and shoot high. Many people have a great vision, but then are willing to settle for just a little part of it. Some aim low, and then shoot even lower, keeping things safe, and never stretching beyond what they are sure they can do. In aiming low, they keep themselves from attaining even a small portion of what they desire. Others aim high, but still shoot low. They speak of their great vision, aim at the extraordinary life they could have, but just when it is time to make the shot they lower their focus and shoot low. Something inside them wants to be sure they won't ever be disappointed.

Disappointment comes with the territory. Not every goal or dream will be fully realized as you imagine that it should. Not every road will lead to your fully manifested vision. However, as you travel each road, you will learn and grow, and be given opportunities to know Self better. Each road will bring wondrous gifts that can lead you on toward your vision, sometimes in astonishing ways. So, aim high and shoot high! Don't be afraid of disappointment. Disappointment is short-term. Life vision is long-term. Go for the gold! Claim your mission, build your vision, and fly!

Questions to Ponder: Intention

Have I fully claimed my soul mission and committed myself to living it in my daily life? If not, how can I take that step?

Where am I in the manifestation of my life vision journey right now? Am I being honest with myself and fully accepting my current circumstances?

Do I live the inner nature of what I wish to manifest? What shifts do I need to make in my "being" in order to fully manifest my vision?

How am I doing in my process of opening to Spirit and soul guidance? Do I perceive that guidance clearly and respond?

Am I ready and willing to take full responsibility for my role in the cocreative process of building my life vision?

MANIFESTATION HOUSE 2: 15

PEACE

→ Is this project in harmony with my soul desires?

→ Am I ready to accept the completion of my project and all that will mean in my life?

→Am I engaging in this project in any way because of what I feel I "should" do or in response to someone else's expectations, or is this truly my desire?

As you begin this manifestation journey, you are no doubt already starting to think about how you are going to create the life you desire. There are always a number of ways to accomplish anything. But not all of those approaches will appeal to you. Not all of them will feel right inside of you. Where are you with your creative process at this point? Is it all feeling good to you, or are there things that you need to accomplish, but that you don't know how to do in a manner that is in harmony with your soul? This can be challenging, especially when you have hard choices to make that can affect other people's lives. However, it is very important for your own well-being and sense of integrity and inner peace. There are times when you should neither speak nor take action until you have the opportunity to sit in your silence and find your inner peace. Then, from your heart, you proceed.

The journey of the second house in the Manifestation Wheel is one of finding peace within all of your being, with the world around you, and with your vision. Long ago, Spirit helped me understand that peace is not the absence of conflict, but rather one's response to the conflict. Fully grasping this concept is critical to the work in the second house. You will never be completely without challenge or conflict in your life, for without them there would be no growth; there would be nothing to "stir the pot" and bring you face-to-face with those parts of yourself that are ready for transformation.

As I begin my work with a client, he or she is often very excited about a particular vision for what he or she wants to manifest. As we begin seriously examining what it actually means to build that vision, however, the client's inner fears, conflicts, and doubts arise. This is a normal part of the process, and to be expected. Soul mission includes our reason for being and what we will give to the world, but it also includes what we will learn, how we will grow, and the transformation that will happen within us, as we go about living that mission. Too often, we come up against resistance or roadblocks to our goals, and interpret them as signs that we are on the wrong track—that we should turn around and find another way. Or, worse still, give up on the goal or vision entirely. Of course, there are times when roadblocks and inner resistance are there to show us that we are going in the wrong direction, but most of the time this is not the case. It is only through our intuitive process and relationship with Spirit and soul that we can truly recognize the difference between a wrong turn and a path that we need to take and from which we need to learn.

In our Western world, we have separated spirituality from everything else in our lives. However, the only place that we can truly create this separation is in our perception. The reality is that who we are spiritually is the core of our being and cannot be separated from any aspect of our being, any thought in which we engage, or any activity of our life. When we do not recognize this unity of Self, we experience conflict and contradiction in our daily lives. We take actions, make decisions, fall into habits and patterns that on the surface appear to be perfectly acceptable. But deep in our souls, we are at odds with that decision or action. Deep in our souls, we are not at peace with how we are living our lives.

The process of coming to peace can be filled with conflict and challenge. We may have to wrestle with aspects of ourselves, and even with Spirit, to get to a place of clarity. Here is the journey of the second house. When we are at peace with the essence of who we are, what we are here to do, the fundamental truths of our being, and how we live our lives in harmony with those truths, the conflicts and challenges that appear can be embraced as opportunities and catalysts for personal development and growth. Therefore, this second house is of utmost importance in the manifestation process. Just as we said in the first house that you must know where the starting point is before you can start, here in the second house you must be at peace with the starting point, as well as the destination.

One sure sign that you are not yet at peace with your vision or its unfolding process is seeking or needing approval from others in order to move forward. If a need for approval arises, pause to reflect on what that need mirrors within you. When you are clear and at peace about your life vision, you need no one else's approval. You are too busy in your passion for what you know you must do.

Finding inner peace means accepting all of the aspects of Self—the shadow parts of ourselves as well as those we are proud of or pleased with. In order to find peace within ourselves we must be willing to look equally at our perfections and our flaws, our good deeds and our poor choices, our dress-up clothes as well as the skeletons in our closets. Any part of ourselves that we deny recognition will eventually find a way to make itself known and heard—usually in some form of emotional eruption. It's better to be able to embrace those shadows and begin the transformation process by accepting them and hearing their story.

We may have a great deal of fear upon stepping into those shadowy parts of self—not knowing what we might find or whether or not we will be able to cope. But in avoidance, we give our power to the shadow. Fear clamps down hard on hopes and dreams, and can choke the life out of them. Think of a time in your life when you told a lie—even a tiny "white lie." Remember how much energy you spent protecting the lie. The same is true with the shadow self. You can spend tremendous amounts of energy protecting yourself from your shadow. By stepping into the shadow, you take back your power, you reclaim your energy. You meet your shadows face-to-face, and invite them to tell their story. As the story unfolds, you come to know yourself better, gain more insight into the significance of your experiences, and reclaim a part of you that had been lost. As you explore your shadows, they become filled with light, and new levels of peace fill your being.

A part of finding inner peace in this second house is accepting personal limitations. Your soul may have chosen certain limitations for this lifetime in order to further facilitate its journey of learning and giving. You may have a physical limitation that restricts you from certain activities, you may lack certain innate skills or abilities, or not have the "total package" for a particular career. But this does not mean that you cannot live your soul mission through a highly rewarding, dynamic, extraordinary life. Ram Dass, writing in *Still Here* after a debilitating stroke, said, "the secret of spiritual practice is that our limits may become our strengths if we learn to work with them skillfully." Your soul has chosen this path for a reason—to pursue its mission in the face of this limitation, present circumstance, or lack of innate skills. What you perceive as challenges are actually gifts. You could not have the full experience your soul seeks without them.

The second house also calls on you to look at dreams that have not yet been, or perhaps will never be, fulfilled—the child you never had, the career that never happened, the soulmate that still hasn't appeared. These circumstances and realities are also a part of the journey. Sometimes there is a much bigger picture of the soul's evolution than most of us are able to see. The journey of the second house includes making peace with the realities that certain dreams remain unfulfilled and may never manifest, even when you can't understand why.

When you can accept these limitations and realities and get on with finding the vehicle that is going to serve your soul mission, you will be much happier, and have a much better chance at a fulfilling life. If, however, you spend your time complaining that others will not give you certain opportunities just because you don't fit a certain mold or have a certain innate ability, or that a specific dream never materialized, you will be miserable. No force outside of yourself can make you live your soul mission or keep you from it. Only you can make that ultimate choice. Limitations and unfulfilled dreams can be gifts—opportunities to discover another way that is uniquely and solely yours. Take them into your heart and make your peace with them. Let your heart show you the path through which your soul can fly.

Questions to Ponder: Personal Limitations/ Unfulfilled Hopes and Dreams

What, if any, do I perceive to be my personal limitations—things about myself that I cannot change, but with which I must work?

What, if any, hopes and dreams to date remain unfulfilled, and, in reality, may never be fulfilled? What must I release or make peace with in order to move forward?

What are the gifts of those limitations? What have I already learned and how have I already grown in ways that I wouldn't have grown without those limitations or realities?

Are there some limitations that, with a shift in thought or perception, I can actually remove? Are any of my limitations self-imposed in order to create the comfortable or safe illusion that I cannot achieve, succeed, or accomplish? In other words, am I creating limitations in my life to assure that I don't have to succeed?

Have I embraced and accepted the true limitations of my life? If not, how can I move toward acceptance and peace?

Acceptance means seeing things as they are, and coming to peace. At that point, you can bring back to your awareness the vision of how you want things to be. Just as the mission can still be lived regardless of the limitations imposed, so, too, can you continue to hold onto your vision. You may have to make some adjustments, but the core of the vision, which is your mission, can remain intact.

Full acceptance of Self is also key to being at peace with and accepting the world around us. When we cannot accept certain aspects of ourselves, then we will not be able to accept those same aspects of another. In order to fully function interdependently (as we talked about in the heart chakra), we must be able to accept all of ourselves and all of others—the whole package. This doesn't mean that we have to like everything we see and accept, but we must acknowledge and accept that it is a part of the reality of our existence, and we must work with it, not fight against it.

The Law of Polarity teaches us that any situation or circumstance contains the full spectrum of possibilities for outcome. Finding inner peace often revolves around being able to see the gift in a situation. Spirit offers this teaching:

*

Within your greatest challenge lies your greatest gift—within your greatest hope lies your greatest fear—within your greatest fear lies your greatest courage. Therefore, your greatest challenges can reveal your most paralyzing fears, your most profound courage, and your true personal power.

Everything that comes to you is a gift box for you to open. Within that box is the full spectrum of possibility. You must keep looking until you find the full spectrum—don't get stuck on one pole. The Law of Polarity states that there is always an opposite whether or not you acknowledge it. If you do not acknowledge it, you become caught in it. There is tremendous power, Love, and healing in the full spectrum. The further the pendulum swings in any direction, the more intensely you experience feelings. But the pendulum will also swing to the other pole just as far. For every action there is an equal and opposite reaction. Keep in mind the full spectrum.

Make a statement to yourself within your meditation and see how your body responds. Have a conversation with the response. For example, you might say, "I deserve to be financially independent." What thoughts and feelings come up as you repeat that affirmation over and over? If there are negative thoughts and feelings, don't push them away. Instead, invite them in. Embrace them, love them, hear them— find out what they have to say.

Full-spectrum living is about allowing yourself the full experience— the full pendulum swing. You can choose to stay in one side and be free there only when you are willing to acknowledge and honor the other side as a real aspect of you.

Focus on the big picture. Let the details take care of themselves. They will then be free to move in creative and astounding ways. If you try so hard to control the details, you are not allowing the full range of possibilities. There is risk involved. But without risk, there can be no freedom.

✳━━━━━━━━━━

Meditation: Facing Your Inner Challenges

Enter into a meditative state. Make a paradigm shift statement to yourself that you know you have an inner challenge with. Make the statement with strength and conviction. See how your body responds. Making no judgment on the response, have a conversation with the it. Listen to its story from a place of Love so that you might resolve the challenge and heal the resistance.

Another area of peacemaking comes with the Law of Change, one of the subsidiary laws of the Law of Vibration. The Law of Change states that because everything is in a constant state of vibration, it is always in a state of change. Change is the constant. Change is what is normal. And change involves risk. When things are always changing, we don't know how they are going to turn out. And the change can get messy and we feel like we are losing control. Many people resist change in their lives. They want the security of things staying the same—always knowing what to expect, no surprises, maintaining the status quo. This is the opposite of full-spectrum living. Change is what brings new life, new growth, new perspectives, new possibilities.

Where are you with change? Are you at peace with the fact that your life will forever be in a state of evolution? Are you at peace with the fact that as you pursue your life vision, step-by-step, you will also change, step-by-step? You considered this topic in chapter 5, when we discussed the Law of Vibration. Look back to your responses then. How do they compare to now? Has anything shifted in your relationship to the concept of change? Are you more at ease, more accepting of change as a natural part of the unfolding of your life?

Finding inner peace means letting go of inner judgment. There are many ways in which we judge ourselves and others. Some are conscious, and we can recognize them and instigate change right away. Others are hidden beneath the surface—judgments that have become so much a part of who we are that we aren't aware we are making them. Releasing judgment begins with Self. And the first lesson in self-judgment is: compare yourself only to yourself—never to others. They are where they are, and you are where you are. Create your own standard of excellence for yourself. After all, you are a beautiful, unique, divine being. Since you are unique, your way or process cannot possibly be like anyone else's. By the same token, everyone else is also a beautiful, unique, divine being. Therefore, their way cannot possibly be like yours. They will march to the beat of their own drummer and you to yours. When we can all find our own peace with that concept, the world will have made a major shift.

Every sorrow, loss, challenge, or hurt contains within it at least one gift for all involved. The gift may be different for each person, but a gift is there. The more adept you become at seeking out those gifts—in fact, at automatically looking for them, fully knowing that they are there—the easier it is to find peace in the midst of conflict and crisis. Seeking and finding the gifts gives us greater faith in the bigger picture and confidence that there is a reason for everything, that there are no coincidences. All is in divine order; that statement is used so often that it can seem trite, but it is absolute truth. Wherever we are, we have chosen to be there. When we can accept that and look for the gifts, inner peace comes more easily. For the moment, we ride the wave, knowing that we are where we are for a reason, and, in time, all will be revealed.

Finding inner peace often involves allowing yourself to grieve. The Sufi poet Rumi wrote, "I saw grief drinking a cup of sorrow and called out, 'It tastes sweet, does it not?' 'You've caught me,' grief answered, 'and you've ruined my business, how can I sell sorrow when you know it is a blessing?" In *Wisdom of the Ages*, Dr. Wayne Dyer responded to those words, saying, "In what we refer to as primitive societies, death is an occasion for celebration. There is a basic knowing, even in times of grief and mourning, that does not question the divine timing of each person's arrival here on earth, or the divine timing of one's departure, either. It is all in order! Perhaps the comfort is the sweetness of seeing that it is all part of the perfection of our universe, which has an invisible organizing intelligence flowing through every cell of creation, including the many painful experiences over a lifetime—then celebrating it all."

Allowing yourself to grieve and mourn loss or change in your life is a part of the inner peace journey of this second house. Change comes in many forms, but regardless of the form, it involves letting go. Sometimes a necessary step in your journey might be letting go of a relationship, a habit, or a belief. Once you commit to letting go, however, there often seems to be a testing period—a time when it seems that we are tempted in every possible way to go back into the relationship, to pick up the habit again, or to fall back into the former belief. These are all just gifts of the universe—opportunities to keep choosing the new path. Every time you choose the new path again, you are stronger and more committed to staying the course. This is another aspect of finding inner peace.

How is your relationship with the world around you? We addressed this issue in the second chakra, in chapter 6. It comes up again here as we look at finding your ultimate inner peace. You know that you cannot change another person, nor can you often change a circumstance. But you can change your perception relative to the person or circumstance. In changing your perception, you have the opportunity to move to peace. The world will not change toward you. It is busy doing whatever it does. However, you can change toward the world. You can change your attitude and shift your perspective so that you approach building your vision and life in a different way.

Questions to Ponder:
My Relationship to the World Around Me

Where am I at peace with the world around me, and where am I in conflict?

How am I at peace or in conflict with world at large?

How can I move to a place of consistent inner peace? What is one step I can take today?

As a part of the healing and peacemaking process, when you experience conflict, fear, or doubt, notice where the feeling lies in your body. Where is this feeling holding on to you, keeping you from being free? Then expand your heart to envelop that part of your body and the feeling itself. Let the pure healing Love of the heart overflow and bring you back to peace. The heart is the alchemical healer of our physical/emotional/spiritual being. Taking whatever you feel into your heart and simply letting it rest there will begin to facilitate healing on every level. For the heart is the seat of the soul. And through your soul, you access every level of consciousness. Peace begins in the heart.

Napoleon Hill, author of *Grow Rich! With Peace of Mind*, said there is a big difference between wishing for something and actually being ready to receive it. As we wrap up our work in the second house, we come to that ultimate question. Are you ready to manifest your vision and embrace all of how your life will be once you are living your vision? Do you know what you will do once your vision is accomplished? What is your pure "gut reaction" to your vision? Being at peace with these questions is vital to your manifestation process.

Questions to Ponder: Finding Inner Peace

What is my "gut reaction" when I look at or think about my life vision? Is my life vision in complete harmony with my soul mission? Am I at peace in every part of my being with the vision that I hold for my life?

Is there any part of my life vision that I am pursuing because I think I "should," or because someone else thinks I should? If so, is this what I really want?

Do I find myself seeking someone else's approval for any part of my life vision? If so, what do I need to examine within myself around this issue?

Am I ready to accept the full manifestation of my vision? What will my life look like when I am living my vision? Does that feel good to me?

In our discussion of the Law of Correspondence, we said that ego and soul are actually one—just different vibrational frequencies of one spectrum. Making peace between ego and soul is another aspect of the journey of the second house. This is also the journey from the solar plexus chakra to the heart. As we work through our personal issues, fears, and resistance, we release the heavy weights that hold us down and keep us in a slow and heavy vibratory state. Our vibration gets higher and finer, and we are able to move closer and closer to pure soul essence, pure Love.

Everything in its essence is Love. Love is the highest and finest vibration there is. It is the creating and sustaining force of the universe. All of creation is Love manifest in form. One part of making peace is, in your mind, stripping everything down to its pure Love essence. Then you see Love in every part of your being. You see Love in every person. You see Love at work in every situation. Taken to its fullest, you just see Love. When you are vibrating pure Love in your thought, action, and being, just think of what you will attract. Think of how your life will be, think of the peace and joy that can be your heart's constant state. I don't mean to make light of this or to say that this is easy. Not at all. Seeing Love in everything and every moment is a huge challenge. But what a great thing to aim for! We spoke at the end of the last chapter about aiming high and shooting high. It doesn't get any higher than "just see Love."

Manifestation House 3:

Energy

→ Is this a project about which I am or can become excited and passionate?

→ What goals or steps do I need to take for its completion?

→ What must I let go of or sacrifice in order to complete this project?

→ Are there others that I need to motivate and excite in order to complete my project successfully?

→ How can I build a sense of momentum and energy focus toward this project?

Dreams and goals are what set very successful people apart from all the rest. Throughout this book, I have said that whatever you can conceive and believe, you can achieve. I have also said that creation is a process of moving from the unseen to the seen, from the inside to the outside. In the first two houses, your work toward your vision was all inside, in the unseen worlds—working with your thought, committing to your vision, and finding inner peace with Self, your vision, and your world. While the inner work continues all the way around the Wheel, here in the third house you begin the outer work, laying the groundwork for building your vision in the seen world. You begin to establish goals and make plans for how you are going to manifest your vision.

The rest of the journey is a magical dance between the seen and unseen worlds, between your thoughts and your actions.

Goals are the secret to success in any venture. Success is simply the steady accomplishment of goals—of doing what you set out to do, step by step. In our culture, we tend to quantify success by the amount of money or prominence it has earned us. However, success as a basic principle has nothing to do with money or prominence—they are just two of many possible symbols or manifestations of success. If your goal was to get your garden planted in a week's time and you accomplished that goal, you have success. If your goal is to perfect a particular skill such as learning to knit or make a piece of furniture and you follow that through to completion, you have success. Furthermore, success within a particular realm will be different from person to person. For instance, if the basic goal is to learn to play the piano, one person's aim might be to learn to play popular tunes for personal enjoyment, while another's might be to perfect a Chopin nocturne for a public concert. Accomplishing either goal means success. Success is defined by each individual. Whatever your goal, you can succeed if you focus your energy and commit to the process of that goal.

Life vision is a very big picture. It has many components and facets, from where you want to live, the sources of your income, and how you will live your soul mission, to the kind of relationship you want to have with a partner or spouse, and what you want your daily life to look like. Goals are steps toward the manifestation of that vision. Vision is the result, goals are the process. Goals should be kept simple, concise, clear, and specific. You should always be able to state any particular goal in one simple, concise sentence. If you can't, then your goal is probably not specific enough. Or perhaps the goal is too big and needs to be further broken down into smaller goals. If you can clearly state what you want to achieve, you can achieve it. If, however, you are not clear in what the goal is or if it is too cumbersome, you will flounder in indecision and inaction.

We tend to want things in our lives because of how we think we will feel once we have them. Therefore, in accomplishing goals and manifesting vision, it is important to go to the feeling first. If you keep in mind the feeling that you will have when you accomplish the goal, you will feed your passion for accomplishing it, and you'll get there much faster. Choose to feel now what you think you will feel once you've reached your goal. Choose to be the person now that you think you will be once you are living your vision. In the first house, we spoke of aiming high and shooting high. Aim and shoot for who you want to be and what you want to feel. The rest will follow.

The more specific your goal, the easier it is to focus on it. However, the specificity of the goal is important for another reason, as well. We've all heard the saying, "Be careful what you ask for because you just might get it." As you set a clear goal and focus your attention on it, you are putting the Law of Vibration and the Law of Attraction into motion. Whatever you focus on hard enough, you will receive. We become or draw to us whatever we think about. If you want your life to be clear, free, and focused, then your thought must be clear, free, and focused. Any thought that is emphasized in the conscious mind will immediately begin to create itself in your outer reality.

The third house gives us the opportunity to begin putting into practice what we have learned about the Law of Vibration. We get to live out the law that like attracts like—that choosing your thought can change your life. Therefore, just by setting a goal and focusing on it, we begin to draw it to us.

The Law of Vibration coupled with the throat chakra ultimately leads us to claiming responsibility on a spiritual level for the creation of our life and the circumstances of our past and present. As we said in our initial throat chakra discussion, by taking full responsibility for your life, you can say, "If I have the power to create this reality, then I have the power to create a different reality!" You can choose how you respond to that fact of life—either you can be paralyzed by it or empowered by it. You can move into blame mode and beat yourself up for what you've created, or go into denial about your role in creating your circumstance, or you can choose to embrace your "result" as something to learn from, and move on to create your next and more desirable reality.

Since your vision encompasses many aspects of your life, create a wish list for each aspect. Then set goals in each area so that you can feel that you are making progress in all areas of your life. Don't worry about how you will accomplish those goals at the moment. In this house, you are just brainstorming, building energy. In the sixth house, you will actually create your action plan and put it into motion.

Meditation Activity: Setting Goals

Go to your Point of Stillness. Then invite Spirit to stand behind you and become your creative partner as you begin to build your life vision. Ask Spirit to help you see your vision even more clearly. Then, along with Spirit, identify the various categories of your life such as personal, professional, emotional, mental, spiritual, and financial and make a column for each in your journal. Create a wish list for each category that will support your life vision.

Then, allow Spirit to guide you as you list goals that can lead to the manifestation of your wish list in each category.

As you think about the goals you have written, there are two fundamental questions you must ask of yourself in order to follow through with the manifestation process:

1. Am I able?

2. Am I willing?

The first question asks whether you have or can access the skills, knowledge, and resources to accomplish your goal. The second question asks whether you are willing to do whatever it takes to commit to the process and follow through regardless of the distractions or obstacles that may appear. You must be able to answer "yes" to both questions if you want to succeed.

The third house is also your place for research. As you set goals toward the manifestation of your vision, you will no doubt find things that you need to learn and skills that you need to develop. Here in the third house you begin to anticipate what some of those things might be and learn all you can about everything you think you might need to know. Take time to gather the facts, develop the skill, and become who you need to be in order to accomplish that goal.

In this house, you also begin to identify the necessary resources for accomplishing those goals. First, you must recognize and acknowledge your own personal resources, such as time, talents, gifts, hobbies, education, money, property, and people. Then look beyond your personal sphere to see from where else you might gather the necessary resources. The world is there to support you if you open to it. Remember the back side of the heart chakra reflects your vision of how the world works, and whether it supports you in your quests or seems to thwart you at every step. If you do not feel supported, take some time to go back to the heart chakra work (see page 98) and open the back side of the heart.

Legendary oil tycoon H. L. Hunt said that there were two steps to accomplishment:

1. Decide what you want.

2. Decide what you are willing to give up in order to accomplish it.

The first step is clear. In the second step, it may be that there is something tangible that you must give up in your life, at least temporarily, in order to accomplish your goal. Or it may mean that what you have to give up is your old thought patterns and habits. Whatever it is that you must be willing to give up, are you willing to do that? Are you willing to move on and let go of the past? And what are you willing to risk in order to accomplish your goals? Are you willing to invest your time and money? How much? If you say that having certain things or developing certain qualities is top priority for you, are you willing to put your money where your mouth is—to make the investment in your future and the quality of life that you desire? How much risk is okay, and how much is too much? There is no right or wrong answer. It is simply whatever feels right to you.

You must consider these questions as you set goals and identify resources. They call out your inner warrior—the aspect of you that is dedicated to your mission, and will stand by it no matter what. Here in the third house we must ask what we are willing to sacrifice in order to live our mission and manifest our vision. We may see all the necessary steps of the process, but are we willing to step up to the plate and go to bat for the life we truly desire?

The third house calls us to draw in the necessary resources and energy for the accomplishment of our vision, and to clear out anything that gets in your way or does not serve your vision. One of the greatest ways to mobilize your forces and raise energy is to get rid of things, ideas, and beliefs that you no longer need. At this point of the manifestation journey, it is time to clean house, both literally and figuratively. This means giving away clothes you no longer wear, books you no longer need, magazines you never got around to reading. Anything that is not fulfilling a positive purpose in your life, either functionally or aesthetically, practically or emotionally, needs to go.

The warrior energy is simple and streamlined. Streamline your life so that you can focus your energies in powerful ways toward the manifestation of your vision and the living of your mission. This becomes a great invitation for whatever you desire to enter—you have created the space. In the words of Rick Jarow in his book, *Creating the Work You Love*, "When your talk and actions are pared down to essentials, you will immediately find yourself taken more seriously. For you transmit the energy of the warrior: the one who is single pointed and willing to sacrifice for the mission. Until your priority is aligned in this way, it will remain weak: the book will remain half written, the song unsung, the house just an idea on paper."

Fantasy and imagination were key tools for identifying your soul mission and creating your life vision, and will continue to be throughout the manifestation process. Having a vivid imagination continues to build your vision and show you the way to its realization. Fantasy is thought set free. Thought creates your life. Therefore, fantasy can create a freer life. Meditation is a great tool for setting your thought free. Every day of your creative life journey, spend time in meditation allowing fantasy to show you the next step—all the many possibilities that are unfolding. Early on in this journey, you cannot possibly see all of what could unfold as you move down the path. Encouraging your fantasy will continually spark your awareness of new possibilities, new doors and windows that are opening all along the way. You have created a mental image of what you want your life to look like as you live your soul mission. Keep fantasizing, keep creating, and inspiration will be a part of your daily experience. Remember inspiration is "in Spirit." You will develop your ability to live in the constant awareness of the interactive presence of Spirit in your life.

The original Greek root of the word "enthusiasm" is *en theos*, meaning "a god within." Everyone has this God within. It is the Law of Mentalism. Stepping into the God within and living life fully from that place brings great excitement and passion to the journey. You will spread joy and love wherever you go, because you will be an embodiment of those attributes. It is merely a matter of choosing to stand in the God-self—to be *en theos*, to be in God. The Greek dramatist Aeschylus said, "When a man's willing and eager, God joins in." Are you willing and eager?

The subconscious mind is greatly influenced by the heart chakra. The heart holds our sustaining passions in life. These are the same fundamental passions that are found in the sacral chakra, but raised now to a much higher vibration or level of awareness. Fundamental or primal passions of the sacral chakra can be short-lived, but heart passion is long-term. While sacral chakra passion is looking for immediate gratification, heart passion understands long-term rewards. When you take your vision to the heart chakra and connect with its passion, the subconscious mind begins to act through the body.

Our mission and vision were born in our hearts. Therefore, what better place than our hearts to bring that vision to life? Heart passion is the most compelling reason we can have for accomplishing anything. Think about your commitment to achieving your vision. Is that commitment in your intellect or in your heart? Is your passion seeking immediate gratification, or are you in this for the long haul?

This takes us back to Martha Graham's "divine dissatisfaction" and "blessed unrest." She was speaking of heart passion—of what you can't *not* do. Whatever you give your heart passion to becomes the focus of your thought. It bears repeating that every part of your life is a reflection of what is going on in your mind and thoughts. Every part. Again, when we really own that, it is incredibly empowering, because if you created it, you can change it. If you don't acknowledge the power you have to create it, you can't tap into the power you have to change it.

You may not have directly created the physical or apparent aspects of your reality, but you created your role or response within it. And that is what you can change. You can choose to change who you are in a situation—to change your role or your response, or to remove yourself from the situation entirely.

Meditation Activity: Building Passion

Go to your Point of Stillness. Then bring your life vision to your awareness, involving all of your senses. Find your heart passion for your vision,
and then sit with it and let it gather enthusiasm and motivation.
Mobilize your energy. Then consider the following questions, writing
your responses in your journal.

What will I do once I have manifested my vision? What do I want my
life to look like then?

Why do I want it? (Be very clear and specific here. You are not ready
for manifestation of your vision if you don't know why it is important to you.)

What parts of my gifts and talents am I using fully? What parts of my
gifts and talents are lying dormant or only partially developed and
utilized? How do they need to "kick in" for the full realization of my
dreams?

What am I willing to stand up and claim that I must be, do, or have
in my life, no matter what? What is my "divine dissatisfaction," that
"blessed unrest" that keeps me marching and makes me more alive
than the others?

Is this the same as what I wrote for my soul mission? If not, are there
some things I need to reconsider?

This third house also calls you to recognize when it is time to break
ranks with "the crowd" and follow your own inner drumbeat. This is the
solar plexus chakra coming into its own. We are not speaking of becoming haughty or childish, taking your toys and going home because you
didn't get your way. We are talking about recognizing when, in order to
truly live your mission and build your vision, you have to step away
from the thinking process of those around you. Grabbing your toys and
running is an act of fear. Claiming your place in the world in service of
your soul mission is an act of courage and truth.

As you find your motivation, establish goals, and identify resources, you are called to step into all of who you are—to blossom into your fullness as a partner in the divine creation of your life. We have already established that the greatest power we have is opening to allow the flow of Love through us in every moment. Therefore, your power is not you, it is what you allow to flow through you. Your responsibility is to open to the flow, and then harness it, focus it, and manage it in service of your mission and vision. How you use it is solely your responsibility—no one else's. The sooner you can step into your Love flow and ride the wave of your divine power, the sooner you are on your way toward manifesting your vision.

Questions to Ponder: Motivation, Goals, and Resources

Do I possess true heart passion and excitement for my life vision? If so, how do I express it? If not, do I need to make adjustments in my life vision so that I can find a true heart passion?

As I begin to build my life vision, are there others that I must motivate and excite in order to fully accomplish that vision? Who are the other people who will play a role in my success?

How can I continue to build a sense of momentum and energy focus toward my vision?

What resources, including time, talent, money, and other people, are going to be necessary to manifest my vision?

Are those resources readily available to me, or must I find or create them? What is my plan?

In what ways do I need to step more fully into my power?

Where in my life do I need to march to my own drumbeat and claim my independence in a way that empowers me to accomplish goals and build my vision?

House 1 Check-in: Does my work in the third house help me see my life vision even more clearly? If not, what do I need to shift?

House 2 Check-in: Does my work in the third house in any way compromise my sense of peace around the manifestation of my vision? Do I still feel at peace with everything that I am developing? If not, what do I need to shift?

Manifestation House 4:   17

Guidance

 → What does Spirit show me that my life will look like when my project is completed? How will it be different from now?

→ What is the pathway Spirit is showing me to take in order to complete my project?

→ What thought patterns need adjustment at this point as I perceive the path? Is Spirit showing me a path I had not considered? Do I have to change my way of thinking in some way in order to follow the path Spirit is showing me? Is changing my way of thinking something I choose to or am willing to do?

→ What new responsibilities must I accept in order to complete my project and the vision that Spirit shows me?

Here in the fourth house of the Manifestation Wheel, we engage the intuitive mind, the inner voice of Spirit, to help us see the future more clearly, and let the future show us the path toward its magnificent unfolding. Through the first three houses, we have created and embraced a vision for our lives, declared our intentions for the future, come to peace with all aspects of the vision, and laid the groundwork for its manifestation. Here in the fourth house, however, we step back from "creative" mode and into "reflective" mode, asking Spirit and soul to show us our future—to give us an even clearer and more expanded picture of what our life can look like when we have manifested our dreams. Through this house, we step more fully into the cocreation of our lives.

Long before entering the Manifestation Wheel, we began this cocreative process by listening to Spirit and soul to help us identify our soul mission—to know who we were called to be in this life journey. From there, we fantasized and dreamed about how we wanted to live our soul mission, and wrote a life vision statement. Now, in the fourth house, we return to Spirit and soul, asking that they take the vision that we have created and show us the glorious splendor that is possible within our vision. If words like magnificence and glorious splendor seem too big for how you feel your life is meant to unfold, keep in mind that the true magnificence and splendor of our lives lies within our hearts, our thoughts, and our relationship to the journey. Every moment offers magnificence and splendor, because every moment offers opportunity for the further unfolding of our divine beauty and essence of being.

Sometimes thinking about the future can trigger unresolved fears or anxieties within us about what the future holds. Those fears and anxieties can create powerful and unsettling images of our future, and override Spirit's guidance if we do not know how to recognize them. The future shown to you by Spirit and soul may very well contain challenges and obstacles you'll have to overcome. However, Spirit will at the same time convey to you a sense of expansiveness, support, and confidence that somehow you will meet those challenges, overcome the obstacles, and continue to grow into the fullness of your potential. A future shown to you by fear and anxiety will feel trapped in a box, have no sense of any other possibility, and feel doomed. Although lifting yourself out of this vision of the future has its own challenges and demands great discipline, it can be done using the tools and principles of conscious and subconscious thought and universal laws that you have learned throughout this book.

In this fourth house you have the opportunity to remove the shackles of fear and anxiety, and create a new reality for your future. Spirit will show you the way, but you must get clear enough to see the path Spirit offers.

The way to get clear is through your Point of Stillness—dropping down below all the chatter and the outer realities of your life until you reach your essence of Love. Once you are in that essence, there are no fears and anxieties. Spirit's vision of your future then easily appears at your request.

Meditation: Spirit's Vision for Your Life

Go to your Point of Stillness. Take as much time as you need to make sure you have really reached that deep, profound stillness that is your essence of Love. Then, using the following questions and process to guide your experience, ask Spirit to show you the magnificent splendor of possibilities within your life vision and your future. You will also come up with questions of your own. Just add them to the list. As you get more comfortable in working with Spirit, you will be shown more and more possibilities without needing questions to prompt or guide the process. Allow yourself as much time as you need for this exercise, and let it take whatever form seems appropriate for you.

To begin, ask Spirit to help you see three years into your future. Place yourself in that scenario, and then, using the following questions as guides, explore your life as if you were there now.

Where am I? What seems to be the principle focus of my life?

What am I offering to the world? What are my creative pursuits and what is their impact?

What is the state of my physical health?

What is my financial situation?

What are my sources of my income?

What have I achieved or accomplished in the last 3 years? How have I accomplished these things? Have I accomplished these things on my own or in cooperation with others?

How much time do I spend on personal growth and development, physically, mentally, emotionally, professionally, spiritually? How is that balanced with the rest of my life? What are the sources of my growth and development?

How much time do I devote to rest, rejuvenation, and refueling? What form does that take?

Now ask Spirit to project you 10 years into your future. Place yourself in that scenario and consider the same questions again. What has changed? How have you grown? What does Spirit show you as the progressive realization of your vision?

Finally, ask of Spirit and your soul the following questions:

What will my life look like when I have accomplished my vision? Help me see details that can guide my manifestation process.

What is the path toward the manifestation of this vision? What is the progression of goals?

What thought patterns and paradigms do I need to shift at this point in order to manifest the vision that You are showing me?

What actions do I need to take now in order to move ahead on the manifestation path?

What new responsibilities must I now accept in order to manifest these expanded possibilities of my future?

How can I start being the person that You show me that I can be now?

We return to the Law of Gender in this fourth house. The Law of Gender teaches us about balance between masculine and feminine energies—between action and reflection, assertiveness and patience. It also speaks of everything having a gestation period, and our faith in the unfolding process. Everything comes in its own time. When we open to Spirit and Its expanded view of our future, we find hope and reassurance that all we desire and feel that we are here to be, do, and have, is possible. We grasp more fully the balance of the yin and yang, the need to alter our steps of action and forward movement with those of introspection and contemplation. And we find the faith to trust the process and keep going even when all we can see clearly is the very next step. I am reminded of these encouraging words from the gospel song, "His Eye Is on the Sparrow:" "Though by the path He leadeth, but one step may I see; His eye is on the sparrow, and I know He watches me." Faith is in the realm of the feminine, while taking that next step in faith is in the masculine.

The Manifestation Wheel offers us this balance. The first house, Intention, is primarily masculine in nature. We actively dream our vision, claim our purpose, and accept all personal responsibility for the fulfillment of that mission and vision. We take the assertive steps to begin a process. In the second house, Peace, we find primarily feminine essence. We turn our thoughts to our inner being, making sure that all is well in our hearts around this mission and vision. The third house, Energy, brings us back to the masculine. We actively set goals as stepping stones toward full manifestation of dreams, find our motivation, and identify the required resources to make it all happen. Here in the fourth house, we return to the feminine as we enter the silence and ask Spirit and soul to show us the way.

Continuing on the Wheel, from the fifth house on, we find the masculine and feminine energies in a wondrous dance together through each house. In Empowerment, there is the feminine embrace, caretaking, and support, but also the masculine energy of guarding, protecting, and standing up for truth and freedom. The sixth house of Action might appear to be all masculine, but effective action itself requires forward motion coupled with pauses to reflect and evaluate. The seventh house, Surrender, involves both masculine and feminine energies as we alternate between playing active and passive roles in the creative process. Finally, the eighth house, Legacy, takes the nurturing and empowering energy of the fifth house to much higher levels.

Through the Manifestation Wheel, we develop the spiritual warrior within us. The warrior embraces both the masculine and feminine energies, allowing them to dance within their being—not merging the two energies, but rather developing each to its fullest potential as equal partners with one another, and then together as a full partners in the cocreative dance with Spirit.

The fourth house is a journey of faith—faith in the wisdom and guidance of Spirit to lead us through whatever steps we must take for our journey. At times, it may appear that even though we thought we made a decision based on intuitive wisdom and guidance from Spirit, the outcome seemed to steer us away from our vision and mission. However, there's no denying the gifts and learning experiences we received in following that "wrong" path—gifts that offer new wisdom and insight into your manifestation process. As I said once before, sometimes you must experience who you are not in order to more fully understand who you are, or take a path that steers you away from your vision in order to more clearly perceive the path that will take you there. Faith is what allows you to see the gifts, learn the lessons, perceive the splendor of it all, and charge ahead with renewed vigor.

The fourth house relates to the brow and crown chakras. In the brow chakra, we transcend time, moving beyond our sense of linear time into a realm where we can move freely back and forth along a time line. The crown chakra is the portal through which Spirit enters our awareness and shares with us Its wisdom and guidance. Spirit shows us the possibilities that lie within our vision in the brow chakra. Through the full development of the brow chakra, we are able to see those possibilities as Spirit shows them to us. We are able to "take the tour" right along with Spirit as our guide, rather than just listen to a description of it. The brow chakra allows us to move with Spirit into other dimensions of reality, and then draw those realities into the present moment in linear time. We are able to see the Law of Gender at work as we look out over the long time line. We more clearly perceive the unfolding process of manifestation, and therefore have complete faith that it will come in its own time.

Confucius said, "Great things have no fear of time." On the other side of the world in a different age, Shakespeare wrote, "How poor are they that have not patience! What wound did ever heal but by degree?" In the 20th century, *A Course in Miracles* said, "Infinite patience produces immediate results." Patience is essential in this process of manifestation. Fully understanding and inhabiting the brow and crown chakras, and embracing the Law of Gender bring us great patience. Patience grows out of faith. When you move into the crown chakra and live in faith, you are in no hurry for anything to unfold. You know it will come in its own time. You have complete faith that each step along the way will be valuable to your experience and add to the fullness of your beingness.

However, there can also be a negative or unproductive aspect of patience. It is possible to tell yourself you are just being patient and waiting for things to unfold when in fact you are really avoiding taking action. Know the difference. Recognize within yourself your own blocks and resistance. Using patience as an excuse will ultimately create inner discomfort, because you will know at some level that you are avoiding living your mission and being an active partner in the cocreative process.

True patience, on the other hand, will feel peaceful and still, because you're standing in complete confidence and faith that things will unfold for the highest good of all.

Questions to Ponder: Patience

Where in my life do I need to develop patience and an awareness of bigger-picture timing?

Where might I be too patient, using patience as an excuse to not act, stifling forward progress and momentum?

How do I find the balance between having the patience to wait when there is nothing to be done and having the courage to act when the time for action has come?

One of the laws of physics tells us that a body in motion tends to remain in motion until it is acted upon by an outside force. In other words, that which is growing will tend to continue growing, and that which is going backwards will tend to keep going backwards, until acted upon by an outside force. How is this law reflected in your life? Are things moving in the direction you desire, or does there seem to be a downward spiral in motion? Are you stepping in as the "outside force" to steer your life out of the undesirable path onto the desired one?

Memories from the past, circumstances and thoughts of the present, and visions of the future all have a role in guiding and creating our lives. The key is balance, and not being attached to any one of the three. Our past is rich in experience and wisdom. However, it is the past. All it can do for us now is show us where we have been and help us recognize where we might want to go in the future. We can only live in the present moment. That is the gift of living in a linear time dimension. Each day is a clean slate, and we can draw or write on that slate anything we wish. The past remains active in the creation of our lives only as we choose. If we remain attached to the circumstances of our past—feelings, surroundings, people, situations—we will continue to live warmed-over versions of those circumstances for the rest of our lives. The other choice is to acknowledge the past, express gratitude for what it has taught you, and get busy living consciously in the present in such a way as to create the future you have been shown. In the present moment, we take conscious action, learn from its consequences, dream, plan, and live with an eye on creating the future.

Once Spirit and your soul have shown you the wondrous possibilities within your vision, the ball is back in your court. Do you look at those future possibilities and say "Yes!" or do you look at your past and say, "But that's not where my life has been leading" and remain caught in the circumstances of your past? Here in the fourth house, you have yet another opportunity to enter the throat chakra, let go of aspects of your past that might hold you back, and leap into your glorious future. Every one of us has a past—a past that includes positive, affirming experiences as well as challenging, painful, or regretful ones. Each day we have the opportunity to review our past, hold on to those experiences that nurture and support our mission and vision, and let go of those that don't. Spirit has shown you the expanded possibilities of your future. You must now choose whether you will allow your past to create your future, or whether you will enter into the present moment and use your powerful conscious mind to cocreate with Spirit the magnificent life waiting for you.

If you want the world to present you with new possibilities and opportunities, you must constantly present the new and evolving you to the world. If you insist on remaining the same, not growing and evolving, how can the world offer you anything different?

Spirit has shown you the future. How do you want to work in partnership with Spirit to create it? How do you want to experience empowerment? Just how fully are you willing to commit to, accept, and embrace the magnificence of you and the resplendent unfolding of a life of infinite possibilities? This is the real question of the fourth house. Are you willing to take the ride? Are you willing to up the ante and move to a completely new level of consciousness and participation in life itself, and say, "I have seen the future and here I come!!" Are you willing to accept the unmatched power and illumination of Love as it flows through you not only for the sublime creation of your life, but for the effect that the energy of your life can have on the world?

What might appear at first glance to be simply a house of looking at the future has now become one of the most profound steps in the journey. Your responses to the "Questions to Ponder" below will determine where you go from here—how fully you manifest your divine human potential—how fully you are willing to live your soul mission.

Finally, before leaving this fourth house, pause to reflect on the first three houses to see if you need to make adjustments based on the path Spirit has shown you. The circular flow and interaction between the houses of the Manifestation Wheel only increases as we move on.

Questions to Ponder: Committing to My Future

How can I more fully incorporate communication with Spirit into my life?

Am I willing to commit to, accept, and embrace the magnificence and glorious splendor of my life?

Am I willing to live my future now? What is my first step?

House 1 Check-in: Does Spirit's vision of my future help me expand my own vision to a larger perspective of possibility? What changes do I want to make in my life vision statement in order to reflect Spirit's vision?

House 2 Check-in: Does this expanded life vision compromise my sense of peace around the manifestation of this vision in any way? If so, what needs to shift?

House 3 Check-in: Does this expanded life vision create more or less enthusiasm and motivation for its manifestation? If less, what needs to shift?

18

MANIFESTATION HOUSE 5:

EMPOWERMENT

→ Does this project have both personal and universal aspects?

→ How can the process and completion of my project nurture me, either directly or indirectly?

→ How can the process and completion of my project nurture others, either directly or indirectly?

→ Is there anything about this project or its process that could cause ill to another?

→ Does this project feel in some way like a gift for my own and everyone else's benefit?

→ Do I need to develop or refine certain leadership skills or characteristics in order to accomplish my goal?

There is an old Irish proverb that says, "It is in the shelter of each other that the people live." This proverb captures the essence of the fifth house of the Manifestation Wheel. In this house, you will examine the leadership aspects of your life vision, and how your soul mission and life vision can empower others, ultimately serving others in your community. As a house of nurture, the fifth house calls you to look at your emotional patterning around interpersonal relationships. Here you have the opportunity to heal any relationship patterns that hold you back from living your vision.

Through the second chakra, we became aware in early infancy that there were others with whom we shared our world. You may remember that it is in the second chakra that the first bands of energy are formed between people as they meet, regardless of the form the relationship will eventually take. During infancy and childhood, our fundamental patterns of how we relate to others were established—we learned to be open and trusting or to withdraw and protect. Our patterning around basic emotional safety or insecurity becomes apparent when, as adults, we look at how we meet others and interact in social situations.

As we clear blocks and create new paradigms around the ways we relate to others, we open a pathway to the heart. We become more open to significant and meaningful connections with those around us. Whereas in the second chakra we were concerned about basic, short-term emotional needs, in the heart chakra we open to a much higher level of consciousness, and consider the long-term ramifications of our emotional choices and relationships. Even in the solar plexus, where we found our place in the world and the roles we are here to play, we were still working on a level of consciousness that was primarily self-serving. Our primary concerns were how we were going to meet our needs and accomplish our goals in the world. In the heart chakra, we develop a desire to serve others' needs as well as our own. We begin to see community as a love and service relationship rather than as a "taking care of basic needs" relationship as seen from the second chakra. The fifth house is the further development of that heart chakra consciousness.

In our introduction to the Manifestation Wheel (in chapter 13), we spoke of the balance between masculine and feminine forces. We said that the first house is primarily masculine in nature, the second house feminine, the third house masculine, and the fourth house feminine. Here in the fifth house we advance to a level of conscious awareness where the masculine and feminine forces begin their dance together. The feminine essence is present in the aspect of nurture, care, and service. The masculine essence steps forward in aspects of leadership and providing for Self and others.

Nurturing, in its purest form, involves tremendous responsibility. Nurturing yourself means taking care of you in every area of your life, and providing opportunities for ongoing growth and development. The nurture of others means fostering the growth of individuals in their path of development—helping them to be all they can be in their own power and strength, not in what or who you think they should be. Nurture is not license for manipulation. It is not about controlling Self or others, or stifling soul journeys in any way. Nurture is about encouraging the free flight of the soul. Nurture is about empowering others to be all they can be. Therefore, as nurturers, one of our greatest challenges is to open ourselves to the highest possible view of who we and others are in divine potential, and facilitate the unfolding of that potential. We may wish that things would be a certain way, that others would make the choices we would have them make, and that all of life would unfold according to our carefully-crafted plan. But that will not always be the case. Listening to our soul and to the souls of others and responding to what you hear helps you to truly nurture the extraordinary potential that lies within each person.

Parenting children is a very special opportunity for nurture. While providing certain structure, protection, and understanding about life is a parent's responsibility, the parent must also constantly listen to the child's soul to hear and recognize the path that soul is here to take. Nurturing then is about providing the appropriate guidance, direction, and support. Each generation has the responsibility of freeing the next generation from limiting paradigms of the past. Parenting, at its highest level, is about listening to your child's soul, and letting it tell you how it needs to be raised.

Samuel Johnson, an 18th-century English writer, said, "The greatest benefit which one friend can confer upon another is to guard, excite, and elevate their virtues." We each have influence over one another, whether it is our intention or not. The thoughts, feelings, attitudes, and beliefs of the people with whom we spend our time will impress themselves upon us, especially when we are not confident in our own beliefs and feelings. We can choose the influences to which we subject ourselves in our day-to-day experience. Think about the people in your life—not just the people you consider to be important to you, but the people that you spend the most time with. These, in fact, may not be the people that you care about the most, but because of the amount of time you spend with them, they will have the most impact on you in your day-to-day life. Take some time for the following exercise in order to gain a clear perspective of how others are influencing your life.

Activity: The People in Your Daily Life

Make a list of ten to twelve people with whom you spend most of your time. These will not necessarily be the people who you love the most or who are the most important to you. These are the people with whom you spend the most hours—fellow workers, colleagues, partners, family, and friends. Then, think about each of these people, one at a time. What are they like? Be objective. The point here is not to judge their integrity or character, but just to observe. As you consider each person, ask yourself these questions:

How does being around this person make me feel? Am I always happy to see them, or do I find myself hoping to avoid them?

Do they have a sense of who they are and what they want in their lives?

Do they entertain big ideas? Do they think "out of the box," or do they live their life within the narrow confines of a limiting belief system? Are they exciting and positive people who seek the unlimited potential in all situations, or is their motto, "We've never done it that way before?"

Are they high achievers, or satisfied with just enough to get by?

Would I point out this person as a potential mentor or powerful positive role model to others?

These might be lovely people with big hearts who you care about, but they may also be going nowhere in their lives. If you are spending a lot of time with them, you face the challenge of warding off limiting thought patterns all the time. This burns up a lot of your energy that could be used for creative pursuits.

After thinking about each of these people, choose several that you feel could honestly teach you something valuable, and the ones you would consider as role models. In the coming days and weeks, focus your attention on how you can spend more time with and learn from these positive people.

If you want to learn and grow, you need to surround yourself with people who are also committed to learning and growth. It is also helpful to have at least a few people in your immediate circle who are farther along in the journey than you, people to whom you can look up, with whom you can toss around ideas and engage in meaningful and stimulating conversation. A part of the work in the fifth house is making sure you have these nurturing and mentoring people in your life, and that you are providing that energy for others.

Questions to Ponder: Nurture

How does my vision nurture me to be all I can be?

How does my vision nurture others to be all they can be?

Is there any way in which my vision manipulates me to be something or someone who, at my essence, I simply am not?

Is there any way in which my vision manipulates others to be something or someone who, at their essence, they are not?

Do I like who I am becoming as I pursue my vision? Am I blossoming into the fullness of my divine potential?

As I look at the lives of those over whom I have some influence, whether they be children, students, employees, spouses/partners, or friends, do I like who they are becoming through my influence? Are they, in my nurture, blossoming into the fullness of their divine potential?

The masculine counterpart of nurture is leadership. Everyone has a different feeling about leadership and whether or not they are leaders. Before we explore this topic together, take some time for the following exercise to see where you are with the whole concept of leadership.

Activity Meditation:
Integrity, Leadership, and Core Values

We begin with another word-clustering exercise. Gather several sheets of blank paper. In the center of one sheet, write the word "integrity" in large capital letters and draw a circle around it. Then, as if free associating, write on this page every word that comes into your mind from the word integrity. Follow the same process you have done in other word-clustering exercises until you feel that you are coming up to a personal issue or revelation. At that point, go to yet another fresh page and write in paragraph form whatever is coming to you.

When you have completed your work with integrity, go through the same clustering process with the word "leadership."

After completing both of these clustering processes, go to your Point of Stillness. Once you have reached the silence, consider the following questions. Take time to sit with each question, and when you are ready, go to your journal to write.

Do I consider myself to be a leader? Am I comfortable with the idea of being a leader?

Do I consider myself a person of integrity?

How does my integrity show itself in my life and in my interactions with others? Are there places where I am not in my integrity? Are there changes I need to make in order to manifest integrity?

What are my core values?

Do I truly live those values, or do I compromise them, either in relationships, career, or other areas of my life?

There are three phases to leadership. The first is following a leader. Before we can become a leader, we follow other leaders to learn, grow, and develop. At some point, we advance to the second phase, personal leadership—becoming the leader of our own lives. The third phase is leading others. We all have varying levels of comfort with being a leader, but the bottom line is that ultimately we all have to become the leaders of our own lives.

Most successful leaders have several characteristics in common. These characteristics are important to consider whether you are developing self-leadership or your skills to be a leader for others. First and foremost, a leader has a vision. Without a vision, there is nowhere to go, no sense of direction. Furthermore, a leader is sincere, passionate, and articulate in sharing his or her vision with others, clearly describing the benefits they can realize from the vision—why it is important that they accomplish the vision. A leader is clear about his or her core values and communicates those values by how he or she lives.

A leader is able to create bridges between people and ideas. With others, a leader must be a mediator at times, the level head who can hear every side of a story, and help those involved to hear one another. When leading themselves, leaders must be able to reach harmony between conflicting inner beliefs or desires.

A leader has a desire, ability, and willingness to serve, for leadership in its highest form is all about service. A leader has compassion that is rooted in strength and a solid sense of grounding, feeling another's situation, but not getting lost in another's circumstance. While compassion is important in working with others, having compassion for Self is also essential to being a good leader. Grounded compassion becomes invaluable as the leader faces the challenging task of being willing and able to identify and articulate the uncomfortable truth—to call reality as it is, and be willing to work with the truth of a situation. Through compassion, leaders are able to help others as well as themselves face and work through their uncomfortable truths.

A true leader has learned to empower everyone around them to be the best that they can be. Empowering others means illuminating for them their strengths and their potentials, and helping them see how to develop them. Whether or not you want to be a leader for others, empowering others is still important, for as you empower others, you empower yourself. You live within an energy of everyone being their best. You create an environment where everyone is always aiming for the highest standard. We are not talking about creating stress and pressure to produce, but rather excitement and desire for developing to your absolute best and offering your best to the world, whether in thought or action.

Finally, a leader is a master at providing momentum for accomplishing the task at hand. The leader inspires, motivates, and creates movement. As momentum builds, everyone involved gets excited. Excitement builds even more momentum. As the energy moves faster and faster, you get so busy keeping up with the pace that you forget to notice when you might become afraid. Momentum is a great tool for blasting through fears and resistance. When things are flying fast, there is no time for analyzing feelings or reconsidering. You are too busy just keeping up.

If you've ever been white-water rafting, you know that when you see the rapids ahead, you have two choices: paddle to the side and get out of the river, or commit to the ride and paddle like crazy! Once you head into the rapids, there is no time to think about how scared you might be. You just have to paddle and stay focused until you reach the other side. As you make it through the rapids, there is a tremendous sense of accomplishment and exhilaration.

Rock climbers say that the most difficult climbs are the ones they remember the least. There was no time to think about what was happening. They were so focused on survival and reaching the top, there was no room for any other thought.

The same is true in the important projects of our lives. The more we stay focused on the task, the less time we have to be distracted by fear or doubt. Blasting through the fear and "doing it anyway" can be a tremendously empowering experience.

Whether you want to become the leader of your own life or be the leader of a thousand-member project team, it is important to develop these characteristics within yourself. The fact that you have worked this far through this book is a sure indicator that you are committed to being the leader of your own life. Developing these characteristics within yourself will prepare you to be a dynamic leader for others, should you ever choose to do so.

Personal commitment is essential for being a leader—commitment to movement and action toward your vision. Too many people want the benefit but don't want to do the work or take the action. The true leader realizes that nothing is accomplished without doing the work. And as we have stressed over and over again, a huge percentage of that work is done in your thoughts. Consider that we are more than half way around the Manifestation Wheel and still have not come to the house of action.

All of our work thus far has been in the unseen thinking, feeling, energetic, conceptual world. It is only after having worked through the "inner stuff" that you are truly ready for action in the outer world.

We've all heard the term "born leader." We were all born to do different things, to live out different missions, and to manifest different visions. However, no matter what talents with which you may have been gifted from birth, those talents must still be developed and refined. The same is true with leadership. When we look at our vision and recognize who we must be and what must be done to accomplish that vision, we see what talents and skills we must develop in order to take on the leadership role and turn our dreams into reality. Look for others in the world who can serve as role models for who you want to be. Whom do you want to emulate in your life? Choose your mentors carefully, and then learn everything you can from them, from both their successes and their mistakes.

The seed of the leader within you is planted in the root chakra. In the second chakra, that seed pokes through the ground and begins to take creative form. In the solar plexus, it blossoms into fully recognizable form and gains confidence in its abilities. As it moves into the heart, all of those leadership characteristics are now fully integrated, and the synergy of Love and Power is given birth.

Questions to Ponder: The Leader in You

Have I developed the self-leadership necessary for manifesting my life vision? Which leadership characteristics (vision, passion, core values, compassion, honesty, integrity, willingness to face the truth) are fully present within me, and which do I need to develop more fully?

Does my life vision require being a leader for others? If so, how?

The fifth house is also about recognizing your role in community-building. It may be a role for which you are widely recognized, or it may be a very quiet, behind-the-scenes role in which very few people know of you or your life. But, as we have said before, your thoughts and activities are energy, and they send out clear messages to those around you. We are all teachers for one another. We all exert influence over others simply by our presence. Does living your life vision create the kind of teaching message you want to share?

In considering community, we ask, "Am I responsible for my brothers and sisters, friends and neighbors, children and parents?" The Law of Mentalism teaches us that we are all one. When we live this law, our consciousness rises to higher and higher levels of awareness, and we realize that the question is no longer about responsibility. We are our brother and sister, our friend and neighbor, our children and parents. We are not responsible for their thoughts and actions, but we are responsible for our thoughts and actions toward them. And since we are all one, our thoughts and actions toward them are thoughts and actions toward ourselves.

Martin Luther King said, "Everybody can be great, because anybody can serve. You only need a heart full of grace, a soul generated by love." We realize our greatness within the context of community, for it is in our relationships with one another that our inner light shines. All of life is about communication on some level—communication with Self, with Spirit, with others. Service is about communication, for when we serve we are sending a message to the world that communicates something of who we are.

In the fifth house, we consider what it is that we are communicating to those around us. What is the message that people are getting? Is it the message that we want them to receive? Is it the message that we want to receive from ourselves? Every message that goes out to another also comes back to Self. Here in the fifth house we look at our forms of communication and service and ask, "Is this what I want? Is this my true intention?"

Questions to Ponder: Service

When I consider my soul mission statement, how do I see my soul mission serving me personally in my life journey? What are its gifts for me? What is its message for me within the context of community and service?

How does my soul mission serve others? What are its gifts for others?

What is the message that it carries about who I am to the community around me?

How does the service of my soul mission, both to myself and others, fit into my life vision? Is my life vision in harmony with my soul mission from a service perspective?

An important consideration in nurture, leadership, and empowerment is how and where you draw boundaries in your life. In all of the activities of this fifth house, there is a fine line between not doing enough and going overboard by doing too much, between offering yourself to others and losing yourself in the process. A part of the work of the fifth house is to recognize the roles you have taken on in your life or the titles by which others know you. Are they the roles and titles that you truly desire? When you consider them from a soul level, are they comfortable for you? Do they enrich your life, or are they costing you? Do they serve your vision? Do they serve the true empowerment and development of those around you? Does your playing the role help them to be all that they can be? These are questions that must be asked in the fifth house, for nurture, leadership, and service can easily fall into a pattern of codependence. We can find ourselves taking on roles or living out patterns that keep us and others around us comfortable and protected from challenges we don't want to face. Or we can find ourselves in roles that we took on long ago, not realizing or thinking about the long-term consequences. These hard questions must be addressed here in the fifth house so that you can enter the sixth house of action unencumbered by roles and titles that are in conflict with your life vision and soul mission.

Setting clear boundaries is one of the greatest gifts you can give both to yourself and to those you care about the most. By honoring your personal space, needs, desires, and vision, you encourage others to honor theirs. You cannot manifest another's vision for them, or protect them from the life lessons they are here to learn. You cannot take on their feelings for them or protect them from hurt. Nor can they do that for you. Understanding and embracing this concept allows you to set boundaries that can ultimately empower everyone involved. It is then up to each individual whether to accept the empowerment.

As you consider how nurture, leadership, and empowerment fit into your life vision, there are some things you might want to think about in order to set clear boundaries. First, examine your true motives for action. Why are you choosing to nurture, lead, or empower? Be clear that you are making choices based on fostering the true divine potential in everyone involved.

Be honest with yourself about what you can and cannot do. When you overspend your time, energy, money, or Self, everyone suffers eventually. Don't compare yourself with what others choose to or are able to do. That is their journey. You have yours. Be true to your journey, your available energy, and your heart.

Keep communication open and honest with everyone in your life. Breakdown or lack of communication is the cause of most, if not all, of the world's major problems. When something needs to be said, speak it clearly, simply, and honestly from your heart. Ask that you be heard from the heart. And offer the same gift to everyone else. When we can listen to one another and truly hear the soul message that lies beneath the words and actions, we can move to a new world order. We will then recognize one another as brothers and sisters in a great, global family.

Know your priorities, and honor them. When you are called to play a role or take on a task that feels in conflict with your soul mission or pulls you out of your focus toward the accomplishment of your life vision, say "no." Let go of things that are not really yours to do. When people ask for something that you cannot give, refer them to someone who can. Honor your vision. Abandoning your vision only leads to frustration and bitterness.

Questions to Ponder: Roles and Titles

What roles do I play in my life? By what titles (mother, teacher, brother, doctor, helper, friend) am I known?

How do I feel about those roles and titles? Are they who I really am? Are they roles that I want to continue playing or giving energy to in my life?

Are these roles and titles a part of my life vision? Are they serving as vehicles for living my soul mission, or are they keeping me from my mission and vision?

Action and words are not the only ways you can nurture, lead, and empower. Sometimes the most powerful gift you can offer to someone or to a situation is to hold them in your heart and support them in your meditation. I came to understand this on an entirely new level in the days and weeks following the September 11, 2001, terrorist attacks on the United States. Security and trust that we had taken for granted in this country was suddenly pulled out from under us. Especially in New York City, there was nowhere to go where people were not in crisis. Under ordinary circumstances, when any one of us experiences crisis in our lives, there is at least someplace to go from time to time to escape—to be with people whose lives are still intact. But that was not the case in New York. Everyone you met had been touched in some significant way by the attacks, either through loss of loved ones or friends, loss of a job, loss of a home, or loss of a sense of safety. Daily activities like riding the subway, going to the post office, riding the elevator to the sixtieth floor of a skyscraper, were all things we took for granted until that day. Even with a commitment to going on with life, we still couldn't help but have a second thought.

As e-mails and phone calls poured in during the days that followed September 11, everyone wanted to know what they could do to help. Emergency efforts were already well under way and monetary contributions to disaster relief were being made as never before in the history of our country. At that point, what we needed in New York City was for someone to just hold the energy for us—something we were having a hard time doing for ourselves. We needed to know that somewhere out there in the world there were people holding us in their hearts and love, because we were struggling to not fall into despair and depression. Hanging on was about all we could do right then. The more we learned of meditation and healing circles around the world sending love and light to New York City, the more our spirits were nurtured, embraced, and supported. That gave us strength to go on.

Never doubt your abilities to nurture, lead, and empower. And don't think it must always be in a prescribed way. You may not be a physical presence, but know that you can still provide support, nurture, and help to others by holding them in your heart. You can offer yourself as a channel for the Love and power of the divine to pour through you toward them; this is one of the greatest tools we have for building community.

Questions to Ponder: Nurture, Leadership, Empowerment, and Service

Are there opportunities for leadership within my vision or soul mission that I have not yet identified?

Does this vision and its process feel like a gift to me and others for everyone's benefit?

House 1 Check-in: Does my work in this house help me see my vision more clearly? If not, what do I need to shift?

House 2 Check-in: After my work in this house, do I feel that my sense of peace around the manifestation of this vision has been compromised in any way? If so, what do I need to shift?

House 3 Check-in: After my work in this house, do I feel more or less enthusiasm and motivation for the accomplishment of my vision? If less, what do I need to shift?

House 4 Check-in: After my work in this house, do I see my future any differently? If so, how? Do I need to shift anything?

19

Manifestation House 6:

Action

 → What is my plan of action?

→ Are there steps in addition to those I listed in the third house that I now see I need to take?

→ Are there others whose help or counsel I must seek in order to complete my project?

→ As I create my plan of action, do I see a need for additional resources besides those I identified in House 3?

→ Are those resources readily available to me, or must I find or create them?

→ What is my time frame for completing this project?

At long last, after five houses of inner work, it is time to pull your act together and take it on the road! Here in the sixth house you build on the third house work of goal-setting and identifying resources by creating an action plan and setting it into motion. Working with an action plan involves time management, daily planning and strategies, setting priorities and sticking to them, and identifying individual projects that will lead to the ultimate manifestation of your vision. It involves stepping into the throat chakra and being willing to live your truth, to "walk your talk." The masculine force of assertiveness and action is balanced in this house by its feminine counterpart, reflection and reevaluation.

The sixth house continues the development of your inner spiritual warrior with the concept of *praxis*, the integration of your belief with your behavior. Praxis means not only knowing our essence and truth, but also living it through the choices we make and the actions we take. Having a skill and not using it is the same as not having it. Having a belief but not honoring it is the same as not believing. Your life can only give to you what you give to it. If you don't plant seeds, there is no harvest. If you don't live from your truth, you don't get results that are in harmony with your truth in return. Be honest about the seeds you plant, call your inner spiritual warrior into action, and create the causes that will lead to the effects you desire.

Praxis is the practical application of "to thine own self be true." Much of the work we have done thus far has been about identifying deeper levels of personal truth. The throat chakra and the sixth house bring us to the universal trinity of creation by first calling us out of concept into form, and then into action. Then, they call us to live every day of our lives in accordance with our truth. This means fully aligning our conscious and subconscious minds. Even though you have done a tremendous amount of inner work by now, stepping into action can still bring up unresolved inner conflicts. We have been on a journey of learning to live by soul guidance, but we are still conditioned by society to "fit into the crowd," to "play it safe," to not "make a spectacle" of ourselves. When we step up to the plate to be all that we can be, we may hear the conflicted message, "Be as good as you can, but know your limitations. Don't get too full of yourself." Or "Don't set your sights too high— people in our family don't make that kind of money." Or "You don't want that kind of success."

Knowing how to do something is a function of the conscious mind. Contrary to what we may think, however, the conscious mind is not what controls or influences our behavior. Following through and putting your knowledge into action, or praxis, is governed by our paradigms in the subconscious mind. Just because you know how to do something doesn't mean that you do it.

We've all experienced situations in our lives where our conscious mind clearly recognizes what needs to be done, but for some reason, we can't seem to take those steps. Something holds us back. The conscious mind may understand the need very clearly and rationally, but if the subconscious thought process is not in harmony with the conscious understanding, you experience resistance and inaction. If we proceed with action against the will of the subconscious mind, it is like trying to drive with the emergency brake on. The car simply will not move. The conscious and subconscious minds must be in alignment for full success in any venture.

Resistance in any situation is usually a message telling you that somewhere in your subconscious mind a red flag has gone up and all is not in harmony within you. In order to get back on a progressive track, you must explore your subconscious thought process to find the red flag, have a dialogue with the thought or belief that is waving it, and choose the appropriate response. Either shifts in your thought and belief will be necessary, or you will need to adjust your outer goal in order to bring it into alignment with your inner beliefs.

Paradigm shifts involve praxis—integrating your knowledge with your behavior—bringing together what you know needs doing with actually doing it. This often means working through issues and past limitations so that you are able to accomplish your present goals. Shifting paradigms is not as simple as deciding you are going to think or believe differently and then just doing it. To experience complete peace and harmony with a belief, you must work through whatever issues arise in response to the desired shift. This is the inner wrestling we discussed in the second house. You must listen to the story of the part of you that holds on tightly to that belief and see how you can reassure it—how you can effect the desired transformation within that part of Self. You may find yourself going back and forth between the second and sixth houses as you seek to release resistance and find harmony between the conscious and subconscious minds, and then proceed in confidence and peace with your action plan.

Conscious and subconscious truths must be in harmony in order for you to progress effectively. We live in a society that looks for someone or something to blame when things don't go according to plan. We are conditioned to look outside of ourselves for the causes of problems. But as the sign on President Harry S. Truman's desk read, "The buck stops here." We come up to the responsibility issue once more. The empowering choice here is to accept that whatever is going wrong on the outside is most likely mirroring a conflict between our conscious and subconscious truths. We can rationalize anything we want, but if we want to make major headway with our action plan, then we must resist the urge to "pass the buck." We must walk through the uncomfortable truth. This is living in integrity—bringing your thoughts, feelings, and actions all into harmony.

The Law of Cause and Effect is a major key to success in the sixth house. When your inner truth is always present in whatever "cause" you create, the "effects" you receive will be in alignment with your desires. However, when you compromise your truth in any action, the results will ultimately reflect your inner discord. Truth is uncomplicated. There is no drama in truth. When you experience inner conflict or disharmony, ask, "How am I denying my personal truth and going with someone else's idea or opinion?" When you honor personal truth, you set an exceptionally high standard for living. This is an orderly universe—what you send out will come back to you. Every thought and action is a cause that leads to a result or effect.

There are generations of thoughts and beliefs programmed into every cell of your being. Those thoughts and beliefs can guide every step of your journey if you let them. Your power to choose, however, can override any preexisting conditioning. Making the choice to follow your own path, to honor your personal truth, may not be comfortable, but it is essential to your success in manifesting your vision.

So here we go—it's time to dive in and make a plan—your initial action plan for the full manifestation of your life vision. This may seem like a daunting task, but keep in mind a couple of things. First, this is your initial action plan—a place to begin. You may adjust, amend, overhaul, and reconsider this plan many times over the course of the next twenty or thirty years. But you have to start some place, and that place is where you are right now. Many pieces may already be in place for you to accomplish your vision. Others you have not yet even conceived. That is as it should be. You will learn and discover as you go along. Not every step of the way will be clear to you as you begin. That's the mystery and the magic of it. Life will keep presenting you with gifts and surprising turns. Admittedly, some can be significant challenges, but if you take the challenges into the silence and work with Spirit to see the inherent lessons and gifts, those challenges will catapult you forward on your path.

Second, through the next few pages you will create your plan in a step-by-step process. When you take both the planning and execution processes of your life one step at a time—remaining focused on the immediate task rather than taking on your whole vision at once—it all becomes quite manageable. Remember that the conscious mind can only focus on one thing at a time. You may wish to accomplish several goals or complete several projects within the same time period, and that can be done, but discipline yourself to give your attention to only one project at a time. Designate certain days of the week or certain hours of the day for each project, and do not let the other projects encroach upon that time. Each project will get its full attention during its designated time.

Having said that, you'll also need flexibility as the creative process unfolds. However, there is a difference between being flexible and lacking discipline. Being flexible means allowing your project to take shape as you cocreate with Spirit, taking each turn in the road as it comes up, while still remaining "on task." Lacking discipline, on the other hand, means allowing yourself to be easily distracted by other things. "Life" happens to all of us—things come up to which we must give immediate attention—but through your discipline and focus, you learn to manage life in such a way that it doesn't become a series of dramas. You no longer live in constant reaction to crises. When you focus your thoughts and intention, focus and order are what you draw into your life. Remember, like attracts like.

In order to begin creating your action plan, you will need a notebook or a stack of paper. Or, you may also choose to create your action plan in the word processing program of your computer. Give yourself plenty of time to work, at least a couple of hours, and you will find this process exciting, inspiring, and empowering. Let the momentum build. If you start to get overwhelmed, take a deep breath and keep going. Push through. Take a short break if you need it, but not too long. You will lose your focus. Commit to creating your initial action plan right now. It will be one of the greatest gifts you will ever give yourself.

Step 1—Vision

Take out your life vision statement and read it again. Are there any changes you want to make at this point—any additions or clarifications? Read it several times and visualize all of its components. Take time to let your vision fire up your passion and excitement about the life you are going to create. When you are charged and ready to go, proceed to Step 2.

Step 2—Organization

If your vision statement is not already divided into categories, such as personal, professional, financial, emotional, and spiritual, take time to do that now. Create a separate page for each category, writing your vision for that aspect of your life at the top of that page.

Step 3—Identifying Goals

Within each category, identify the goals that can lead to the manifestation of your vision. You have already identified some goals in the third house. Use them as a starting point, and then take off from there.

In some categories, there may be several pathways that could lead to your success. If you find yourself seeing more than one possible path, write them all down in separate columns and set goals for each. Leave space on the page after each goal. Be creative. Each pathway that you imagine to your eventual success will spark new ideas. The process can help you climb out of your box and see possibilities you never imagined before. Don't worry at this point about how you will accomplish these goals, or even in what order they should come. Just get them on paper.

Complete this process for every category. Because you will probably be further along in the manifestation of your vision in some categories than in others, you will find that you have a lot to write and many goals to accomplish in some categories, and less in others. That's normal. Don't make this harder than it is. This is the creative part of action planning. Just have fun with it. Work with Spirit and create your plan.

Step 4—Identifying Projects within Goals

Now that you have identified the goals that can lead you toward manifesting your vision, it is time to identify the specific projects necessary to accomplish those goals. You will achieve success by breaking your goals down into small projects that you can complete within relatively short periods. By taking this step, you create a completely doable step-by-step process that will lead to accomplishing your vision. Keep the projects simple. If they get too complex, they will overwhelm you, and you will not even start. When you realize that a project is too big, break it down into smaller steps.

If you find that a goal is so large that you have no idea where to start, break that goal down into smaller ones. What is a smaller goal that, once accomplished, could lead you to the larger one? Instead of focusing on what you don't know how to do, focus on what you do know, or who you know who could help you see the path. Then you will be on your way once again.

Review the goals you have written in each category and write down specific projects toward each goal. Don't worry about which you should do first at this point. Just identify the projects.

Step 5—Prioritizing Goals and Projects

Go back to each category and prioritize the goals you have written. What is the order in which you must accomplish them for the manifestation of your vision? Which are the most important to you? What seems to be the flow that will lead you to manifestation? Place your goals in priority order within each category.

Once you have prioritized the goals within each category, go back and prioritize the projects within each goal.

Step 6—Identifying Resources

Under each project, write the resources necessary for its accomplishment. Will you need time, money, advice, or help from particular individuals? Will you need to develop a new skill or incorporate new technologies in order to complete that project? You did some work in this area in the third house. Again, let that be your starting point, and then take off from there. Identify everything you will need, at least as you can see it now, in order to complete each project.

Step 7—Putting Yourself on the Line

Look back at your life vision in each category. Where are you going to have to risk something, to put yourself on the line, in order to manifest this vision? What is it going to cost you? Are you willing to take those risks? Are you willing to call forth the spiritual warrior within you, garner your strength and courage in the face of obstacles and opposition, either from within or from people around you? Where do you feel that the risks are too great and you need to reconsider your plan? Getting comfortable with considering risk and discerning the possible payoff and personal or community cost is an important part of your action plan. List the potential risks, costs, and concerns associated with your action plan, and write beside each one your thoughts and feelings.

Step 8—Set Time Lines

Go back to each project you have written and estimate how long it will take you to complete that project. Once you have estimated the time for each project within a goal, estimate how long you think it will then take you to accomplish that goal. Finally, based on the time lines for each project and goal, estimate how long you think it will take to manifest your vision in that life category. Remember you are working on long-term vision here, so don't worry if your time lines add up to ten or even twenty years. Also, don't worry about how much time you have in your schedule now to complete these projects, or about which categories you should concentrate on first. Just create time lines for each project, goal, and category.

Step 9—Set Priorities among Categories

Once you have completed all of steps 1 through 8 in each category, you get a true sense of how you are going to manifest your life vision. The time lines are far from set in stone—they may start shifting tomorrow. But you have a place to start—a sense of where you are going and how you are going to get there.

At different times in our lives, we focus on different things. Balance in all areas of our lives is important, but there will be times when we intentionally choose to let things get a little out of balance for a short time in order to make great strides in a particular area. What is important here is the consciousness with which we make that choice. As long as we are fully aware of stepping out of balance, have a clear sense of when we will reinstate the balance, and discipline ourselves to follow that plan, everything is fine. When we let go of the importance of balance and let our projects take over our lives, we get into trouble. Stay focused and keep your intention clear in each choice you make.

Given that understanding, look back over the categories of your life vision. Which ones are calling out to you for immediate attention? Which ones can move you forward toward your overall life vision the fastest? What needs to be the primary focus of your life right now? What should then follow as the secondary focus? What categories of your life vision are taking care of themselves for the moment? This doesn't mean you can ignore them—they will still need your nurture—but they may not need as much attention as others.

Once you have identified the one or two categories that are going to receive your greatest attention for the immediate future, it is time to zero in on them and get moving. If you identified multiple paths that could lead to accomplishing your vision in a particular category, look back over your time lines and goals necessary within each path. Which path feels right to you? Which one does your intuition tell you is the right one? The path may even end up being a combination of two or more paths. If that is the case, take time to create that combination path now.

STEP 10—WORK YOUR PLAN

Congratulations! You have an action plan! Now let's see how to work it.

The first step is to take your individual goals and put each one on its own Manifestation Wheel. The Wheel can continue to give structure to your process, down to the smallest project. With some goals you will be able to zip around the Wheel in a matter of minutes. With others, it may take several hours or days. The process of the Wheel assures that you address every aspect of the goal for its complete accomplishment. If you get stuck somewhere along the way, the various houses of the Wheel and the knowledge you have gained throughout this book about how life works will give you the tools to break through. As I said in chapter 13, the farther you go in your manifestation journey, the more Wheels you are likely to have going at once.

An action plan is worked hour-by-hour, day-by-day, week-by-week. In other words, how you organize your time is crucial to accomplishing anything. Your ability to create and manage time and set priorities will determine your success at manifesting your vision. You must live each day within the context of your life vision. In a balanced existence, all aspects of your life are being fed and nurtured. So taking a day to hike in the woods, two weeks to travel to a place you've always wanted to go, or a few days spent enjoying family and friends, can be just as important to your life vision as completing a career project or meeting a financial goal. Everything in balance.

So what is time management? Put simply, time management is about minute-by-minute awareness of how you are spending your day. Make your choices consciously. Every choice will have a consequence. Work the Law of Cause and Effect in your favor. Be proactive in the creation and management of your time. Work your agenda rather than someone else's. That doesn't mean that you aren't there for others or don't respond to their needs. But, again, keep everything in balance. When you are good at time management, you don't lose yourself in another's situation, or let another take advantage of your generosity and rob you of your personal progress.

If time management is a challenge for you, for the next week make a log of how you spend your time. Be specific. Chart every minute. Don't make broad, sweeping time statements. The more specific you are, the clearer you will see how you are using your day. At the end of the week, spend an hour or so looking back at your time log. Just as you did in the checkbook and calendar exercise on pages 183-187, see what your real time priorities were. Then identify the adjustments that you need to make. How can you create a structure that serves all of your time needs? Then look at the projects you have put on your plate for your immediate attention and create a time structure that serves you.

Create a daily schedule that makes success possible, while at the same time allowing time for the rest of your life to remain in balance. Recognize where you need to learn to say "no"—where you need to draw the line and reserve your energy for accomplishing your goals.

And, at the same time, identify where you need to say "yes" and create a structure to accommodate that need.

Time management is not just about scheduling and priorities, however. The master time manager also recognizes the importance of creating empty space in the day—space for entering the silence, space for magic to happen. Space gives room for Spirit to speak to you and guide you. It also gives room for ideas, people, and circumstances to present themselves at the perfect time for the continued unfolding of your vision. Just as in chapter 8 where you wrote your life vision a second time, opening up space for Spirit to enter in and create something even more magnificent, the mastery of time management includes space for Spirit interaction in daily life.

Time management is part of developing your craft of living—how you design and live your life in such a way that your vision flows into reality. It means taking care of each thing as it comes along—not letting things pile up by avoiding or ignoring them. Time management means knowing what to respond to and when, which battles to fight and which ones to let pass, and how to claim time as your own.

Finally, you must create space in your life for whatever it is that you want to manifest. For instance, if you want to manifest more time for your family, but you insist on scheduling appointments 7 days a week from 8:00 A.M. to 10:00 P.M., there is no space for the family time to materialize. If you want to create a new job, but you don't tell anyone you are interested in another position or allow time for a search and interviews, the new job probably will not appear.

We must create space for what we want in our lives. Once we have created the space, we must then project ourselves and our vision into that space. Specialized photography has shown that as the root of a plant grows, it projects its energy out into the space it will inhabit before it actually grows into that space. The heart of a fetus begins as a cell that has a beat long before a heart has formed. The idea was there first—again, the universal trinity of concept, form, action. What do you want in your life? What is the goal that you must accomplish? Create the idea, open the space for it to materialize, fill that space with your energy and intention, and then take the action necessary to complete the manifestation.

Through your action plan, you are now empowered to manifest the life you desire—to find fulfillment and reward in a life inspired by soul mission and lived in freedom. From this point, all you have to do is *do* it. You have to follow through—discipline yourself to stay the course. You've done your inner work, you've cleared away energetic blocks and belief patterning, and you've learned to become the master of your thought. Now the time has come to put it into practice, to walk the walk of this amazing journey called your life. You have claimed your life as your own, and opened the gates to the magnificence and splendor of your being. This doesn't mean that everything is an easy ride from here—no challenges, no conflicts, no heartaches. But you now have tremendous tools to get you through whatever comes.

Rick Jarow wrote, "We work through our doubts and questions, and we grow through our resistances. This is how creative careers are built—not by smooth sailing, but by the willingness to negotiate troubled waters." Our greatest resistance often comes just as we are about to reach a point of tremendous breakthrough or powerful initiation. On some level of consciousness, we realize that once we pass through that gate, our lives will never be the same, and so we resist, reluctant to give up something of the past or what we know. However, that is precisely the time to take a deep breath and walk on in. In the traditional Celtic cross tarot spread, the next to the last card position represents both your greatest hopes and fears. The Chinese character for crisis means both opportunity and danger. So it is in our journey. Within our greatest possibilities are our greatest fears, because in order to step into our greatest possibilities, we have to step into our greatest Selves. The Law of Mentalism reminds us once again that you are the human manifestation of an aspect of God. Hear the call to your greatness, step forward, and claim your magnificence.

The chakras can be very helpful as a tool for identifying the source of your resistance or fear. What is the nature of your resistance? Are you having trouble staying present, claiming your personal power, connecting with Spirit? See the table on page 265 to match the appropriate chakra with the nature of your resistance. The key is to go straight to the place in the body where the resistance lives and do your work to clear the block. Meditating from within the chakra, ask questions and have a dialogue with the emotional and avoidance issues that arise as you breathe in that area of your body and address your feelings.

Ask Spirit for guidance in working through your fears and doubts.

Identifying Chakra Location
of Resistance or Avoidance Issues

Resistance to	Chakra
Being fully present, fully engaged	Root
Emotional or sexual connection or chemistry with others; lack of creative energy	Sacral
Personal power and strength; sense of individuality Ability to make your own choices and decisions	Solar Plexus
Love; aligning with the rhythms of the universe	Heart
Living your truth; taking responsibility for your life; letting go of the past; taking risks	Throat
Opening to your vision; clear perception	Brow
Connecting with Spirit	Crown

One last but important aspect of the sixth house is gratitude. As you create your action plan and then begin your work, be grateful for all that life brings you. Gratitude increases the flow of energy in your life in every way, including your communication with Spirit. A regular practice of gratitude can be like opening the floodgates of abundance a little wider each day. Give thanks for the opportunity to share your gifts and to experience all that life offers. Express your gratitude for your home, your family and friends, the money that flows through your life, the challenges you face and the gifts within those challenges, the experiences of your day. As a part of your time management, create a space each day to sit quietly, breathe, and give thanks. You will see the abundance of your life greatly increase.

Again, congratulations! You have just completed a huge step that very few people ever take the time to do. You have created a plan. Put your plan into action now, and create the life you desire!

Questions to Ponder: My Plan of Action Review

House 1 Check-in: Does my work in this house help me see my life vision more clearly? Is there anything that I need to change?

House 2 Check-in: Have I in any way compromised my sense of inner peace? If so, what do I need to shift?

House 3 Check-in: Does my work in this house create more or less enthusiasm and motivation for my life vision? If less, what do I need to shift?

House 4 Check-in: Does my work in this house affect my vision of the future? If so, how? Do I need to shift anything?

House 5 Check-in: Is my plan of action one that continues to nurture and add value to my life and the lives of others?

MANIFESTATION HOUSE 7:

SURRENDER

➡ Am I creating space for Spirit in my life?

➡ Am I willing to surrender this project to Spirit and step up to a higher level of the cocreative process?

There comes a point in the manifestation process where it appears that you've done all that you can do. You've done your inner work, created your action plan, put the plan into motion, and accomplished goals. Now, either your vision is going to manifest, or it's not. However, you are now at the threshold of the most magical and amazing part of your manifestation journey. In the seventh house you "give your vision up to the fates," send your vision-child out into the universe and see how it grows up. You turn it over to Spirit, and a new level of cocreation begins.

When we enter this surrender stage of the cocreative process, we realize on a completely new level that we are not alone. We not only have partners in the physical dimension who can help us achieve our goals, but we have Spirit. In the seventh house, we are called to give up our insistence on independence and step into the higher consciousness of interdependence. We are called to surrender our ego need to "do it on our own" and enter into direct soul interaction and exchange.

A koan is a nonsensical riddle that, when meditated upon, can shed new light upon something in our lives. Take a few moments to meditate on the following koan in order to more fully understand the concept of interdependence.

Meditation: Interdependence

Go to your Point of Stillness and reflect on the koan, "I have to do it by myself, and I can't do it alone." Does this statement have any meaning in your life? How does this koan help you understand how you allow the concept of interdependence to exist in your life?

The seventh house is about developing your interdependent relationship with Spirit. In building your action plan in the last house, we talked about creating space in your daily life for Spirit to enter and let magic happen. Now in the seventh house, you actively work with the space you created, entering into a rhythm that alternates surrender to Spirit with direct action in response to Spirit's guidance. Just as action was the theme of the last house, surrender is the theme in this house. It is often one of the most difficult aspects of a manifestation journey because it means giving up control. However, it does not mean the end of your involvement.

Surrendering your vision to Spirit opens the door to a new level of manifestation. You enter creative partnership as perhaps you have never known it. Just as a child reaching adulthood doesn't mark the end of a need for parenting, as your vision develops a life of its own it doesn't mean the end of manifesting. The child grows into an adult and has its own life to live—a life that the parent can no longer control. The parent must surrender the child to the universe, accepting that they have done all they can do to raise that child, trusting that Spirit will continue to guide their child, and that through its upbringing the child has learned how to walk in the world. The role of parent shifts from provider, caretaker, and nurturer, to wisdom-keeper, adviser, and supporter.

So it is with your vision. You have been provider, caretaker, and nurturer for your vision. You have taken all the steps you could, and the vision is taking on a life of its own. Now you give it to Spirit. Spirit becomes the air current on which your vision can fly, lifting it to ever greater heights in its development. You take on a new role now as co-pilot with Spirit on a magical and mystical flight. "Freedom" takes on a new meaning. Creation and manifestation become an extraordinary exchange between you and Spirit. You engage in a creation relay in which you pass the vision over to Spirit and Spirit runs with it for awhile. Then Spirit passes it back to you, and the manifestation process continues as you hand the vision back and forth. As you continue developing your relationship and partnership with Spirit, you feel guided in each step of the way.

Rick Jarow says, "Surrender is not an abdication of will or power, but a deepened intimacy with living." That deeper intimacy comes through surrendering to the Laws of Rhythm and Gender. The Law of Rhythm says that everything has a flow and a cycle. The Law of Gender says that everything comes in its own time—that there is a gestation period for anything to come to fruition. It takes tremendous faith and trust to surrender to these laws. When you surrender, you enter into the realm of the Great Mystery, where there is no rational proof of anything, no scientific theories to fall back on. There is only your belief and understanding of the laws of the universe. Spiritual forces that we will never fully understand are at work in our human experience. However, as these unseen forces kick in, things just happen.

You may think of surrender as a passive process, and in fact, it is. But surrender is also an active process. As you begin to see where Spirit is taking your vision, how the manifestation process is unfolding, you must pick up the ball and run with it again when Spirit passes your vision back to you. Spirit will take care of the "behind the scenes" activities— putting all the unseen pieces in place. The passive element of the seventh house is to be willing to trust that process, while the active element is to see that everything is in place for manifestation in the seen world— that you have taken care of everything that is your responsibility.

The fourth house took us into the brow and crown chakras in order to look at our future. We talked briefly about transcending linear time, moving freely back and forth along the time line. Here in the seventh house, we realize that what we experienced in the fourth house was only the beginning of a new world of possibility and reality. We learn in this house that we can travel in our consciousness to the simultaneous time/space dimension of the crown chakra. In the fully developed crown-chakra consciousness, time and space are one. We can step into a level of reality where everything that has ever happened or will ever happen is happening now. In the simultaneous time/space dimension, there is no such thing as time or space as we know it in the physical dimension. Everything simply exists as energy, without restriction of physical form. This also means growing into fuller understanding of the Law of Correspondence. Through the brow chakra, we can learn to shift easily between the many layers of consciousness or reality, and then in the crown chakra bring all those layers into one.

Although we may not realize it, we are constantly stepping in and out of a linear time/space awareness. Any time that we expand into the intuitive mind, we have shifted to another realm. In our journey together, we first began making the shift in chapter 4 when we entered the silence. Meditation is the gateway to this boundary-free dimension. As you develop your meditation skills, you can become a master at time/space travel, breaking the bonds of time and space to gain new perspectives and access other realities. Even in daily life, whenever you daydream or fantasize about something, you have stepped out of linear space/time and into a dimension with fewer boundaries. Through many houses of this Wheel, you have shifted out of a strictly linear time/space dimension in the process of doing your work. Though grasping the concept of shifting time and space may seem impossible to the rational mind, once you are willing to temporarily suspend rational thought and expand into your intuitive mind, it is all very simple. A boundary-free time/space dimension is the domain of the intuitive mind. The more adept you become at living intuitively, the more easily you shift back and forth between the linear time/space dimension and the boundary-free world.

Meditation: Time/Space Travel

Go to your Point of Stillness. Once you are settled in this deep meditative state, imagine a very long, straight highway with nothing alongside it. The highway stretches beyond the limits of your sight in both directions. Now allow your imagination to turn that highway into a time line. Traveling back and forth along this highway represents the passage of time from the distant past to the distant future. Imagine that everything that has ever happened or ever will happen lies somewhere on this linear time highway.

Now allow your imagination to show you the point on the highway that represents this present moment in time, and place yourself in that spot on the highway. Notice that from your present spot you can see a short distance in front of you as well as behind you. This is as much of the linear time line that you are able to perceive from a rational mind perspective.

Now lift out of the box of your rational mind and float several hundred feet above the highway. Suddenly the length of the highway or time line that you are able to perceive becomes much greater. You can see much farther into the past and into the future. The higher you lift above the highway, the greater expanse of linear time you are able to perceive. From this high vantage point, however, another magical thing happens. You are not only perceiving the past and the future, but as you perceive it, it is all happening at once! The higher you rise above the highway, the more you lose a sense of the highway as a time line and the more it becomes simply a very long road with millions of people, places, and events happening all at the same time in the same highway space. This is crown chakra awareness. There is nothing difficult about opening to that awareness—simply a willingness to let go of what you've always been taught was real. The only challenge is to temporarily suspend rational thought—to surrender to higher consciousness and a greater reality.

You may wish to remain in this high awareness for awhile, either in your silence, or writing in your journal. The more you practice this meditation exercise, the more adept you will become at rising quickly above the linear time highway and shifting to a simultaneous time/space view. Then you will be able to jump back and forth between these two perspectives easily. With this skill, you gain the ability to perceive life from a universal perspective, no longer trapped within the confines of the linear time/space dimension.

Manifesting from this level of awareness is a fantastically liberating experience. You move into a new level of patience and understanding of process. When you begin to recognize your own human and divine greatness, you also begin to move into a consciousness of absolute faith that it will happen. There is no longer any need to hurry. You live within the Law of Gender, knowing that your job within the cocreative process is to use all of the universal laws to their fullest in service of your divine unfolding, and that all will, in time, be revealed and manifested.

In chapter 6, we spoke of the root chakra containing the seed of our potential. Here we can refine that understanding to see that the root chakra contains the seed of our human potential, while the crown chakra contains the seed of our divine potential. The more we are able to integrate the physical and the spiritual, to grasp the Law of Mentalism which tells us that we are equally human and divine, the more we will understand our potential greatness. We will also understand that if we insist on doing it alone, reaching our greatness is impossible. Without recognition of Spirit as cocreative partner, we cannot fully develop in the crown chakra, and therefore never fully know our potential as human manifestations of divinity.

In order to enter into this house of surrender, you must have completed your work of the first six houses. If you haven't done your work, you cannot be a full partner in the cocreative process. Spirit needs you as Its hands and feet—you must do Spirit's work in the physical dimension. And you need Spirit to do the necessary work in the unseen dimension. Perhaps you've heard the expression, "Let go and let God." That is the essence of the seventh house. Let Spirit carry your vision for awhile. Then when it is time for you to take it back, Spirit will guide you in each step.

In the fourth house, you had a conversation with Spirit, asking to be shown the greater possibilities within your vision. We now move to a new level of interaction. The seventh house is no longer about just talking with Spirit. The seventh house is about working with Spirit, knowing and expecting that miracles will occur, that the unexplained will appear, and that your vision will manifest in some form. Ask Spirit to help you be in the right place at the right time. Ask that the right circumstances appear and that you will recognize them and know the role you are to play.

As you move more deeply into the work of the seventh house, it is like moving full steam ahead into miracle land. The right people do begin to show up, the right opportunities do come to you, all the pieces do begin to fall into place, and you are constantly amazed that you are in the right place at the right time.

You are now working in a much higher vibrational frequency. You are no longer working only with the physical realm. You have called in the full power of the spiritual forces to be your partner. Along with this step comes a realization that you alone are no longer creating the picture of your life or manifesting the vision. It becomes Spirit-infused. Spirit takes over and brings a new creative force to your vision and your life, catapulting you ever farther into the full realization of your potential. You began to see this in the fourth house, but there you were still only looking at possibilities. Here in the seventh house you are living them, and possibly even exceeding them.

In the bigger picture of cocreative manifestation, you realize that your vision no longer belongs only to you. You realize that it is just the vehicle for your personal journey within the larger collective journey of creation. When you enter the higher levels of cocreation, you surrender your personal vision to the spiritual vision of our evolving universe. This doesn't mean you will have to settle for less—quite the contrary. It means that you are expanding into the universal consciousness and actively participating in the ongoing creation and evolution of the cosmos. You see your mission and vision within a much larger context, and move into a synergistic dance with the universe. You open to a realm of consciousness where your vision becomes fully aligned with Spirit and creation. You are no longer focused on the personal nature of your vision, but on its universal nature. Life opens to new levels of freedom and ecstasy.

Questions to Ponder: Cocreation with Spirit

Am I creating space for Spirit to enter into my life? If not, how can I?

Am I engaging in the cocreative process with Spirit by engaging Spirit as my partner in creation? Have I made the transition from talking with Spirit to working in partnership with Spirit?

Am I surrendering my vision to Spirit, trusting in the unseen divine process of manifestation?

How am I now understanding the playing out in my life of the Laws of Rhythm and Gender on a higher level?

Am I seeing miracles begin to happen in my life—wonderful synchronicities of things falling into place?

House 1 Check-in: How do I see my mission and vision within the larger context of the ongoing creation and evolution of the cosmos?

House 2 Check-in: Has my work here in any way compromised my sense of inner peace? If so, what do I need to shift?

House 3 Check-in: Do I have more or less enthusiasm and motivation for my life vision? If less, what do I need to shift?

House 4 Check-in: How has my work in this house impacted my vision of the future? Do I need to shift anything?

House 5 Check-in: Through my work in this house, do I continue to see how my vision will nurture and add value to my life and the lives of others?

House 6 Check-in: As I enter higher levels of the cocreation process with Spirit, does my action plan need any adjustment? If so, what adjustments do I need to make?

MANIFESTATION HOUSE 8:

LEGACY

→ Do I feel I'm in harmony with the universe as I go through the process and complete my project?

→ Does the completion of my project contribute to a positive living environment on the planet?

→ What impact will my project have on future generations? Am I in some way making life better for them?

A Native American proverb says, "In all your deliberations, consider the impact on the Seventh Generation." The final house of the Manifestation Wheel calls us to expand our view of our life vision to a global perspective. Here, we consider our vision from the perspective of our legacy for those who follow. Robert Hargrove wrote in *Masterful Coaching*, "Most of us act as if we were dropped on the planet from the heavens with the expressed purpose of living our lives as fully, successfully, and happily as we can. It seldom occurs to us that we are responsible for passing this world on to the next generation in better shape than we found it. It seldom occurs to us that our way of living is not sustainable and we are existing off the capital of future generations. It often doesn't occur to us that our legacy to our children should not just be a few material possessions but the raising of our collective vision from a foundation of socially constructive values deeply embedded in our society, communities, and schools." The eighth house is about giving your best toward the future of our global community.

This may be a much bigger picture than you have ever considered. Yet when you remember that the universe is a vibrating energy system, and that your personal vibrational frequency contributes to the make-up of planet Earth's vibration, you can begin to wrap your mind around the idea that you do have a voice—that your life does matter. Your every thought goes out into the universe as a vibration. Each word that you speak has an impact on the energy around you. Every action that you take either reinforces the energy patterns that are already in place or shifts them to something new. Your choices for the present create your future, and contribute to the collective future of all. In this last house, you consider the gifts that your life vision offers to the world, and ask, "Am I contributing to the positive evolution of the world? Am I honoring our planet Earth, her needs, and resources? Am I contributing to raising human consciousness?"

As we consider how we want to create the future, the eighth house also calls us to consider our past—to look at our family heritage and cultural traditions and ask, "What am I being called to perpetuate?" Perhaps you feel a soul desire to honor and sustain something from the past—a tradition, a belief, a practice. There may be aspects of your heritage to which you feel a strong allegiance, and a desire to carry them forward in history. You may also feel that aspects of your heritage have run their course, yet need to be remembered and honored for their importance in their time. Are there ways in which you feel called to honor aspects of the past and carry them into the future?

On the other hand, there may be other aspects of your heritage or culture that you feel called to change—certain beliefs, practices, or traditions that are standing in the way of progressive growth and development. In our initial discussion of paradigms in chapter 9, we discussed our responsibility to free future generations from limiting belief systems of the past. Do you find limiting beliefs within your heritage or tradition from which you choose to free yourself, so that the next generation can start with a clean slate?

If you have never considered your life from this universal perspective, doing so now might seem overwhelming. You might say, "But my vision is just to raise my children well, provide for the needs and desires of my family, perhaps travel a little, and be able to contribute to causes I care about." You might feel that your mission and vision are insignificant in the big scheme of things. Not so. The eighth house still applies. Regardless of the size of your vision, it is still an energy system that reaches out to the universe and spreads its vibration.

What is the contribution you wish to make to the future? We are not talking about money, possessions, or time. We are talking about thought—energy vibration. Your mission, vision, or gift can be anything as long as love and purity of intention are its foundation. The most powerful gift you can give to the world is a pure vibration of love through your thoughts, words, and deeds.

This last house on the Manifestation Wheel brings us back one last time to the Law of Mentalism and the understanding that we are all one. The more we can let go of national and ethnic borders and begin thinking globally, the sooner we can live the Law of Mentalism as a global community. As outer space exploration continues in this century and beyond, our global consciousness will no doubt eventually expand to universal consciousness. We will understand how our choices and decisions here on Earth affect the entire universe. It may take longer for the effects to be felt in some faraway galaxy, but as time continues to accelerate and the distances between planets gets shorter through outer space travel, those effects will take less and less time.

In chapter 4, Spirit offered a wonderful teaching on inner space. In this house, as we focus on our mission and vision from a universal perspective, we are also called to explore even more deeply our inner universe. As Spirit said, "Inner space is the final frontier . . . inner space is the real magical galaxy. The stars, solar systems, and planets that dwell within you are the new frontier to explore . . . There are unknown yet inhabited regions within you." Our inner and outer worlds are reflections of one another. Every exploratory step in one world carries us deeper into the other. No matter how far the pendulum swings in one direction, it will swing in the other. Exploration of outer space can be a profoundly spiritual experience when we open our minds to see the outer space reflection in our inner world. At the same time, the deeper we are willing to go in our personal inner journeys, the more profoundly and clearly we understand others' journeys.

The time line with which we worked in the last chapter also exists deep within us. Within our heart chakra lies access to all that ever has been and ever will be. When we go deep into our hearts, we can begin to perceive a future world and recognize the gifts we can give. Again, our choices, thoughts, and actions of today create the world of tomorrow.

We begin building this universal consciousness with an awareness of our own community, state, country, and ultimately, our world. If you could see the world as bands of energy connections, you would see an amazingly intricate web that is woven between people, thoughts, places, and even spirits who are no longer in physical bodies. You would understand interdependence between Earth, plants, animals, and humans, and, as a result, know the importance of taking care of all of creation. Every part depends on all the other parts. We live in a world where every creature, every plant, and every person serves a function. All of creation has a purpose. The eighth house calls us to feel the interconnectedness of all of creation, and to live our lives in a way that honors and sustains life for all.

Meditation: The Web of Creation

Go to your Point of Stillness. Then allow your awareness to float up and out of your body—about 100 feet above the space where you are now. Float here for a few moments and begin to perceive the web of energy bands between you and others with whom you share your space, and even the space itself. Let go of any preconceived notions about how the web should appear, and allow your inner senses experience the energy.

Rising much faster now, float on up above your city. Pause there for a few moments to perceive the web of energy bands in the city. Then float on up above your region of the country. How do you perceive the web here? Continue rising until you can see the curve of the Earth. How do you perceive the web of energy bands that exists between all aspects of creation? You may perceive bands of energy from one person to another, from a person to a place, and even from a person on earth to a person in the spirit world. As you continue to rise, you may also perceive bands of energy between planets, stars, moons, and celestial bodies.

Don't be concerned if the first time you do this meditation you don't perceive a lot. Just as in working with shifting time/space dimensions, we are working only in the intuitive mind, which requires suspending your connection to the rational mind. As your awareness grows in the coming months through using the tools you have learned here and elsewhere in your spiritual journey, you will notice that each time you return to this meditation, you perceive more layers of reality. This meditation is a great tool for sensing the vastness of our interconnected web.

The eighth house ultimately calls us to a very high level of self-realization and acceptance. The full journey of this house means acknowledging and accepting Self as a divine force of nature that has a purpose—a mission that will in some way make the path better for generations to come. In this house, we are called to fully accept our responsibility as cocreators of the universe. Spirit plays a huge role in that creative process, and so do we. Our words, thoughts, and actions shape our present and our future—not just for us individually, but for the entire global family.

Acknowledge your greatness, your inner divine force. Respect your role as cocreator, and call your life into being in its highest possible form. Live your life as a human manifestation of the greatness of God.

Questions to Ponder: Legacy

How does the process and manifestation of my vision add to a positive environment for living on Earth?

What impact will the process and manifestation of my vision have on future generations? Through the accomplishment of this vision, am I in some way making life better for the generations to follow? If so, how?

How can I be more conscious of my thoughts, words, and actions as having vibrational effects on the universe? How can I be more responsible in doing my part to create a positive future?

What parts of my family heritage and cultural traditions do I feel called to keep alive? Are there memories of the past, either personal or cultural, that I feel called to preserve?

What from my heritage or culture do I feel must now be changed for the positive evolution of the human family and our Earth?

What is my personal legacy to future generations?

House 1 Check-in: When I look at my vision from this global perspective, do I see it more clearly? Is there anything that I need to change?

House 2 Check-in: Has this global perspective in any way compromised my sense of inner peace? If so, what do I need to shift?

House 3 Check-in: Do I have more or less enthusiasm and motivation for my life vision? If less, what do I need to shift?

House 4 Check-in: How has looking at life from this very large perspective affected my vision of the future? Do I need to shift anything?

House 5 Check-in: Through my work in this house, do I continue to see how my vision will nurture and add value to my life and the lives of others?

House 6 Check-in: As I move into a much more global awareness, do I see the necessity for adjustments to my action plan? If so, what adjustments do I need to make?

House 7 Check-in: Has my sense of Spirit's presence in my life changed after my work in the eighth house? If so, how?

In Conclusion:

The Journey Forward

ONCE MORE, congratulations! You have made it around the Manifestation Wheel with your life vision, and should be well on your way to living your dreams. You have learned to honor your mission and keep it as the basis of every action, choice, and decision—a constant guide and sounding board off of which to bounce the many considerations of your life. Let this become the way you live each day. The more you honor your soul, holding Self in the absolute highest regard and respect, the greater your gift to those around you and to the world.

One of the most powerful gifts of the Manifestation Wheel is that as you move through the houses, doing your work and growing into your vision, you experience a constantly expanding awareness. The Wheel accepts us wherever we might be in our growth and development process, and becomes our personal evolution program. No matter what project you may place on the Wheel, you are certain to expand in your sense of Self and your relationship to the world around you. The Manifestation Wheel raises your awareness toward a global and, ultimately, universal consciousness.

Universal consciousness is where the soul wants to play. Always seeking freedom, our souls are anxious to remove any obstacles that might hold us back from free flight. The Manifestation Wheel moves us toward a richer experience of full-spectrum living—toward dancing freely in the universal realm of all possibility.

Even after you have worked your way around the Wheel, you will no doubt still meet challenges, have your peace threatened, question your legacy, or "hit the wall" in some way. This is normal, especially when working on large projects that demand growth and change in you. Take these challenges as signs that you are reaching new levels in your personal development and manifestation process. Go back to the appropriate house and work through whatever has come up. It may take more than one trip around the Wheel to accomplish major life manifestations. But the result is the full magnificence of you!

Ralph Blum quotes the *Daily Word* in *The Book of Runes*: "I no longer try to change outer things. They are simply a reflection. I change my inner perception and the outer reveals the beauty so long obscured by my own attitude. I concentrate on my inner vision and find my outer view transformed. I find myself attuned to the grandeur of life and in unison with the perfect order of the universe." The further we go in this journey to magnificence, the more we realize that all of life really is experienced according to our personal perceptions. When we concentrate on our inner vision and project that vision out into the world, we create the life we desire.

So where do you go from here? You have gained many tools and great understanding for your journey through your work. Keep doing what you are doing. Use the tools. Cultivate the understanding. And keep coming back to these pages. As I said in the Introduction, this book is like the owner's manual you never received when you came into this world. Unlike the owner's manual for your car or an appliance, however, this book has a particularly magical quality—it evolves as you evolve. That is to say, each time you come back to these pages, you will read them in a new way, as if the words have changed. They will serve you for many years to come—again, not because my words are so important, but because of what they stir up in you. Each time you return to the book, you will be in a different place in your life, and therefore bring a completely new set of perspectives and experiences to the work. Therefore, much of the work will seem fresh and new, yet, at the same time, comfortably familiar, like a true heart friend that perhaps you haven't seen for awhile. You find comfort and safety resting in one another, yet a freshness and inspiration borne out of all you have each learned since your last dance.

There are specific times that I would definitely recommend coming back to this book. During times of transition, challenging decisions, or life changes, let these pages bring you clarity, strength, and support for your journey. When you are confused or things aren't flowing as you might like, or when you sense that there is an inner block to your outer progress, return to the exercises here to identify the block or find your path again. Let your intuitive senses guide you to the section of the book that will be the most helpful.

However, this book is not only to be used as a tool to get you past a block or help you through transition. Come back to it when your life is really flying! Let these pages help you move up to the next level, challenge you to go farther, to step into the next growth phase. As we said before, the soul seeks its own greatness, and will not give energy to anything less. Therefore, it is our charge to give energy only to the absolute best for our lives. Choose and commit to the path that sets your soul free!

Finally, may you manifest your perfect dreams, know the magnificence of your soul, and, by living your mission and vision, find the greatest possible fulfillment in all of your days!

SOUL MISSION ✳ LIFE VISION

MENTORING PROGRAM

The Soul Mission ✳ Life Vision Mentoring Program is designed to empower you to become all that you can be—personally, professionally, emotionally, spiritually, and financially. Programs are custom designed to fit your needs, and may include:

one-on-one coaching sessions

project consultations

workshops and retreats

tele-classes

personal intensive residencies

group coaching

teacher training and certification

supporting publications, videotapes, audiotapes, and tools

Alan Seale and the dynamic leaders of the Soul Mission ✳ Life Vision Mentoring Program become your creative and supportive partners for masterminding and manifesting the life you desire. Through your committed work with Alan and his team, you spread your wings and fly!

To learn more about this extraordinary and unique program, visit Alan Seale's Web site at:

www.alanseale.com

e-mail: *info@alanseale.com*

or write to:

Soul Mission ✳ Life Vision

P. O. Box 506

Jeffersonville, NY 12748

BIBLIOGRAPHY

Blum, Ralph. *The Book of Runes*. New York: St. Martin's Press, 1987.

Boldt, Laurence G. *How to Be, Do, or Have Anything*. Berkeley: Ten Speed Press, 2001.

Bolles, Richard N. *How to Find Your Mission in Life*. Berkeley: Ten Speed Press, 1991.

Chopra, Deepak. *The Way of the Wizard*. New York: Harmony Books, 1995.

Cohen, Andrew. *Embracing Heaven & Earth*. Lenox, Ma: Moksha Press, 2000.

De Mille, Agnes. *Martha: The Life and Work of Martha Graham*. New York: Random House, 1956.

Dyer, Wayne. *Wisdom of the Ages: 60 Days to Enlightenment*. New York: HarperCollins, 1998.

Fisichella, Anthony. *Metaphysics: The Science of Life*. St. Paul: Llewellyn, 1988.

Gibran, Kahlil. *The Prophet*. New York: Random House, 2001.

Hargrove, Michael. *Masterful Coaching*. San Francisco: Jossey-Bass Pfeiffer, 1995

Hill, Napoleon. *Grow Rich! With Peace of Mind*. New York: Fawcett Columbine, 1967.

Jarow, Rick. *Creating the Work You Love*. Rochester, VT: Destiny Books, 1995.

Jones, Laurie Beth. *The Path: Creating Your Mission Statement for Work and for Life*. New York: Hyperion, 1998.

Karpinski, Gloria. *Barefoot on Holy Ground*. New York: Ballantine Wellspring, 2001.

Kinder, George. *The Seven Stages of Money Maturity: Understanding the Spirit and Value of Money in Your Life*. New York: Dell Publishing, 1999.

Leonard, George and Michael Murphy. *The Life We Are Given*. New York: G. P. Putnam's Sons, 1995.

Nemeth, Ph.D., Maria. *The Energy of Money*. New York: Ballantine Wellspring, 1999.

Osbon, Diane K., ed. *A Joseph Campbell Companion*. New York: Harper Perennial, 1991.

Ouspensky, P. D. *In Search of the Miraculous*. London: Routledge & Kegan Paul Ltd., 1950.

Proctor, Bob. *The New Lead the Field Seminar* (tape and workbook series). Niles, IL: Nightingale Conant Corporation, 2000.

———. *You Were Born Rich*. Phoenix: Life Success Production, 1997.

Ram Dass. *Still Here*. New York: Riverhead Books, 2000.

Ray, James A. *Science of Success: How to Attract Prosperity and Create Life Balance through Proven Principles*. La Jolla, CA: Sunark Press, 1999.

Robbins, Anthony. *Awaken the Giant Within*. New York: Simon & Schuster, 1991.

Ruiz, Don Miguel. *The Four Agreements*. San Rafael, CA: Amber-Allen Publishing, 1997.

Seale, Alan. *Intuitive Living: A Sacred Path*. York Beach, ME: Weiser Books, 2001.

Shannon, William H. *Silence on Fire: The Prayer of Awareness*. New York: Crossroad, 1995.

St. John, Noah. *Permission to Succeed*. Deerfield Beach, FL: Health Communications, 1999.

Straub, Gail. *The Rhythm of Compassion*. Boston: Journey Editions, 2000.

Three Initiates. *The Kybalion: A Study of the Hermetic Philosophy of Ancient Egypt and Greece*. Chicago: The Yogi Publication Society, 1912.

Thurston, Ph.D., Mark. *Soul-Purpose*. New York: St. Martin's Paperbacks, 1989.

Walsch, Neale Donald. *Conversations with God, Book 1*. New York: G. P. Putnam's Sons, 1996.

———. *Conversations with God, Book 2*. Charlottesville: Hampton Roads Publishing Company, Inc., 1997.

———. *Conversations with God, Book 3*. Charlottesville: Hampton Roads Publishing Company, Inc., 1998.

Washington, James M., ed. *A Testament of Hope: The Essential Writings and Speeches of Martin Luther King, Jr.* San Francisco: HarperSanFrancisco, 1991.